What People Are Saying About Chaim Bentorah and *Hebrew Word Study*...

You are going to love reading *Hebrew Word Study: Revealing the Heart of God*! For decades, I've had the privilege of learning from the wit and wisdom of Chaim Bentorah. His insights into the Hebrew language deliver interesting and life-changing perspectives that I've seen only from his work.

—*Lester Sumrall*
President, HEIR.TV

Chaim Bentorah has studied Semitic languages for many years, and his approach to, and use of, the esoteric Hebrew in his Bible studies is inspiring and enlightening. His stunning research and manner of presentation have greatly deepened my own personal devotional study. He puts great emphasis in his word studies on understanding the heart of God without promoting specific doctrines. His writings are original and practical, with application for everyday life, and there are many insightful lessons for all audiences. His mastery of the Hebrew and Aramaic languages is cutting-edge and relevant, providing messages of hope, strength, and peace for the perplexing times in which we live.

—*Mark Siljander*
Former US Congressman & UN Ambassador
President, Bridges to Common Ground
Author, *A Deadly Misunderstanding*

Chaim Bentorah's rich insights into the Scriptures are incredibly life-changing. He writes in a way that makes the Bible come alive!

—*Kari Browning*
Director, New Renaissance Healing & Creativity Center,
Coeur d'Alene, ID
Author, *Unsealing Ancient Mysteries*

I have had the privilege of being on the receiving end of the amazing fruit that Chaim Bentorah is producing in regard to understanding the passionate heart of the Lord by gaining a basic understanding of the Hebrew alphabet and words. And I've seen firsthand hearts being opened to know Jesus better through Chaim's work. Apart from just being a great guy, Chaim Bentorah is a true friend of the Bridegroom. I highly recommend his books as a tool to attain greater intimacy with the Lord.

—*Marvin Adams*
Executive Director, IHOPE (Indiana House of Prayer & Equipping)

In *Hebrew Word Study: Revealing the Heart of God,* Chaim Bentorah's writings are deep, insightful, and totally addictive. I found myself probing the depths of the ancient Hebrew scripts and etymologies with an unexpected twenty-first-century twist. There's nothing comparable to Chaim's unique approach to unraveling the mysteries in the Scriptures with his unabashed human touch. Put on a pot of coffee, sit back in your favorite easy chair, take a deep breath, and plunge into another mighty adventure!

—*Peter Scott Snyder, BA, MA, PhD*
Missionary to China

HEBREW WORD STUDY

REVEALING THE HEART OF GOD

CHAIM BENTORAH

WHITAKER HOUSE

The forms *Lord* and *God* (in small caps) in Bible quotations represent the Hebrew name for God *Yahweh* (*Jehovah*), while *Lord* and *God* normally represent the Hebrew name for God *Adonai*, in accordance with the Bible version used.

Hebrew Word Study:
Revealing the Heart of God

Chaim Bentorah
www.chaimbentorah.com
chaimbentorah@gmail.com

ISBN: 978-1-62911-697-6
eBook ISBN: 978-1-62911-698-3
Printed in the United States of America

Whitaker House
1030 Hunt Valley Circle
New Kensington, PA 15068
www.whitakerhouse.com

Library of Congress Cataloging-in-Publication Data
Names: Bentorah, Chaim, 1950– author.
Title: Hebrew word study : revealing the heart of God / Chaim Bentorah.
Description: New Kensington, PA : Whitaker House, [2016] | Includes bibliographical references and index. | Description based on print version record and CIP data provided by publisher; resource not viewed.
Identifiers: LCCN 2016021456 (print) | LCCN 2016020067 (ebook) | ISBN 9781629116983 (E-book) | ISBN 9781629116976 (hardcover : alk. paper)
Subjects: LCSH: Hebrew language—Word formation.
Classification: LCC PJ4603 (print) | LCC PJ4603 .B46 2016 (ebook) | DDC 221.4/47—dc23
LC record available at https://lccn.loc.gov/2016021456

8 9 10 11 12 13 14 15 16 **w** 30 29 28 27 26 25 24

Dedication

To Michelle Foss and Laura Bertone,
who came to me when I needed a friend.

Contents

Author's Note

Please refer to the alphabetical Glossary at the end of this book for definitions and explanations of historical, cultural, and linguistic terms followed by an asterisk * when they initially occur in the text. Some of these terms may first appear in plural form. For clarity, in the case of a term consisting of two words, two asterisks ** will follow the second word of the term, and in the case of a term consisting of three words, three asterisks *** will follow the third word of the term.

As with other Semitic languages, the original Hebrew alphabet is consonantal, with no separate letters for vowels. Nevertheless, vowel sounds were used in the Hebrew language, because it is impossible to pronounce a word without using the sounds represented by *a*, *e*, *i*, *o*, and *u*. In rabbinic Hebrew, the letters aleph, hei, yod, and vav can be used to denote a vowel. Additionally, around the seventh century AD, the Masoretic text introduced the *niqqud*, which are a series of dots and dashes placed near a consonantal letter to indicate a vowel. The normal pattern is: consonant, vowel, consonant, vowel. I use the *abajab*, or the consonantal alphabet, and follow a rabbinical tradition of defaulting to using the *a* whenever any vowel is needed, except in cases where I am explaining a certain word usage or grammatical expression. Additionally, while many academic texts use left-handed apostrophes for the aleph and right-handed apostrophes for the ayin, this text has been streamlined, using right-handed apostrophes for both.

Finally, in the Scripture quotations, braces indicate my own translation, brackets indicate words added or substituted for clarity and/or flow, and boldface type indicates my emphasis.

Foreword

Have you ever wished you could know God better? I would love to walk in the garden and converse with God as Adam did; alas, the reality is that our most authoritative source for understanding Him is what is written in Scriptures that came from the heart of God into a human language that we can't understand, and were then translated into yet another language that we can understand. This book is designed to bring us beyond just reading various translations of the Bible to discovering the very heart of God.

The old adage "Something was lost in translation" holds more truth than we often care to admit. Each language of the world has its own unique semantic domain, or meanings understood by each word used. For example, I can say the word *house*, and it will raise a variety of images in your mind. If I were to use the equivalent word, *rala*, among the remote Amanab people in the tropical rainforest of Papua, New Guinea, they would have a completely different set of images—none of which would match the image that is in your mind. In other words, the most accurate translation of even one simple word can convey many different meanings.

At the core of any translation effort is the desire to convey into the receptor language—as much as is possible—everything intended by the speaker. When it comes to Bible translation, reverence for the inspiration of Scripture causes us to conclude that a technically accurate translation is preferred. Modern, paraphrased versions of Scripture are considered to be more for devotional use.

In this book, you will find a wonderful blend of the same respect that ancient rabbis had for the holy Word of God, combined with the skill of a contemporary Hebrew teacher who reveals through the language itself—by closely looking at the words we have received from God—a devotional understanding of what was in His mind. What we discover is the heart of God; and, in the process, we get to know Him better.

—*Andrew Minch*
Papua, New Guinea, Translation Consultant
Wycliffe Bible Translators

Preface

Many years ago, as a graduate student, I studied under a highly respected Hebrew professor. I learned that he would get up early every morning and study the Word of God for three hours in the original Hebrew,* Aramaic,* and Greek.* I aspired to be like my professor, and indeed it has been my habit for these many years to arise early and study the Word of God in the original languages for a minimum of three hours a day. This is just a minimum. There have been periods when I would study the Word of God eight to ten hours a day.

You may wonder how a person can study the Word of God so much. Some people can barely read through the Bible in one year, and they consider that an accomplishment. However, these same people can take a popular novel that is longer than the Bible itself and polish that off in a week's time.

One secret to sustained studying of God's Word is this: if you fall in love with the Author of the Bible, you will feel there is not enough time in the day to study His Word. Also, as your love for Him deepens, He will reveal His secrets to you. I have found the Word of God to be a well that never runs dry.

Of course, having been a teacher of Classical Hebrew** and Aramaic does help. I have learned the freedom that we have through allowing the Holy Spirit to guide us. I have learned that our Bible lexicons* and dictionaries are not the final word. I have also learned that with over one hundred twenty different modern English translations of the Bible, all putting their own spin on various passages of Scripture, I can allow the Holy Spirit to guide me in any number of these different spins.

The reason for this freedom is that Classical Hebrew is an ambiguous language. It has only seventy-five hundred words, as opposed to Modern Hebrew, which has a quarter million words. Accordingly, every word of Classical Hebrew can have multiple meanings. Just looking up a word in a Hebrew dictionary, in a lexicon, or in *Strong's Exhaustive Concordance* will not really tell you how a word is to be used in a particular verse. Much of the translation process involves a close examination of the context, the culture of the day, and the idioms* in order to determine which of the many possible English words to apply to any given Hebrew word in a specific verse. I learned from Jewish rabbis that you must also put a Hebrew word into its emotional context. Hebrew is an emotional language—a language of poets—and thus there is an emotional context involved in many passages of Scripture.

I was even taught through rabbinic literature** how to translate letter by letter. You will find some of that approach in this book. I do not advocate using the traditional meanings behind Hebrew letters to assist in a word study on an academic level; however, for one's own personal devotional study, using the meanings behind Hebrew letters to better understand a Hebrew word and to put it into its context is a tool that could prove to be of value, if for no other reason than to cause one to meditate on the Word of God. Therefore, when I apply the traditional meanings behind Hebrew letters, my conclusions are not to be considered authoritative but rather the ponderings and musings of an old teacher seeking to understand the heart of the God whom he has learned to love over his many years.

Accordingly, this book is not an examination of the common usages and applications of various Hebrew words. Those books are plentiful enough. Instead, it seeks to walk the road less traveled, to examine the secondary and optional meanings of certain Hebrew words, to seek the origin of a word and to plug it into the context and see if it fits. If it does fit, then maybe there is a deeper spiritual message to be found.

In no way does this book seek to undermine any of our modern translations. It is this writer's belief that all of our modern English versions of the Bible were translated by men and women skilled in the biblical languages and in linguistics. Every word in the more than one hundred twenty modern English translations was prayerfully considered, and it is my position that even though different translations may contain different meanings, expressions, and nuances, they all reflect the inspired Word of God. They also demonstrate the ambiguity of the Classical Hebrew language and the infinite greatness of God.

Let me illustrate: If you look at a drop of water with the naked eye, you see just one drop of water. But if you put that drop of water under a microscope, you see a whole world of life within it, things that you could never see without the magnification. So it is with the Word of God. You may see just one word, but put that word under a spiritual microscope, and you will see a whole world of life within it that you hadn't even begun to imagine. The Jewish Talmud* teaches that there are "seventy faces" to Torah.* That is, every verse could have seventy different shades of meaning. The Word of God is pictured as a gemstone that is taken out to the sunlight. When the light reflects off the gemstone, it displays many different colors.

To be sure, there is a literal meaning to every verse, and the Talmud does warn that we are never to wander away from the *pashat*, or the literal meaning. Yet the literal interpretation is like the surface of the ocean. It is beautiful and vast, but if you dive beneath that surface—similar to observing that drop of water under a microscope—you will find a brand-new world filled with amazing wonders. This, again, is how it is with the Word of God. Its surface meaning is vast and beautiful. Many books have been written declaring the beauty of the surface meaning. This book, however, seeks to dive beneath that surface, to explore options, alternatives, and secondary meanings that are often not applied to a passage of Scripture and to challenge the reader to see if he or she can discover a depth of truth, a message from God, that he or she has not yet explored.

I am aware that many insights in this book are not found in your average Christian library, but you will find them in the depths of Jewish literature, such as the Talmud, the Mishnah,* the Midrash,* and other works of Jewish scholars over the past three thousand years. The Jews, of course, are the people of the Old Testament and the guardians of the Hebrew language. For centuries, Christians have shunned the works of Judaism because the Jewish people as a whole did not accept Jesus as their Messiah. Christians have felt that if the Jews would not accept Jesus as Messiah, then what could they have to offer to Christians? But just because they have not accepted Jesus as their Messiah does not mean that their mission as God's chosen people has been withdrawn.

With the founding of the country of Israel in 1948, and with Christians' growing understanding of the role that the Jewish people play in God's prophetic plan, Christians have been warming up to the Jewish community and recognizing the vast storehouse of knowledge of God and of His Word that they have built up over the last several thousand years. Only in recent generations have Christians come to understand that being the chosen people means more than having been selected by God as the people through whom the Messiah would come into the world; it also means that their role is to demonstrate to the world the holiness of God, the loving nature of God, and how to love Him in return. Christians are discovering that their roots lie in Judaism, that their Savior Jesus Christ was Jewish, and that the first Christians were Jewish. Suddenly, Christians are approaching the Jewish community hat in hand and "[taking] *hold of the skirt of him that is a Jew, saying, 'We will go with you: for we have heard that God is with you*'" (Zechariah 8:23).

I make no apology for my references in this book to the Talmud, the Mishnah, and other Jewish works. I have studied them for forty years and have even studied them in the Aramaic. I have found great wisdom in them and an understanding of God that I generally find lacking in the Christian community. Most important, I have learned that God has a heart—a heart that is easily broken.

I was born and raised in orthodox, evangelical Christianity. I am a Christian, and I cling to the tenets of my faith that were instilled in me as a small child. I have read and reread the ninety studies in this book, and I personally do not believe that any of them would in any way step outside the boundaries of my evangelical faith. If you feel there are passages where I have done so, I want to hear from you. I can be reached through the contact information at the back of this book. I want to know where I may have strayed from the paths of the fundamentals of our faith. I sincerely doubt, however, that you will find any conflict with our orthodox Christian beliefs. If you do, then I was misunderstood, and I will stand to be corrected.

This book, compiled from daily word study devotionals that I have written over the years, will introduce you to a world you have probably not visited before. Again, the Hebrew language is a language of poetry and pictures. One can read many depths of meaning into a well-written poem. The Jewish poet Hayim Nahman Bialik once said that to study the Holy Scriptures in any language other than the original Hebrew is like kissing your bride with a veil between your face and hers. I hope this book will remove that veil so that you will see just how beautiful the Word of God really is and that you, too, will seek to truly know and understand our God so that you will not inadvertently wound His heart.

You begin your journey to the heart of God by looking
for the obvious.

Never take anything of God's creation for granted:
from the highest mountain or the mightiest storm to the smallest
ant or even a blade of grass.

All cry out to us from the very heart of God.

—*Chaim Bentorah*

Study 1

Refuge: *Sagav* (שׂגב)

"The Lord *also will be a refuge for the oppressed,*
a refuge in times of trouble."
—Psalm 9:9

Jacques Lowe was the personal photographer for President John F. Kennedy. He had over forty thousand negatives of photographs of Kennedy and his immediate family in his collection, but only four hundred photos were ever published. Jacques Lowe was a very careful and meticulous person, and he took exceptional care of his negatives and photographs. If a museum or a library needed one of his photos, he personally developed it himself. When it came time to find a safe place to store his negatives, he researched every possible option available and eventually decided that the safest place for them in the whole world would be a vault at the J. P. Morgan Chase Bank in New York City. Today, none of those forty thousand negatives exist. You see, this vault was located in the World Trade Center and was destroyed in the terrorist attack on September 11, 2001.

A Place of Ultimate Safety

David, the author of our study verse, lived a life on the edge as a warrior and a king. He was probably more aware than anyone else that, even for a king, there was no truly safe place on earth. Yet when David said that the Lord is *"a refuge for the oppressed"* and *"a refuge in times of trouble,"* he was referring to a place of ultimate safety. The Hebrew term translated *"refuge," sagav* (שׂגב), which means "to be high," is a very unusual word to be used in the sense of a refuge. The picture is of a refuge in the heavens or in outer space—a place that is inaccessible.

The term *"oppressed"* is from the Hebrew word *'adah* (עדה), which means "to be crushed under by affliction" or "to have a heavy weight on top of something." The word for *"trouble"* is *tsarar* (צרר), which means "to be bound up"; it could also come from the root word *batsar* (בצר), meaning "a pruning." God is a refuge for us from those who seek to crush us or to hold us down, or from those who have us bound up in fear. The meaning of *sagav* (שׂגב), or *"refuge,"* does not only give a picture of God surrounding us and protecting us, but also of Him lifting us up and carrying us away from all the problems and stresses that have us bound.

Taken to a Height Above the Storm

I remember a time when I was on a plane, and the aircraft passed through a storm, so that we were buffeted about by strong turbulence. The pilot announced he would take the plane up a couple hundred feet. After that, we were flying above the storm. We had entered a place where it was calm and peaceful. When I looked out my window, I could still see the storm raging and the lightning flashing below us. This is what *sagav* (שׂגב) refers to; this is the shelter that David is speaking about. It is not a situation where we are going *through* a storm or being protected *in* it; rather, God is taking us to a new height where the storm cannot reach us.

As a shepherd—and probably afterward, even as king—David spent a lot of time looking up into the sky, especially viewing the stars and the planets in the evening hours. To him, those heights were the safest place that anyone could be. No one could touch you if you rose to such an altitude. Like David, we will sometimes face problems that have the potential of crushing us, thus provoking great fear that binds us up. At those times, perhaps we can sit back, as David did, and picture God taking us to a new height.

The promise in Psalm 9:9 is that when the storms of life threaten us, the Lord is our refuge; He makes us inaccessible to the storms. We may think we can find shelter in some natural haven, or in the "arm of flesh." But just as Jacques Lowe was mistaken when he thought he had found the safest place in the world for his photographs and negatives, we will soon realize that it is a mistake for us to trust in human strength. Even the vaults of the Chase Bank could not offer protection from life's turbulence and perils. The only real protection or shelter for us, as David knew, is in the arms of God, which simply lift us up and away from the storms of life, where we can rest in Him; from there, we can look down in peace from the height of His care even as the storms rage below us.

Study 2

Ravished: *Livabethini* (לבבתני)

"Thou hast ravished my heart, my sister, my spouse; thou hast ravished my heart with one of thine eyes, with one chain of thy neck."
—Song of Solomon 4:9

"Have you ever been in love? Horrible, isn't it? It makes you so vulnerable. It opens…your heart and it means someone can get inside you and mess you up."[1]
—Neil Gaiman

I once had a rabbi tell me that Song of Solomon is a very difficult book to read. The book is pure poetry, and, as such, it is very hard to find the right English words to match the emotion and power of the original Hebrew. Additionally, once we have been able to decipher the poetic song, our hearts will break over the revelation of how much God truly loves us and longs for us, and how we have so lightly treated His passion toward us.

Nearly every modern translation of Song of Solomon 4:9 puts a different spin on it. There is no literal translation for it, and no direct link to the English language. The French and Italian languages,

1. Neil Gaiman, *The Sandman, Volume 9: The Kindly Ones* (New York: DC Comics, 1996), part nine, 7.

which have a poetic nature to them, can do a much better job of rendering this passage than we can in the scientific and precise English language. But since English is really the only language that most of us reading this book know, here goes.

God Joins His Heart with Ours

Let us look at the words *"Thou hast ravished my heart."* This is one of the most beautiful—and, at the same time, one of the most heartbreaking—words that I have ever run across in my forty years of studying biblical Hebrew. You see, this phrase is only one word in Hebrew: *livabethini* (לבביני). It comes from the root word *levav* (לבב), which means "heart."

The first thing to understand is that this is one of the rare cases where the double beth (בב) is used. The ancient Jewish sages used to teach that the beth (ב) represents not only the home but also the heart. As the saying goes, "Home is where the heart is." A double beth (בב) represents God's heart and our hearts joined in a love relationship. It is a picture of two hearts opening up to each other and becoming equally vulnerable.

Do you want to understand God's heart? Consider your own heart, for it was created in His image. Is your heart not wounded when someone you care about simply ignores you? Do you not grieve when someone you look forward to being with calls five minutes before your scheduled time together and says, "Oh, sorry, I am too busy for you right now"? What do we do to God's heart when we ignore Him or are too busy to spend a moment in prayer?

Be Gentle with God's Heart

Extrabiblical literature uses the word *livabethini* (לבביני) to denote pulling the bark from a tree. I really did not understand this connection until my study partner looked up what it means to remove a tree's bark. We often think of trees as towering giants that are difficult to kill. You might be surprised to find out that removing bark can actually be harmful to a tree. Tree bark damage is not only unsightly, but it can also be deadly.

Essentially, the bark of a tree is its skin. The main function of the bark is to protect the phloem layer, which is like the human circulatory system. It brings the energy produced by the leaves to the rest of the tree.

I remember the times when I was a child and my friends and I would go the forest preserve and strip the bark off trees and playfully throw it at each other, never realizing that we were hurting those trees—wounding them and possibly killing them.

So, what is Solomon expressing when he says to his beloved, "*Livabethini*" (לבביני), or "*Thou hast ravished my heart*"? He is saying that with just one glance from his beloved, he has fallen hopelessly in love with her. She has stripped him of the hard shell that he had built around his heart to protect it, and he has made himself vulnerable. He is a king with the most powerful security force in the world surrounding him to protect him, yet one little peasant woman, with a mere look, has caused him to open his heart and say, "I am giving you the ability to break this heart. You have my heart in your hands—please be careful with it. There is no one to protect my heart from you; only you can protect it."

If we are the bride of Christ, and He is our Bridegroom, does it not follow that He is saying to us, "*Livabethini*" (לבביני), "You have ravished My heart"? If He is saying that, He is also indicating, "Although I am God, and although I may be to you a towering giant who seems invulnerable, I am stripping the bark off My tree; I am voluntarily making Myself vulnerable to you; I am giving you My heart. You have the ability to deeply wound My heart; no one but you can protect it, so please be gentle with My heart."

Study 3

Deep Things: *'Amaquth* (עמקות)

"He discovereth deep things out of darkness, and bringeth out to light the shadow of death."
—Job 12:22

My study partner has a friend who related a dream to us in which she was in the ocean, sinking down. Jesus came and took her hand and led her to the bottom of the sea. On the way down, a shark came along; Jesus put up His other hand, and the shark turned away. Then an eel appeared, and again Jesus held up His hand, and the eel turned away. Finally, they reached the bottom, and a light appeared, revealing a treasure chest filled with pearls and gold.

The friend indicated that God had given her Job 12:22 in relation to her dream. I found her dream to be a perfect illustration of this verse—as it reads in the original Hebrew. When I first read it in the King James Version, it created some questions in my mind.

God Will Reveal His Secrets

The first thing I questioned is why God had to "discover" something. Does He not already know everything? The word in Hebrew translated here as "*discovereth*" is *magalah* (מגלה). This word comes from one of two possible roots. It it either gimmel, lamed, lamed, forming *galal* (גלל), which means "to discover"; or it is gimmel, lamed, hei, forming *galah* (גלה), which is used to express the idea of revealing a secret. I believe the latter is more fitting to the context.

The term *"deep things"* is translated from the Hebrew word *amaquth* (עמקות), which also means "that which is unsearchable." Thus, God is revealing secret things that are unsearchable. The word for "*darkness*" is *chashak* (חשך). To understand this word, we need to know some linguistic history. About seven hundred years after the birth of Christ, a group of scribes* known as the Masoretes,* wanting to preserve the Hebrew language, added a system of dots and dashes to indicate vowels and grammatical usages. The Masoretes introduced two variations of the letter shin: שׁ and שׂ. The first shin, שׁ, has a dot on the right side of the letter. This indicates an "sh" sound, and it is called a "shin." The second shin, שׂ, has a dot on the left side of the letter. It makes an "s" sound (as in *sun*) and is called a "sine." It can also change the meaning of a word.

For the word *chashak* (חשׁך), the Masoretes put the dot over the shin on the right side. However, there are rabbis who argue that the dot should have been placed over the left side, making the letter a sine, and thus the word should be *chasak* (חשׂך), which means "that which is restrained." This would render the first part of Job 12:22 as follows: "God is revealing secret things that are unsearchable and that He has restrained." More than likely, the original Hebrew is a play on the two words for "darkness" and "restraining." In other passages, I believe it can and should be read both ways.

In the last part of this verse, we have the words *"and bringeth out to light the shadow of death."* The words *"shadow of death"* are translated from just one word in Hebrew, *tsalemaveth* (צלמות), which is considered by many translators to be a compound word. It is made up of *sal* (צל), from the root word *tsalal* (צלל), meaning "shadow," and *moth* (מות), meaning "death."

Keep in mind that the original Torah was written as one very long word. In fact, the sages teach that the Torah is just one word. In the original text, there was no separation between letters, and there were no vowels. In other words, if the English sentence "The cat ran home" were to be written in the style of ancient Hebrew, without spacing between the words and without vowels, it would appear like this: "thctrnhm." Without vowels and word separation, it appears almost impossible to read. Similarly, that is the reason for much of the ambiguity in Classical Hebrew, and why it is often difficult to translate ancient Classical Hebrew into a modern, precise language like English.

The Masoretes introduced a separation between letters to indicate individual words, and a separation to form verses and chapters, as well as dots and dashes to indicate vowels. My point is this: In the compound Hebrew word for *"shadow of death,"* the last letter, taw (ת), could easily be the first letter of the first word in the next sentence. That would put the verb in the next verse in the future tense, meaning "He will increase," or "He will make great," rather than *"He increaseth"* (Job 12:23), or "He is making great."

If we take that taw (ת) from *tsalemaveth* (צלמות), *"shadow of death,"* and put it in the next word, we are left with just one word, *tsalemav* (צלמו), rather than a compound word, *tsalemaveth* (צלמות). Thus, instead of *"shadow of death,"* we would have a word that means "that which is obscure," or "His secrets."

Abiding in His Light

Next, let's look at the word for "light," *ha'or* (לאור). This word has the preposition* *lamed* (ל) as a prefix,* and there is also an article attached. We should render the last part of this verse as "He brings His secrets to the light." The light does not go to His secrets; He brings His secrets to the light. If we abide in His light, He will bring His secrets and mysteries to us, similar to a waiter serving us dinner.

I find that there could be a secondary rendering** of this verse, so that it might read, "He reveals His secrets, which are unsearchable, from that which He has restrained, and will bring to the light His secrets."

The secrets and mysteries of God cannot be found by searching for them, because He has put them in "restraint." However, if we abide in His light, He will bring them to us and reveal them to us. To learn the secrets of God, therefore, we must abide in His light; or, as I like to say, we must abide in His heart.

When my study partner's friend mentioned that God had given her Job 12:22 in relation to her dream, my study partner replied that he thought God had also given her this verse as a way to describe meditation. That would make sense. To meditate is just to sit at God's table, resting in His light and letting Him serve you a meal of His secrets and mysteries.

Study 4

Love: *Chav* (חב), *Racham* (רחם)

"For God so loved the world, that he gave his only begotten Son, that whosoever believeth in him should not perish, but have everlasting life."
—John 3:16

"Then Peter, turning about, seeth the disciple whom Jesus loved following; which also leaned on his breast at supper, and said, Lord, which is he that betrayeth thee?"
—John 21:20

Most of us are familiar with the three words in Greek that express three levels of love: *agape* (unconditional love), *phileo* (brotherly love, friendship), and *eros* (erotic love). The Hebrew language also has several different words that are rendered as "love." There are basically four common words that are translated as various forms of love, although they also have other renderings: *'ahav* (אהב), "love"; *racham* (רחם), "tender mercies"; *dodi* (דודי), "beloved," as in spousal love; and *ra'ah* (רעה), "brotherly love," or "friendship."

It would be wrong to try to make a parallel between the Greek words for love and the Hebrew words for love. However, this does create a real problem for translators, because love is at the very root and center of Scripture. The Septuagint* uses the word *agape* for the Hebrew word *'ahav* (אהב). This is probably the closest word in the Hebrew to the meaning of *agape*, but it is far from a perfect match. I suppose we could say that *ra'ah* (רעה) is like *phileo*, since it is a word for friendship, and that *dodi* (דודי) could, in a certain context, be like *eros*. Yet these definitions would not be accurate because they are too limited. *'Ahav* (אהב) is used in cases where *agape* would not fit, and *ra'ah* (רעה), although rendered as "friendship," is also rendered as "shepherd" and "consuming passion" and was often used by David to express his love for God. Oddly, *ra'ah* (רעה) is also used for evil in the sense in which one has a consuming passion for something that is not of God (such as when people abuse drugs or alcohol). So, in many cases, it would be very inappropriate to consider *ra'ah* (רעה) as equivalent to *phileo*. Additionally, Solomon used the word *dodi* (דודי) with his beloved to express a sexual desire, but this word does not carry the lustfulness or self-gratification of *eros*.

The fourth Hebrew word for love mentioned above is *racham* (רחם), which is often expressed as a romantic love or rendered as "tender mercies." It is rarely used in the Old Testament, but it is frequently found in the Aramaic New Testament, where it has a similar spelling and sounds the same in Aramaic as it does in Hebrew.

Does God Have Favorites?

In the Greek New Testament, we find that the word used for "*love*" in "*God so loved the world*" (John 3:16) is *agape*. In the Peshitta—the Aramaic Bible—the word for love is *chav* (חב), which is similar to the Hebrew word *'ahav* (אבה) and means "love." However, in John 21:20, where we read about "*the disciple whom Jesus loved,*" the Greek again uses the word *agape*, but the Peshitta uses the Aramaic word *racham* (רחם), which is identical to the Hebrew *racham* (רחם).

Most Bible scholars today believe that Jesus and His disciples did not speak Greek but rather the Northern, or Old Galilean, dialect of Aramaic. Aramaic is very difficult to translate into another language. There is a growing school of thought that the original manuscripts of the Gospels were written in Aramaic and then translated into Greek about twenty years later. Even if the Gospels were originally written in Greek, the words of Jesus would still have needed to be translated from Aramaic into Greek. We have Aramaic manuscripts that date earlier than our earliest Greek manuscripts, which were lost around AD 300 (about the time of Constantine). If Jesus and His disciples used two different Aramaic words for love, then the writer and/or translator, putting the words into Greek, would have been stuck with only one possible word that would fit for both words, and that word would be *agape.*

So, again, when Jesus said, *"God so loved the world"* (John 3:16), He used the Aramaic word *chav* (חב), but when John wrote the phrase *"the disciple whom Jesus loved"* (John 21:20), he used the word *racham* (רחם). These are two entirely different words that both mean "love." Initially, the most logical conclusion from all this would be that we are dealing with two levels of love, and this would suggest that God either loved the world more than He loved this disciple, or that He loved this disciple more than He loved the world. In other words, we face the old dilemma of whether there are degrees to the love of God.

Is it true that God loves everyone—but has favorites? Did He love the patriarch Joseph more than He loves me, which is why Jospeh got to be prime minister of Egypt, and I am just a dusty old teacher? Did God love Moses more than He loved Miriam and Aaron, which is why He spoke face-to-face with Moses but not face-to-face with Moses' brother or sister?

Note that John 21:20 does not merely say *"the disciple whom Jesus loved"* but *"the disciple whom Jesus loved following."* In Greek and Aramaic, this phrase is more properly rendered as "the disciple whom Jesus loved who followed Him."

Loving and Being Loved

The key difference between *chav* (חב), as used in John 3:16 as God loving the world, and *racham* (רחם), as used in John 21:20 of the disciple whom Jesus loved, is that *chav* (חב) is a love that is not necessarily returned. *Chav* (חב) speaks of a love that flows from just one person and is not always completed. For love to be completed, it must be returned.

Racham (רחם) is a completed love. Love can be pretty lonely and painful if it is not returned. For example, a teenage girl can moon over some handsome rock star who doesn't even know she is alive, and she can feel depressed, sad, and brokenhearted; she can *chav* (חב) him. But if that rock star were to look into her eyes and say, "I love you," she would immediately be transported to cloud nine, where birds sing and flowers look beautiful again. Love can exist if it is not returned, but it cannot sing until it is shared.

When I was a pastor, I performed many weddings, and I was always delighted to watch *chav* (חב) turn into *racham* (רחם) as I spoke the words, "I now pronounce you husband and wife." At that moment, the reality sets in on the couple that they have now declared to the world that they love one other and are committing their lives to each other. With that declaration, they realize that they love and are being loved in return—*racham* (רחם).

You see, God loves the world, but the world does not love Him in return. It is when we love Him in return that His love is complete; it is when we love Him in return that He is able to rejoice over us with singing. (See Zephaniah 3:17.) Salvation is not just about getting saved and going to heaven. It is about completing the love that God has for us, bringing joy and celebration to *His* heart—which has been loving us for years.

Therefore, when we receive God's offer of salvation and turn to Him in love and say, "I love you," His love is made complete, and He rejoices. Why do the angels rejoice over one person who repents? (See Luke 15:7, 10.) The same reason you cry at a wedding. You are rejoicing over seeing the joy of two people (not just one) who have found each other in love and who share that love, returning it to each other. The angels rejoice for the same reason we read the works of Jane Austen, Elizabeth Barrett Browning, and Grace Livingston Hill—because we love a good romance where two people love each other!

It is not that God loves one person more than another. He loves all equally. It is just that very few people will love Him in return and complete His love, bring Him the joy of His love, awaken Him in that love, and cause Him to sing with joy in that love.

In my exploration of God's heart, I believe the most defining element I have discovered is not only a passion in God's heart to love, *chav* (חב), but also a longing to be loved in return, *racham* (רחם). You and I—humble, little, frail human beings—have the ability to bring joy to the heart of the God of the universe simply by saying to Him, wholeheartedly, "I love you."

Have you told Him today that you love Him? Is God's love for you just *chav* (חב)—one-sided? Or is it *racham* (רחם)—completed, shared? Do you want to bring to the all-mighty, all-powerful God a feeling of joy and make His day? Tell Him you love Him.

Study 5

A Hug: *Devek* (דבק)

"You shall fear the Lord *your God; you shall serve Him and cling to Him, and you shall swear by His name."*
—Deuteronomy 10:20 (NASB)

I would like to focus on just one word in the above verse: *"cling."* In the Hebrew, this word is *devek* (דבק). To render it as "to cling" is really to sell it short, since the idea is not like clinging to a rock or a tree during a storm so you do not get blown away. This word is an expression of love and respect—an embrace or a hug. In the context of this verse, I render the word as follows: "You shall fear the Lord your God; you shall serve Him, and you shall *hug* Him…."

The Gift of the Sabbath

Rabbinic literature teaches that a *devek* (דבק) is a high and deep stage of spiritual development in which the seeker attaches himself or herself to God and exchanges individuality for a profound partnership with Him. The force behind a *devek* (דבק) is a love of God and a desire for intimacy or closeness with Him. Is that or is that not the definition of a hug?

This would explain why many Orthodox Jews** view the requirements of the Sabbath as the *gift* of the Sabbath. The requirements are not a burdensome bother, filled with restrictions, but an opportunity to draw closer to God in order to enter into a *devek* (דבק) and receive a hug from Him. The "dos and don'ts" of the law are thus opportunities to connect with Him. This is why David said in Psalm 1:2, *"But his delight is in the law of the LORD; and in his law doth he meditate day and night."*

How could anyone get so excited about laws? The Orthodox Jews could because reading, studying, and meditating on the law of God was an opportunity to enter into a *devek* (דבק) and receive an embrace from God.

Why Do You Go to Church?

Consider the gift of the Sabbath. Why do you keep the Sabbath? Why do you go to church? Some people see it merely as a family or social obligation, or maybe as a way to win favor with God so they can receive some blessings, get some good luck, or secure a passport to heaven. But for others, observing the Sabbath is an opportunity to draw closer to God.

You cannot get to heaven by keeping the law. You can get to heaven only by receiving the finished work of Jesus Christ. The law, however, enables you to come to know this Jesus who is taking you to heaven. When you start to really know God and understand His heart, your love for Him grows; and when you love Him, you begin to desire a *devek* (דבק).

When reading Deuteronomy 10:20, therefore, we must take note that God is not calling us to cling to Him like a parasite or a leech. This thing is two-sided. God will cling to us if we will cling to Him. He will give us a hug if we will give Him a hug. The picture is that of two lovers embracing each other. *Devek* (דבק) is not a group hug. It is a hug between two individuals—you and God. When God embraces you, it is as if there is no other being in this universe but you. He gives you His full, complete attention in a *devek* (דבק).

God does not live within time. He does not know the barriers of the past or the future. Thus, He can move back and forth through time as easily as we walk through air. He can spend each second and moment with you, and then just move through time and spend each second and moment with me. I believe that is how He is omnipresent. You have His complete and full attention every second of your life. He has nothing else to do but stand in front of you with His arms open wide, waiting for you to step into those arms so He can give you a *devek* (דבק), or a hug.

We usually come to God with a handful of "give me's." Yet if you wanted to protect the heart of the person you love most, the easiest thing to do would be to give that person a hug. Similarly, to protect the heart of the God whom you love, you need to take a little time to enter into a *devek* (דבק) and allow Him to give you a hug, and then give Him a hug in return.

Fear the Lord, serve the Lord, and—while you are at it—give Him a *devek* (דבק).

Study 6

Rest: *Shabbat* (שׁבת)

"So the people rested on the seventh day."
—Exodus 16:30

When I was a pastor, it was not unusual for me to hear a delinquent member of my congregation say, "Well, my New Year's resolution is to honor the Sabbath day." What they meant is that they resolved to attend church every Sunday. That is a good resolution, but there is more to honoring the Sabbath than just attending church. I would like to examine the Hebrew word for "Sabbath"—*Shabbat* (שׁבת)—and see if there are any suggestions that could enhance our efforts to honor this special day of the week. We will be taking a journey through the Hebrew alphabet,** where we will explore the word *Sabbath* in its Semitic root** form and see how it is related to similar words in the Hebrew.

What Does It Mean to "Rest"?

God had commanded His people to *"rest"* on the seventh day. (See Exodus 16:23.) The phrase *"so the people rested"* in Exodus 16:30 is translated from the Hebrew word *yisheveth* (וישבתו). It is from the root word *Shabbat* (שׁבת), which means "to rest" and "to cease." We learn in Genesis 2:2 that God Himself *rested* on the seventh day.

(I mean, all that creating things into being must have worn poor God out! Surely, He needed a *rest*—I know I certainly would have.) Actually, the English rendering for the word *Shabbat* (שׁבת) as *"rest"* can be a little misleading. It does not mean to rest in order to regain your strength; it means to *cease* from your activity, or to interrupt your normal activity to accomplish something.

This leads to an important question: What are we to accomplish on the Sabbath? As *yisheveth* (ישׁבתו) is used here in Exodus, we have a sort of play on words*** with *yashev* (ישׁב), which means "to dwell" or "to sit down." *Shabbat* (שׁבת) is also related to the word *bashavathu* (בשׁבתו), which means "to bond." Thus, this time of *resting* is meant for *bonding with God*. You don't bond with God by worrying or fretting over the pressures and problems of the past week. You bond with Him, for example, by exploring the Hebrew alphabet and discovering the riches of His heart and mind.

The word *Shabbat* (שׁבת) is spelled shin (שׁ), beth (ב), taw (ת). (Keep in mind that Hebrew reads from right to left.) In the ancient Hebrew language, every word is built upon a three-letter root word. Some words are interrelated when they share the same first two letters. In this case, the first two letters of *Shabbat* (שׁבת), are shin (שׁ) and beth (ב). I believe that all the other words that start with shin (שׁ) beth (ב) relate in some way to the shin (שׁ), beth (ב), taw (ת) of *Shabbat* (שׁבת), or "rest."

Am I just sermonizing and reading into the text, or did God really have such a divine plan with the Hebrew language? Let us take a journey through the Hebrew alphabet to see if all the other shin (שׁ) beth (ב) words are related. As we journey, I will let you be the judge. Colossians 3:15 tells us to let the peace of God rule our hearts. In the Greek, the word for *"rule"* is *brabeueto*, which means "to umpire." You do not need an umpire to call the obvious plays; you need an umpire when there is a question or a dispute, such as whether a ball player is safe or out during a play. So, I will throw this claim out there and just leave it to you. If you find a peace in your heart that all these words are related, perhaps God is prompting you with a little extra insight to keep in mind when you seek to honor the Sabbath day.

Twelve Ways to Celebrate the Sabbath

In addition to *Shabbat*, there are twelve words in Hebrew that begin with shin (ש) beth (ב). Accordingly, we are to take one day a week and *rest* or *cease* from our normal activities in order to do twelve things. When you celebrate the Sabbath next Sunday or Saturday or whichever day you consider to be the seventh day, remember the twelve other shin beth (שב) words that tell you what you are to do or what God wishes to accomplish with you on this seventh day when you cease from your normal activity.

Here are the other twelve words that begin with shin beth (שב):

1. Shin beth (שב), aleph (א) = *shava'* (שבא): "God's passion." The first letter of the alphabet is aleph (א) and represents God. Shin (ש), beth (ב), aleph (א), or *shava'* (שבא), refers to God's passionate love. The first thing you are to do on this day of rest is to just sit back and let God love you, enjoying His passionate love.

2. Shin beth (שב), beth (ב) = *shavav* (שבב): "Kindle a fire." The next thing that should follow on the Sabbath is *shavav* (שבב), which is to allow this passionate love of God to kindle in you a fire of love and affection that you can return to Him.

3. Shin beth (שב), hei (ה) = *shavah* (שבה): "To take as captive." When you and God express love to each other, He will take you as His personal "captive." *Shavah* (שבה) is the same word used when a groom comes for his bride, takes her from her father's house, and carries her to his father's house to make her his bride and to enter into intimacy with her. So, the next thing God wants to do after He has expressed His love to you, and you have expressed your love to Him, is to *shavah* (שבה), or to take you away as a bride to His bridal chamber to spend a time of intimacy with you.

4. Shin beth (שב), chet (ח) = *shavach* (שבח): "To soothe, calm, relax." When God takes you away as His bride, the first thing He will do is what a bridegroom will do for his new bride—he will seek to make her comfortable and relaxed, to assure her that everything is all right, that he will make certain nothing will happen that will shame

her or harm her. During this time with God, you will become *shavach* (שׁבח); the pressures and stresses of the prior six days will settle down and be soothed, and you will find your frayed nerves being calmed.

5. Shin beth (שׁב), teth (ט) = *shavat* (שׁבט): "To measure." Once you are in the bridal chamber, God will measure you. He will lovingly gaze upon you as a husband would gaze upon his bride and measure her beauty. Then he will softly, quietly, whisper to her that she is beautiful. This is the moment when God reminds you that through the sacrificial death of His Son Jesus Christ, all your iniquities and sins have been cleansed, and He has made something beautiful out of you.

6. Shin beth (שׁב), kap (כ) = *shavak* (שׁבכ): "To mingle, interweave, have intercourse." After a time of just enjoying your beauty as His bride, God will then share a more passionate intimacy with you.

7. Shin beth (שׁב), lamed (ל) = *shaval* (שׁבל): "To grow." During this time of intimacy, God and you will grow closer together, more in love and more passionate with each other.

8. Shin beth (שׁב), mem (מ) = *shavam* (שׁבמ): "To share hidden secrets and hidden knowledge." When two lovers are being intimate, speaking lovingly to each other, they cannot help but share their deepest secrets. They will share things that they would express to no one else. Thus, during this Sabbath rest, God will share the secrets of His heart with you as His bride, as you share the secrets of your heart with Him as your Bridegroom.

9. Shin beth (שׁב), nun (נ) = *shavan* (שׁבן): "To be tender and delicate." (The word *shavan* (שׁבן) uses the final form** of the letter nun.) During this time of intimacy, having trusted each other with the deep secrets of your hearts, you enter a period of just sharing intimate words with each other. This will be a time when God speaks tenderly to you as His bride. He will speak of love. He will call you His dearest, His most precious, His treasure, and other gentle, loving, sweet names.

10. Shin beth (שׁב), ayin (ע) = *shava'* (שׁבע): "To become satisfied, fulfilled." After a time in which God and you share love, intimacy,

and the secrets of your hearts, you, as His bride, will feel a great, overwhelming sense of satisfaction and fulfillment.

11. Shin beth (שׁב), sade (צ) = *shavats* (שׁבצ): "To weave or intermingle together to create something beautiful." During this time of intimacy, God as Bridegroom and you as His bride will intermingle together, will weave together, to create something beautiful from your relationship.

12. Shin beth (שׁב), resh (ר) = *shavar* (שׁבר): "To examine in order to make pure." As the Sabbath concludes, and God has cleansed you, shared His secrets with you, and made you an intimate part of Him, He will then do a final examination of you as His bride and declare that you are indeed pure and holy before Him.

Thus, as you consider your observance of the Sabbath, perhaps you sense a peace in your heart that *Shabbat* (שׁבּת) should be a time of intimacy with God, of growing closer to the One who loves you. Perhaps you will take another trip through the Hebrew alphabet and let God tell you what you mean to Him, and tell Him what He means to you.

Study 7

Awaken: *Quts* (קוץ)

"As for me, I will behold thy face in righteousness: I shall be satisfied, when I awake, with thy likeness."
—Psalm 17:15

There is a quite a bit of dispute over the syntax* of this verse. You can easily see this if you compare how it is rendered in our modern translations. Some say, as the King James Version indicates, that David will be satisfied to *bear* the likeness of God, and others say that David will be satisfied to *see* the likeness of God. Literally, the Hebrew reads, "I will be satisfied in an awakening of your likeness," which could go both ways.

What Was David Saying?

I believe there are two keys to identifying the proper syntax. The first is that there is no conjunction* separating the two thoughts: *"I will behold thy face in righteousness"* and *"I shall be satisfied."* That does not mesh with David's usual style of writing, but this psalm is specifically attributed to David, so there had to be a good reason why he left out the conjunction. The word for "awakening" in Hebrew is *quts* (קוץ). This could be an awakening from sleep or from death. Without the conjunction, David could only be referring to an awakening from death, which would be in keeping with his poetic style. The first thought indicates his state in life, and the second indicates his state in the afterlife. Hence, he did not use a conjunction.

More telling is the verbal use of *quts* (קוץ). This is found as a hiphal* verbal form in an infinitive* construct state. The infinitive construct is the most likely reason why many translators render this as David *seeing* God's likeness rather than *being in* His likeness, because the pronominal* ending would indicate the subject under the infinitive construct. Did you follow all that? No? How about if I just say that this could be rendered as: "I will be satisfied in awakening to your likeness"?

David is saying that while he is alive on earth, he will *behold God's face*. The Hebrew word for "*face*" is *pani* (פני), which is often rendered as "God's presence." The word for "*behold*" has two possible roots. If we say the root is *chazah* (חזה), which means "to see" or "to perceive," we would have to render *pani* (פני) as "face"—thus saying that David is actually seeing the face of God. However, if we say that the root is *'achaz* (אחז), which means "to seize" or "to grab hold of," we would then more correctly render *pani* (פני) as "presence," which would make more sense. Rather than David seeing the face of God, he is seizing or holding on to the presence of God.

That is why I can relate to the following rendering much more easily: "As for me, while I live on this earth, I am going to hold on to the presence of God. When I awake into heaven, I will be satisfied to see His likeness," or "to see Him face-to-face." The word for "*satisfied*" in Hebrew is *sava* (שבע), which is also the word for "seven" and for "complete filling" or "completeness." Thus, in heaven, we will be made complete, or be completely filled—not only by experiencing God's presence but also by actually seeing Him.

Awakening to See Jesus Face-to-Face

I have read stories from people who said that Jesus appeared to them and sat down and spoke with them. Whether these stories are true is not for me to say. I can only say that as I surfed the Internet and ran across these stories and read people's testimonies, I found myself filled with jealousy. Or maybe what I was feeling was not jealousy, but rather a longing to have Jesus appear to me so we could sit down together and talk. I find myself getting angry with these people who seem to easily sit back and tell of their experience with Jesus. I feel like shouting at them, "How dare you talk about such an experience to a starving person!" My listening to someone describe being transported to heaven and meeting Jesus, or how Jesus walked into their bedroom and had a chat with them, is the equivalent of sitting across from someone who is eating a steak dinner and commenting on how juicy and tender each bite is while I chew on a thin celery stick. I feel like saying, "Fine, eat your steak, but keep your comments to yourself!" Then I find myself getting angry with God and asking Him, "Why do You appear to people who seem to barely open up Your Word and who don't hunger and seek after You, but You never walk into my bedroom?"

I guess that is why I must translate Psalm 17:5 as I do. For me, I will embrace God's presence with all my heart, knowing that one day soon I will awake and see Him; then I will sit down with Him and have that long chat. And it will be far greater than what was experienced by those testimony-givers who had divine visitations on earth. In each case, Jesus appeared to them but eventually left; it was a temporary visitation. But when that day comes, and I see Him face-to-face, it won't be merely a vision, and Jesus will not leave the room after a little while. I will see Him and *will continue to see Him for eternity.* I will be *"satisfied,"* complete.

In the meantime, there is one thing I can control. I can continue my journey to the heart of God. Even if Jesus did appear to me in a dream or in a vision, that would not necessarily mean I knew His heart. I don't believe David ever had a vision of Jesus, but he knew that one day he would awake and see Him for eternity. He had something even more exciting than a vision of Jesus—he knew and understood His heart.

Study 8

Song: *Shur* (שׁוּר)

"A Song or Psalm for the sons of Korah, to the chief Musician upon Mahalath Leannoth, Maschil of Heman the Ezrahite."
—Introduction to Psalm 88; verse 1 in the Hebrew text

I often challenge my Hebrew students to choose any passage in the Old Testament to study, no matter how unlikely it is that they will find some spiritual value in it. I guarantee that by the end of the class, they will find a deep, hidden spiritual truth there. However, the above is one portion of the Hebrew Scriptures by which I was almost proven wrong.

Nearly every Bible reader wonders about the strange words in the headings of some of the psalms but soon shrugs them off as archaic musical connotations and moves on. But wait a minute. This is the Word of God. Every letter, word, and sentence comes from God for a reason, so there must be a reason for such introductions.

"Do Not Open Until in Despair"

I read Psalm 88 many times but could never understand what redeeming value it had, because it is so filled with despair. Yet Psalm 88 is like a little gift package that is labeled, "Do not open until you are *really* in despair."

If you should find yourself in deep despair over spiritual warfare that you have been battling, and you are telling God that you are tired of being a good soldier, of trying to move forward, of fasting and spending hours studying the Word, of praying constantly but seeing very few results, and that you are ready to crawl under "yon rock from whence you came," you may want to spend some time studying this psalm. You may find that you relate to the writer's disappointment, despair, and suffering.

Psalm 88 was written by a man who cried out to God but heard no reply. It ends with this statement: *"Lover and friend hast thou put far from me, and mine acquaintance into darkness"* (verse 18). This is not a happy ending. I heard some preacher say that every psalm may begin with despair, but it ends in joy. Yet that is not the case with this psalm. One can really question why it is in the Bible in the first place, as it offers no hope or encouragement. It is the cry of a man who has spent a lifetime praying but has never received an answer to his prayer.

Yet the introduction to this psalm seems to provide the answer to his cries. In our English Bibles, this heading is not given the dignity of being called verse 1. In the Hebrew Bible, however, there is no separation between it and the words of the first verse. As part of the inspired Word of God, I consider it to be verse 1. It's important not to skip over it and miss what it has to say to us.

The first thing we learn is that this portion of Scripture is both a song and a psalm. The conjunction "or" between "Song" and "Psalm," as given in the King James Version, is not in the original. The word for "Song" in Hebrew is *shur* (שׁור), which means "song," and the root word in Hebrew for "Psalm" is *zamar* (זמר), which also means "song." Yet *shur* (שׁור) is a song of peace, joy, and celebration of the power of God, while *zamar* (זמר) is a song of praise that comes when one is being pruned or tried by God.

Another fact we can note is that Psalm 88 was written by a man named Heman the Ezrahite. We are not sure if this is the Heman the Ezrahite that we read about in 1 Kings 4:31, whose wisdom was almost on par with that of Solomon's. The experience of the Heman in this psalm does not fit the profile of any other Heman in Scripture. Names in Jewish literature tend to be more descriptive than identity-based, as they are in our culture. This may be a Heman the Ezrahite that is not mentioned anywhere else in Scripture. However, in Jewish literature, I have found a description of a Heman that does fit the profile of the Heman of Psalm 88. Jewish literature and tradition teach that this Heman was a gifted musician and vocalist—but he was also a leper. From reading the psalm, we learn that he developed leprosy as a young man, such that he never knew the joy of playing with friends, or the touch of a woman, or the satisfaction of sharing his talents before a congregation. Instead, he was doomed to a life of solitude, of living in poverty, and of being shunned by all.

Yet this psalm was written in praise to God, and then it was given to the sons of Korah, who made up the temple choir, and to the chief musician. It says it was given upon *mahalath* (מחלת), which some say is a musical instrument. No English translation is provided for *mahalath* (מחלת), and it is uncertain if the root word is *chalah* (חלה), which means "to be exhausted," "to be diseased," "to be weak," "to be feeble," or "to be afflicted," or if it comes from the root word *chul* (חול), which means "to be in pain," "to tremble," or "to shake." Either way, it was given in great distress to the choir and to its director.

The next word is *leannoth* (לענות), which comes from the root word *'anah* (ענה) and means "to be humbled by affliction." This word is in a *piel** infinitive form and suggests this rendering: "He has been humbled like no other man." The following word is *maschil* (משׂכיל), which comes from the root word *sakal* (שׂכל) and means "to prosper" or "to understand." This word is in hiphil participle* form, so we could render it as "He has caused him to understand," or "He has caused him to prosper."

Knowing God's Heart

Here, then, is the picture we see in this psalm. Heman is a diseased, broken, poverty-stricken beggar. He has called out to God all his life to be healed of his leprosy, but he has not been healed. Nevertheless,

God has still done a wonderful work of healing in him. He has healed his soul. Although God gave him a beautiful voice, Heman was not allowed to sing in the temple because of his affliction. However, he could sing on the street corner; and, if Jewish literature is correct, that is what he did. He stood on the street corner, a dying, broken, poverty-stricken man, never having known the love of a woman, the joy of having children, or times of celebration with friends. But he had God, with whom he could share the deep hurt of his heart in complete humility. His pure honesty opened God's heart, so that He gave Heman the understanding that his suffering had brought him to the point of humility so that he could know God's heart.

Heman is still singing on that street corner today. Do you hear him? I do. I hear him singing a joyful song of praise and worship. I even see him nod at me, as if to say, "You think you have it rough? Check me out, and yet I still praise and worship God. So, what's wrong with you?"

Nothing, Heman, nothing is wrong with me, except that I have neglected to worship and praise my God.

Study 9

Heart: *Levav* (לבב)

"Keep thy heart with all diligence;
for out of it are the issues of life."
—Proverbs 4:23

If anyone understood the conflicting nature of the human heart, it was Solomon. The wisest man who ever lived did some pretty foolish things when it came to matters of the heart. He must have been an old man when he wrote the above verse, for he was obviously writing out of his own personal experience.

What Is the Heart?

To study this verse, we first need to understand just what the heart is. The word used here is *levav* (לבב), which is the most common Hebrew word for "heart." It can refer to the physical heart or to many other things, such as thought, reasoning, judgment, will, design, affection, love, anger, hatred, courage, fear, joy, sorrow, and life. What do all these things have in common? They all determine our behavior, the direction in which we go, and the choices that we make. If we give our heart to God, what are we doing? We are giving Him complete control over all the decisions we make and all the directions we take in life. His thoughts become our thoughts, His reasoning becomes our reasoning, His will our will, His judgments our judgments—and so forth. To truly give God our heart, we must know and understand His heart. That is why Solomon exhorts us to keep our heart with all diligence; for if our heart belongs to God, to abuse it would be to abuse something that belongs to Him.

The Hebrew word for *"keep"* is *shamar* (שׁמר), and the word for *"diligence"* is *netsor* (נצר). Both mean "to keep" or "to watch over," but they come at it from different angles. *Shamar* (שׁמר) means to keep watch as in "to guard" or "to beware," while *netsor* (נצר) means to keep watch as in "to guard and conceal" in order to scrutinize. So, Solomon is telling us that the part of us that reasons, makes choices, feels love, fear, hatred, passion, and so on, is to be carefully watched over in order to keep us from making foolish choices.

Join Your Heart with God's Heart

How do we keep from making foolish choices? By scrutinizing our hearts. How do we scrutinize our hearts? The Word itself tells us. The word for *"diligence," netsor* (נצר), is spelled nun (נ), sade (צ), resh (ר). Nun (נ) represents faith, sade (צ) speaks of humility, and resh (ר) signifies the Holy Spirit. By faith, we humble ourselves to the will of the Holy Spirit. When we give our hearts to God, He unites them with His.

A devoted husband seeks to scrutinize his wife's heart because if he breaks her heart, his heart will break also. If he brings her sadness, he will be sad; if he brings her joy, he will be joyful. Yes, there is self-interest in pleasing the one we love, but it is not *selfishness*, for we have joined our hearts with that person. Selfishness involves a heart separated from that of another. Thus, when a husband scrutinizes his wife's heart, he is protecting his own heart as well as hers.

Therefore, when a husband joins his heart with his wife's, he will feel her joy and her sorrow. So, too, when we join our hearts with God's heart, we will feel His joy and His sorrow. To scrutinize our hearts will be to scrutinize God's heart. To protect God's heart will be to protect our hearts.

"For out of [the heart] *are the issues of life."* That phrase is a tough one to translate. The Hebrew word for *"issues"* is *yasta'* (יצא), which conveys the idea of "seasons," particularly springtime, since spring is often viewed as a period of new life. You could almost say, "For out of the heart come the seasons of life." Wherever we allow our heart to move will determine if the season is winter or spring. If our hearts are united with God's, it will always be spring.

Still, we must remember that if our hearts are united with God's, not only are we joyful when He is joyful, but we are sad when He is sad. Consequently, as we draw closer to God, we may find that we are filled with a sense of sadness. This might not make sense to us, because we tend to believe that the closer we move toward God, the more joy and peace we should feel. Yet if there is something in our heart that displeases God, should we not feel His displeasure? And if He is sorrowful over people's injustice or pain, should we not feel His sorrow?

We tend to forget that we are in an ongoing relationship with God. And, as in all relationships, there are times of both joy and sadness. If we follow the advice of Solomon and *shamar* (שׁמר), or *"keep,"* our hearts with *netsor* (נצר), *"diligence,"* our hearts will begin to unite with God's. Our hearts will not always be joyful, nor will they always be sad, but they will be closer to God's own heart.

Study 10

Worship: *Shachah* (שׁחה)

"For thou shalt worship no other god: for the Lord, whose name is Jealous, is a jealous God."
—Exodus 34:14

There are only three words in Hebrew for the concept of "worship." One is *'atsab* (עצב), which is used just once in Scripture for worship and conveys the idea of sorrow. Another is *'abad* (עבד), which means "service" and is sometimes used for "worshipper." However, when all is said and done, there is only one word in Hebrew for worship, and that is *shachah*, which simply means "to bow down" or "to fall prostrate" (at least that is what your lexicon will tell you). *Shachah* is the word used in the above verse.

There is not too much more we can glean from *shachah* (שחה) except to view how it is applied in Scripture, where we see it used as paying homage—either to God or to someone or something else. This verse from Exodus suggests that bowing down to another god makes God jealous. So, there must be something pretty bad about bowing down before some other god. We can assume that such an act means to give of yourself and your devotion to—as well as to depend upon—the one to whom you bow. In the past month, I have attended many worship services but have not once seen someone bow to God. In fact, the posture is usually the opposite, with everyone standing with arms outstretched. I rarely see *shachah* (שׁחה) in worship services.

What Is Worship?

Worship is such an important word in our Christian vocabulary, but we apparently have very little insight into the dynamics of what worship really is. We appear to be doing what seems to work or what tradition tells us worship is. In high-church services, worship is the recitation of liturgical traditions. In mainline churches, it is an order of service that lasts about an hour. In Pentecostal or full-gospel circles, it is the lifting of one's hands and the singing of choruses about love and mercy. Yet the word *shachah* (שׁחה), or "worship," means *to bow down or to prostrate yourself before God.* In essence, it has nothing to do with music or with uplifted hands; in fact, it really has nothing to do with praise and thanksgiving, since these are just manifestations of worship.

The Hebrew sages chose a particular combination of letters to express the most intimate aspect of our relationship with God. The word *shachah* (שׁחה) is spelled shin (שׁ), chet (ח), hei (ה)—at least, the Masorites spelled it with a shin (שׁ). Some Jewish scholars will argue that it should be a sine (שׂ). As I mentioned in a previous study, a shin (שׁ) is identified by a dot on the right side of the letter, while a sine (שׂ) has a dot on the left side of the letter. In the original Hebrew text, there were no dots at all; they were added later for clarity and pronunciation. If *shachah* were spelled with a sine (שׂ), the word would mean "to swim" or "to have an overflow." Nevertheless, both shin (שׁ) and sine (שׂ) represent *wholeness*, *completeness*, and *nearness to God.*

The next letter in *shachah* (שׁחה) is chet (ח). Traditionally, the chet (ח) represents *an intimate joining of man to God.* If we assume that the first letter is a sine (שׂ) rather than a shin (שׁ), we can see how worship is pictured as "swimming." When you swim, you are surrounded by water. You can worship while reading Scripture by yourself, while studying the Word of God with other believers, while singing, or while sitting quietly before God. Any time God has your full attention, He can surround you with His presence and His love, just as water surrounds you when you are swimming.

Moreover, if you were to put shin (ש) and chet (ח) together, you would find that the word expresses *worship*. The final letter in the word *shachah* (שחה) is hei (ה). The hei (ה) speaks of the breath of God, of the presence of God, and of God's feminine nature. Hence, worship is any act that joins man with God into a completeness surrounded by the presence of the Spirit of God.

A Sacred Trust

When I was in graduate school, I studied the ancient Ugaritic* language. This language was rediscovered in 1928 and, next to the Dead Sea Scrolls,* has been the single most important tool for Hebrew scholars in clarifying biblical Hebrew texts. It was written in the cuneiform abtar** system, yet its grammar and style is clearly Hebraic and is to Classical Hebrew what the Anglo-Saxon language is to our modern English language.

During my time as a graduate student, there were only about five thousand people in the world who actually studied the Ugaritic language. I know this because we had to get our textbooks from the Vatican, and I was told they printed only five thousand copies. This textbook had a paper cover, with the pages attached by strings. I remember translating a poem about a goddess who fell in love with a mortal man and had an intimate relationship with him. The word used to describe this relationship was a form of the word *shachah* (שחה), which became in the Hebrew language the word used for worship. The ancient concept of *shachah* (שחה) is that of a god sharing his or her passion with a human being, and the human sharing his or her passion with the god. Perhaps a good definition of worship would be God sharing His passion with us as we share our passion with Him.

When two lovers share their passion with each other, the very nature of such sharing declares they have an exclusive relationship with one another that they do not have with anyone else. They have given their hearts to each other. To share such passion with anyone else would violate a sacred trust built into that relationship.

This is why God *"is a jealous God,"* and His *"name is Jealous."* If you give your heart to Him, He will give His heart to you. When you give your heart away to someone, you make yourself very vulnerable. You have given that person the power to abuse your heart and even to break it. When God gives us His heart, He entrusts us with a lot of power. He gives us the power to abuse and break His heart. We Christians have a tendency to be very careless with the heart God has entrusted to us. Yet it would seem that, according to Exodus 34:14, that heart is easily broken.

Study 11

God Sows: *Jezreel* (יזרעאל)

"And the earth shall hear the corn, and the wine, and the oil; and they shall hear Jezreel."
—Hosea 2:22

If there is any chapter in the Bible that expresses the heart of God, it is Hosea 2. There we have a picture of the prophet Hosea, who was married to an unfaithful woman and yet deeply loved her. He longed for her to return—not just to fulfill her duties as a wife and a mother, but also to reenter a love relationship with him. God had called Hosea to marry this unfaithful woman, and He had put a deep love in Hosea's heart for her so that he could prophesy about God's love for us.

How often we give our heart to God and then chase after other gods, such as money, a career, or earthly pleasures. When we do this, we are much like Hosea's wife in our relationship with God. Yet in Hosea 2, we see the deep love of God; we see His longing and desire for His people to return to Him—not just to call Him *baali* (בעלי), meaning "my master," but to call Him *'ishi* (אשי), meaning "my husband."

Prosperity, Joy, and Healing

What's interesting is that, in the midst of a declaration by God in which He speaks of betrothing us to Him again as a young love, He talks about the earth hearing the corn, the wine, and the oil, and then hearing from *Jezreel* (יזרעאל). Talk about throwing a bucket of water on a hot romance! In the midst of declaring His love, God starts to talk about agriculture.

But the motif* of agriculture gives us a wonderful poetic expression, because there is a double meaning in it. *"Corn"* is symbolic of prosperity. *"Wine"* often represents joy. And when God speaks of *"the oil,"* He uses a unique word in the Hebrew, *yastar* (יצר), which refers to a pure, shining oil, an anointing oil. It is not the oil used in ceremonies but a pure essential oil used to anoint a wound.

Here God shows us that His heart has been deeply wounded by our unfaithfulness; yet He is saying that not only will He restore us to our former prosperous position with Him and to our joy in Him, but He will also *heal us.* When we wander away from God, we also suffer a wounded heart due to our sinfulness. And rather than thinking of His own hurt, God is thinking of the hurt we feel when we have been wounded. We can see a picture of this by looking at the prophet Hosea. He has been deeply hurt by his wife's unfaithfulness. He has a broken heart, and as he says these words of Hosea 2:2 to express the heart of God, he is also expressing his own heart toward his wife. To this woman who has brought him so much pain and heartbreak, Hosea is thinking only of the hurt she must have experienced, and he longs to heal that hurt.

God Will Do the Planting

Then God says that we will *"hear Jezreel." Jezreel* (יזרעאל) means "God sows." That image is fitting for this poetic expression in which God uses an agricultural motif to express His desire to restore us. But by using the word *Jezreel* (יזרעאל), He is saying that He, and no one else—especially not those phony gods we pursue—will be the One to give us prosperity, joy, and healing. It won't be our money-market accounts, our jobs, or our material possessions that provide us with these things. We will find them all in Him, for He will do the planting.

There is also a secondary meaning in the use of *Jezreel* (יזרעאל). Jezreel was the place where Gideon defeated the Midianites and where Saul defeated the Philistines; and it was in Jezreel that Jehu ordered the wicked Queen Jezebel to be tossed out of her window to her death. Jezreel is a picture of victory and of deliverance from our enemies, as well as from idolatry. God will restore our victory over all the phony gods that we pursue, and we will find our complete and total joy in Him.

But note that this passage is not saying this will necessarily happen; it is only expressing the heart of God toward us. Often, when we find ourselves in a weak moment, we give in to sin and blow it. Then we come crawling back to God, thinking He must be very angry with us, and expecting Him to really take the whip to us. So, we bravely face the music and wait for Him to punish us. That is what we think because that is what we would do in our fallen human nature. But if we can just catch a glimpse of the heart of God as shown in Hosea 2, we will find that even when we are in our worst, most backslidden condition, He longs to restore us to His prosperity and His joy. He wishes only to heal our wounds and to forever remove our false gods from us.

Study 12

Anger: *'Aneph* (אנף)

"And the Lord *was angry with Solomon,*
because his heart was turned from the Lord *God of Israel,*
which had appeared unto him twice."
—1 Kings 11:9

Every modern translation I read uses the word *angry* in the above passage. Well, you can't blame God for being angry with King Solomon after Solomon pulled the stunts he did. God gave him vast wisdom, wealth, and power, and all He asked of Solomon in return was to keep a few commandments. But what did Solomon do? He went out and married foreign women who persuaded him to build shrines on Mount Olivet for their gods Milcom and Chemosh.

The Septuagint indicates that these idols were built to "Milcom," but in the unpointed text,[2] the word used is *mlk* (מלך), which could refer to *melek*, a king, or to Moloch, the notorious false god who demanded human sacrifice. Even if it is not a reference to Moloch, there were occasions when the god Chemosh demanded human sacrifice. Regardless, having shrines to either god planted the seeds that led the people to actually offer child sacrifices toward the end of the kingdom period, even though prophets such as Micah condemned

2. See the entry for "vowel pointings" in the Glossary.

this terrible practice in God's name. (See Micah 6:7.) The people were desperate, and because of the pagan influence of these other religions on the Hebrew faith, they felt that if they sacrificed their own children to God, He would reward them with His favor. They could not understand what the prophets were teaching: God wanted their faith and their obedience, not their erroneous sacrifices—especially not human sacrifices.

A Heart Turned Away from the Lord

Notice what our study text gives as the reason for God's anger: Solomon's heart was *turned* from God. Solomon had started out with a heart toward God, and God had appeared to him and told him he could ask for anything he wanted, and it would be given to him. Solomon did not ask for wealth or power, but rather for wisdom to lead the people properly. God appeared a second time to Solomon at the dedication of the temple, even though by that time, Solomon was beginning to fall into sin. History refers to this temple as *Solomon's Temple* and not as *God's Temple*, because Solomon did not build the temple entirely according to God's will. He built it on the backs of slaves, financed through heavy taxation; moreover, he used bronze where he should have used gold, and gold where he should have used silver. The temple was more of a monument to himself than it was to God, yet God appeared and declared that His presence would reside in the temple as long as the people followed certain rules—which they didn't.

An Angry, Irrational God?

So, now we arrive at the point where Solomon has pushed God too far, and God is angry with him. I don't know about you, but God's response sort of frightens me. I mean, if God is capable of anger, it is possible that I could make Him angry. I know from having been in ministry for many years as a pastor and a teacher that I sometimes say and do things that make people angry, even though I certainly never intend for that to happen. I wonder just how far we can push God before He finally responds with fire and brimstone.

An earlier passage, Exodus 32:7–14, indicates that God flew into a rage because His people were worshipping a golden calf, and He declared to Moses that He would destroy the people and begin again by making a great nation out of him. It appears that Moses had to jump into the fray and calm God down, saying in effect, "God, You're upset. You don't know what You're saying. Here, sit down, relax, have a piece of my bagel, and think about what You're doing. What would Egypt say? What would the world say?" It seems that God finally cooled down and said, in effect, "Moses, when you're right, you're right. I don't know what came over Me. I won't destroy them." At least, that is the way it sounds in our English translations. When you read that passage in English, you almost cannot help but get a picture of an irrational God who flies off the handle because people are paying their respects to another god.

"The Lord's Heart Was Broken"

Let's see if we can gain a clearer picture of what was happening by examining the Hebrew word translated *"anger"* in both our study verse and the passage from Exodus, but focusing on our text about Solomon. That word for *"anger"* is *'aneph* (אנף), which is found in a hithpael* (reflexive) perfect (past) form. It is interesting to note that there is a beth (ב) in front of the word *"Solomon."* This could indicate the preposition *in*, which would be more compatible with a hithpael or reflexive form than would the word *with*, which the beth (ב) could also refer to.

Additionally, since this is in a hithpael (reflexive) form, it would suggest that due to what Solomon did, God was *'aneph* (אנף), or angry, with Himself—and not with Solomon. However, using the English word *anger* in this context, indicating that God was angry with Himself, does not make much sense.

Consider for a moment what the word *anger* currently means in the English language. It refers to an emotion that can have varying degrees of strength, the cause of which might range from mere frustration to actual hate. Therein lies the problem with translating *'aneph* (אנף) as *"anger."* The word *'aneph* (אנף) is not actually rooted in our idea of anger but has its origins in *the snorting of a camel.* A camel will snort when it is frustrated or angry. When a Bedouin's camel starts to snort, he does not interpret this as his camel hating him or wanting to do him harm but rather as an expression of frustration. What is often the cause of this frustration? A feeling of helplessness. Someone is pushing the animal to do something that it has done its best to do but cannot accomplish. This is the proper use of the word *'aneph* (אנף), particularly when it is used in a hithpael (reflexive) form.

But even the word *frustration* falls short of the true nature of *'aneph* (אנף). Rather, think of a wife who has done everything she could to show her husband how much she loves him, only to see him walk out of the house and seek the comfort of another woman. What that wife feels is *'aneph* (אנף). Yes, she feels anger, but she also feels hurt, heartbreak, frustration, sadness, grief, rejection, and even fear. If she truly loves her husband, she wishes him no harm, but she fears what his infidelity will do to him and to their children.

Thus, considering that the English word *anger* often carries the idea of wishing someone harm, it would be inappropriate to use it in this passage. God meant no harm to Solomon, for He loved him and had appeared to him twice. In Hebrew, the word translated *"appeared," ra'ah* (ראה), is used in a niphal* form, which is also reflexive. So we would say that God had made Himself known to Solomon with His presence, or that He had made Himself intimate with Solomon.

Accordingly, the word I think is indicated here instead of *anger* is *heartbreak*: "The Lord's heart was broken because Solomon's heart was turned away from Him."

We need not fear God being angry with us in the sense that He would wish to bring us harm. However, there is something even greater for us to fear than the possibility of personal harm. When we end our journey to the heart of God, will we find His heart in shattered ruins because of our spiritual infidelity? That thought is much more fearful to me than the idea of an angry God who wishes to do me harm.

Study 13

Pressed: *Ma'aq* (מעק)

"But ye gave the Nazarites wine to drink; and commanded the prophets, saying, Prophesy not. Behold, I am pressed under you, as a cart is pressed that is full of sheaves."
—Amos 2:12–13

The prophet Amos was a contemporary of the prophets Isaiah, Micah, and Hosea. He came from a little farming community in Judah known as Tekoa, which was just a little south of Bethlehem. Yet he was called to prophesy to the northern kingdom of Israel. He prophesied circa 750 BC, which was just three years before the first invasion of northern Israel by the Assyrians.

It took twenty-eight years for the Assyrians to finally conqueror the entire nation of Israel. In one invasion in 740 BC, they carried away the people of the tribes of Reuben and Gad, as well as the half-tribe of Manasseh, and then spent the next fifteen years picking away at the remaining seven-and-a-half tribes. Finally, they conducted a three-year siege against Samaria, the capital city of Israel, and in 722 BC, the city fell under the Assyrian ruler Sargon II.

Falling on Deaf Ears

During this time, God's prophets warned His people of a coming captivity. Amos 3:7 says, *"Surely the Lord God will do nothing, but he revealed his secret unto his servants the prophets.*" In other words, God wouldn't act without revealing His plans to His prophets. Yet, as we see in Amos 2:12, the prophets were silenced by the people. Prior to 740 BC, the nation of Israel had been at the zenith of its prosperity. The Israelites had managed to reclaim all the land they had lost, so that their borders extended to a point not seen since David and Solomon. Additionally, they were major exporters of wine and oil. However, although the nation as a whole was rich, the average person lived in poverty and near starvation. Many people lived as sharecroppers and were forced by wealthy landowners to produce products for export rather than grow food to feed their own families. The gulf between the rich and the poor was at its widest point.

The prophet Amos was a shepherd who also tended sycamore fig trees, and he knew the people's sufferings firsthand. When God gave him a vision, he went to the rich and the powerful and delivered God's message of the coming natural disasters and of the conquest by foreign powers.

Amos had a vision of an earthquake, which occurred two years later. The fulfillment of his prophecy gave him quite a bit of credibility and resulted in his gaining disciples who spread his message. Unfortunately, the message fell on deaf ears, as it was a message of doom at a time when the Assyrians had retreated due to internal conflict and Israel was experiencing its greatest financial boom. Only a handful of people believed the message of the prophets. These people became the "remnant," the ones to whom God gave a *"song,"* as mentioned in Isaiah 5:1–7.

The prophets faithfully preached a message of repentance. Amos's message was threefold. The first part of the message was against the wealth and prosperity not only of the rich merchants but also of the religious leaders who became richer at the expense of the poor, who just became poorer. The second part of the message was about the lack of justice toward those who were doing the right thing—those who sought to help the poor, the innocent, and those who otherwise could not help themselves. These righteous people were thrown into prisons, tortured, and beaten because they were a threat to the rich and powerful. Amos's third message was directed toward religious ritual that was devoid of true faith, performed only to win some favor with God rather than to seek the heart of God.

A Desire to Protect God's Heart

As a farmer, Amos used a strong agricultural motif. In Amos 2:13, he declared that God was so hurt by the rejection of the message of His prophets and the rejection of the dedication of His servants that He felt like a cart that is pressed down because it is full of sheaves. The Hebrew word translated *"sheaves"* is *'amar* (עמר), which has a double meaning. It does refer to stalks of grain tied together, but it is also used for those who are *self-seeking*. In Hebrew, the word *"pressed"* is *ma'aq* (מעק), which has the idea of *burdened with pain*. God was saying that the rejection of the message of His prophets by those who are self-seeking had *burdened His heart down with pain*. He had sent the prophets and the Nazarites to warn the people and to be an example to them, but the people had rejected them.

Today, there are many people who feel they are called to be prophets and are giving messages similar to those of Amos. I do not oppose any message that calls a nation to repent, and I will indeed support such a message. However, I would like to point out one trait that Amos possessed that our modern-day prophets should give serious consideration to in regard to their own callings. Amos 2:13 shows us that Amos knew the heart of God. He was not preaching a God of anger and wrath but a God who had a *broken heart*.

What made Amos different from many prophets was that he prophesied not only on behalf of the suffering, but also from a desire to protect the heart of God. So, the next time you speak out against the sin in our nation, ask yourself why you are speaking out. Is it from fear that you will be swept up in judgment and lose your comfortable lifestyle? Or is it because you feel the heart of God breaking, and you want to protect His heart?

Study 14

See: *Ra'ah* (ראה)

"But he himself went a day's journey into the wilderness, and came and sat down under a juniper tree: and he requested for himself that he might die; and said, It is enough; now, O Lord, *take away my life; for I am not better than my fathers."*
—1 Kings 19:4

The verse right before our study text says, *"And when* [Elijah] *saw that, he arose, and went for his life"* (Kings 19:3). I find the Hebrew word for *"saw"* here to be quite important in regard to my own personal journey to the heart of God. Let's look at the context of this word.

Elijah was responding to Jezebel's threat to lop off his head within twenty-four hours. Some translations say that Elijah became afraid and ran, while others say he became aware of the threat and ran. I have heard many preachers say that Elijah was not afraid, but that he took off running as a matter of defense and to be alone with God. The passage does not specifically say that he ran away out of fear.

Fearing and Seeing

The problem arises in the word translated *"saw"* in 1 Kings 19:3, which is *yara'* (ירא). This word comes from one of two roots—either *yara'* (ירא) or *ra'ah* (ראה). The first root word means "to fear" as in *terrorized* or *scared to death*. The second means "to see." In many cases, *ra'ah* (ראה) is used for spiritual sight or insight.

The Masoretic text added the vowel pointings* that direct us to the root word for *ra'ah* (ראה), which signifies *to see, both in a natural and spiritual sense*. It has been said that the scribes did this because they did not want to show any weakness in Elijah's faith. Fear, of course, would be a major weakness, because, as the saying goes, "The opposite of faith is fear." Sitting around wanting to die does not sound like a declaration of faith. Then again, if Elijah had wanted to die, why would he be so afraid of death that he ran off into the wilderness?

But in 1 Kings 19:3, we learn that Elijah *"saw"* what Jezebel had planned for him. This would most likely be a spiritual insight, and receiving this insight caused him to run away as a defensive action. But he was also terrified by what he *"saw."* These two sides of the coin, being terrified and taking defensive action, are joined by Elijah's words, *"I am not better than my fathers."*

The issue with the fathers was a matter of faith and trust in God. Elijah was not despondent due to Jezebel's threat but because after all the miracles God had performed—proving that He would provide—Elijah had still allowed fear to take control of him. He saw himself as no better than his ancestors; although they had walked in the daily miracles of God in the wilderness, when it was time to enter the Promised Land, they were overcome with fear, so that God could not let them enter in.

When We Allow Fear to Take Control

We can only imagine what kind of relationship Elijah had with God. However, I am certain that the prophet was filled with remorse over having wounded the heart of his God by his lack of faith. His relationship with God was so close that he had witnessed firsthand the miracle of the withholding and the releasing of rain (see 1 Kings 17:1; 18:1–2, 41–45), the miracle of the bread and the meat (see 1 Kings

17:1–6), the miracle of fire from heaven (see, for example, 1 Kings 18:16–39), and more, but he still let fear take control.

Elijah did not necessarily ask God to take his life; he asked Him to take his *nephesh* (נפש), or his soul. Like many other Hebrew words, this term has a wide range of meanings, including one's physical life and one's free will. Perhaps this was the point at which Elijah finally decided to give up his will to God completely and ask Him to take control of his *nephesh* (נפש), the central area of his will, his emotions, and his passion.

When Satan, the father of the "Jezebel spirit," points his finger at you and says, "Look at you—you lost your job. What's going to happen now? You will be homeless; you will starve…doom, doom, doom," then all your faith and confidence in God is suddenly shaken, just like Elijah's was. You find yourself running in fear; and finally, when you are sitting under that juniper tree, you end up in despair—not over all your problems, but over your lack of trust in God. You are not only disgusted with yourself, but you are also feeling bad because you think you have let God down and have wounded His heart with your lack of faith. After years and years of seeing God's faithfulness, you discover that you are no different from the unfaithful children of Israel. Just as you are ready to enter your promised land, you encounter a giant, and you crumble in fear. So, like Elijah, you cry out, "'*It is enough.*' Lord, take my will, my desires, my hopes, my dreams, my very soul, because I am so tired of living in this fear and lack of trust in You!"

Which "Dog" Will You Feed?

My grandfather used to tell the story of an old Native American man who became a Christian. Someone once asked him what it was like to be a Christian. He said, "It is like having two dogs inside of me fighting, one good and one evil." When asked which one would win, the old man said, "Whichever one I feed the most."

Just like Elijah and that old Native American man, we have two "dogs" fighting inside of us—a dog of fear and a dog of faith. For a while, we let the "arm of flesh" feed us and take care of us. But when that arm of flesh fails us, and we must turn to God to feed us, our faith falters because for too long we have been feeding the dog of fear rather than the dog of faith. Which of those two dogs fighting it out inside of us will win? The one we feed the most.

Study 15

The Lord Will Prosper: *Yativ YHWH* (ייטיב יהוה)

"Then Micah said, 'Now I know that the Lord *will prosper me, seeing I have a Levite as priest.'"*
—Judges 17:13 (NASB)

After the story of Samson in the book of Judges, we have a rather odd account. Chances are you were never taught this story in Sunday school, and you may never even have heard it talked about in a sermon. Yet it is included in Scripture, and its message seems quite clear.

The story centers on a man from Ephraim named Micah who stole 1,100 pieces of silver from his mother. It is curious that the Bible mentions the specific number of silver pieces. Jewish tradition teaches that this mother was Delilah, who had received 1,100 pieces of silver in exchange for ratting on Samson. Of course, Delilah was a Philistine, and this was apparently an Israelite woman—but then, Delilah did have a thing for Hebrew men, so who knows?

Another idea is that the number "one thousand" in Hebrew is designated by the word *aleph* (אלפ), which is in a hiphal (causative) demonstrative form. In this form, coupled with the word *ma'ah*

(מאה), which means "one hundred," it would then have the idea of *bringing forth thousands.* We learn in verse 3 that Micah's mother had intended to consecrate this silver to God—or to her perverted concept of God. The letter aleph (א) in the Canaanite script is a picture of a bull's head. This was a representation of the god Apis, upon which the golden calf the Israelites made in the wilderness was based. The Egyptian god Apis (and his Canaanite/Philistine counterpart) was believed to increase your offering a hundredfold if he found it acceptable.

Attempting to Revoke a Curse

We learn in Judges 17:2 that Micah's mother had cursed the loss of the silver. When Micah confessed his wrongdoing, his mother declared that she would *"restore"* (Judges 17:3), or *"return"* (NASB), it to him. The word translated *"restore"* or *"return"* is *shub* (שׁוב), which is in a hiphal (causative) form and would more correctly mean "to cause to recall or revoke." In other words, she would revoke her curse.

The word translated *"curse"* (NASB) is *'alah* (אלה)—not to be confused with the Arabic *Allah. 'Alah* is rarely rendered as the word *curse,* since it really means "to call upon God." The mother called upon God to restore her silver, which she was going to offer to her erroneous concept of Him in order to get a multiple blessing. Sounds crazy, doesn't it? Sort of like using money God has given you to buy a lottery ticket, and then asking Him to help you choose the right number so that you will win.

This mother had such a mishmash concept of God—Jehovah mixed in with pagan beliefs—that she might have been planning to offer this silver to her idols in hopes that the "good deed" of her son's confession of having stolen it would prove to be an acceptable offering, and that God might see fit to return it in a greater proportion. Not unlike a "seed-faith" offering.

Micah had undergone a change of heart and returned the silver to his mother. However, I think he had a little nudge. Leviticus 5:1 (NIV) tells us, *"If anyone sins because they do not speak up when they hear a public charge to testify regarding something they have seen or learned about, they will be held responsible.*" After his mother invoked her *'alah* (appeal to God), Micah felt that God was really going to get him, so he confessed before the lightning bolt descended. Once the silver was returned, the mother took two hundred pieces of it and made them into a graven image. Again, there is this crazy mixture of paganism with the true worship of Jehovah. She was using a portion of this silver to make an idol.

Trying to Bribe God

Still, why only two hundred pieces? This was a fifth of the 1,100, and according to Leviticus 6:5 (NASB), "*anything about which he swore falsely; he shall make restitution for it in full and add to it one-fifth more. He shall give it to the one to whom it belongs on the day he presents his guilt offering.*" These two hundred pieces of silver were meant to be a *guilt offering*. So, again, how does the mother offer it? She makes an idol out of it, then uses the rest of the nine hundred pieces of silver for its original intention, which was to bribe God (being perfectly frank here) for a blessing. The nine hundred would go to maintain the place of worship—to pay the light bill, so to speak.

The story gets even crazier. Jewish tradition teaches that Micah then builds a little altar and makes an ephod, most likely using some of the silver from the remaining nine hundred pieces, and consecrates one of his sons to be a priest and to set up a little backyard worship center, where the object of worship was an idol made from the silver that Micah had stolen and returned. Then Micah just sits back, waiting for the Lord to give him a big fat blessing for all his good works. The bottom line is that Micah begins to worship his own good deed, hoping that such a deed will bring him good fortune.

But wait—this story gets even more wild. To really add the frosting to the cake, along comes a real, honest-to-goodness Levite. The Levites were members of the priestly tribe. This Levite, however, was homeless. Levites were generally well-cared for, and they did not become homeless unless they had a really shady background. Nonetheless, this man was a Levite, and Micah gave him a good job offer to be a priest for his backyard temple, thinking that the man could add some real professionalism to his do-it-yourself altar.

Micah then declares, in effect, what many of us might say if we hired a pastor who was a seminary graduate, fully approved by an accrediting association and ordained by a prominent denomination: "The Lord will indeed prosper me now!" Micah says that God will prosper him now that he has a real Levite priest working for him. Such a priest will really give him credibility with God, and when that increase comes, boy, will it be bountiful! The Hebrew word translated "*prosper*" is *tov* (טוב), meaning "good" or "in harmony with God," combined with a double *yod* (ייטוב), which indicates that this is in a hiphal (causative) form. In other words, Micah feels this situation will actually cause the Lord to be in harmony with him and to prosper him. The Hebrew word for "LORD" here is *Jehovah*.

Ridiculous, don't you think? Yeah, about as ridiculous as thinking that if you spend some of your tithe money to buy a ticket to fly to a convention where there is a so-called true man of God preaching, and you give another big portion of your tithe money to this man as an offering, he will lay hands on you; and, of course, if you have an honest-to-goodness holy man pray for you, then God will surely bless you and give you the miracle you want.

Of course, we Christians today are too sophisticated to do such things. That Levite priest was no more than a Levitical rabbit's foot to Micah, and we would never consider our preachers or religious teachers to be a Levitical rabbit's foot, would we?

We learn later that poor Micah did *not* receive any blessing or miracle. In fact, he lost everything, ending up empty-handed. (See Judges 18.)

As Foolish as Micah?

Maybe the reason we were never taught this story in Sunday school and have never heard any sermons preached on it is that we don't believe we could ever be as foolish as Micah was. We would never actually worship our good works! We would never believe that, when faced with a real need, we would "hire" a preacher to lay his hands on us as we held our good deeds up to God and said, "With all these good things I have done, and with this godly man laying hands on me, I know that You will prosper me now and give me my miracle." And we would never believe that God would surely respond by saying, "Oh my goodness, you have done such wonderful things for Me, and now that you have an honest-to-goodness ordained preacher praying over you, I will surely bless you. How could I *not* answer your prayer—you've earned it!"

No, I am sure none of us would be that foolish in our thinking. We all know better. Such a story has no application to any of us today.

Study 16

A Word Came: *Devar Hayah* (דבר היה)

"And it came to pass after many days, that the word of the L*ORD came to Elijah."*
—1 Kings 18:1

"And behold, the word of the L*ORD came to him."*
—1 Kings 19:9

"And after the fire a still small voice."
—1 Kings 19:12

As I continue on my journey to the heart of God, I am becoming more sensitive to Scriptures that indicate God speaking with man. In 1 Kings 18:1, when God spoke to Elijah, we have the phrase *"the word of the* L*ORD came to Elijah."* In 1 Kings 19, we read not only that *"the word of the* L*ORD came to Elijah"* (verse 9) but also that God spoke to Elijah in *"a still small voice"* (verse 12).

The first two verses are rendered as *"the word of the* L*ORD came to…."* In both of these verses, the Hebrew term translated *"word"* is *devar* (דבר). The sages used to say that *devar* refers to words spoken from the heart. So, the "*word*" that was being spoken came from God's heart.

God's Word Can Become a Part of Us

While the first two verses read the same in our English version—"*the word of the* L*ORD* *came to…*"—they are actually quite different in the Hebrew. In 1 Kings 18:1, the word translated as "*came*" is *hayah* (היה), and in 1 Kings 19:9, the word "*came*" is not even in the original text.

Although *hayah* (היה) can be translated as "came," in its Semitic origins, it meant "to be," "to become," or "to exist." This is important, because God was communicating to Elijah that he had to present himself to King Ahab, which would be no easy task. Ahab had a price on Elijah's head. Even Obadiah, the king's servant, feared for his own life in merely having to report to the king that Elijah was on his way. Yet Elijah promptly took off for the palace without so much as a bulletproof vest. He was headed for certain death.

In most of our daily decisions, seeking God's guidance through an inner feeling tends to work just fine. We say, "I feel like God is telling me to [attend this meeting; not attend this meeting; buy this car; not buy this car; go on this trip; not go on this trip; and so on]." It is likely that none of those decisions would carry serious consequences if we happened to be wrong about it. But suppose you were to come upon a drive-by shooting, and the Lord said to you, "Walk in front of the bullets"? It would take more than just an inner feeling that God was telling you to do this for you to obey. Similarly, if there was a home near you in which all the family members were ill with the Ebola virus, and God told you to go to that home and pray for the sick, you would want more than just an inner feeling that you should go there. That is why I feel we need to use a different word for *hayah* (היה) than "*came.*" I would tend to use one of the secondary meanings for this word—"to exist"—and I would render this verse as, "The word of the Lord existed for Elijah," or "Elijah became a part of the word of the Lord." The word of the Lord had become such a part of Elijah that he could do nothing else but go in response to it.

God's Word Can Come as Personal Instruction

However, note again that in 1 Kings 19:9, we have the same expression, *"The word of the Lord came to...,"* but the word *hayah* (היה) is not in the original Hebrew. The literal rendering would be "The word of the Lord unto him" or "The word of the Lord for him."

I really don't know what Elijah experienced in these various instances of hearing from God. However, it is clear that God spoke differently in each case. In the first instance, the word was very clear—so clear that Elijah became a "part" of it. It had to be clear, because it was a life-and-death situation. In the second case, the word was just *unto* or *for* Elijah. In this case, God was giving Elijah some personal instruction; hence, the word did not carry the force of the word that had come to him previously.

God's Word Can Come as Intimate Communication

Additionally, we find in 1 Kings 19 that God spoke to Elijah in a *"still small voice"* (verse 12); and right after that, He spoke to him in a *"voice"* (verse 13). It appears that God has levels of communication that depend upon the circumstances. In each case, Elijah didn't have to second-guess whether he was hearing from God; he seemed to recognize God's voice no matter what the circumstances.

In James 5:17, we learn that Elijah was a human being just like us. He prayed that it would not rain, and it did not rain. Could we not do the same? If God made His voice clear to Elijah, why would He not make it just as clear to us? Surely God does, but perhaps it comes in direct proportion to the need at the time.

Sometimes, His word must be *hayah* (היה), becoming a "part" of us, so that it is perfectly clear at times when the consequences hang in the balance. Other times, when He wants to share something intimate with us, He may speak in a still, small voice. For example, suppose a husband and wife are riding along in their car, and the wife sees another car sliding across the lane in their direction, so she screams to her husband, who is at the wheel, "Look out!" He reacts in time, and they avoid a collision. But then, later that evening, when they are alone in their bedroom, the wife may smile playfully at her husband and, before planting a good-night kiss on him, say, "Look out…." The first "Look out" is *devar hayah* (דבר היה), and the second is that *still, small voice*.

Sometimes, God does not speak in a whirlwind or in an earthquake or in a fire. (See 1 Kings 19:11–12.) Sometimes, He wants to speak to us in a soft, gentle, loving way, and we must be ready to respond appropriately.

Study 17

His Mercy Endures Forever: *Ki Le'olem Chasedo* (כי לעולם חסדו)

"And when he had consulted with the people, he appointed singers unto the LORD, and that should praise the beauty of holiness, as they went out before the army, and to say, Praise the LORD; for his mercy endureth for ever."
—2 Chronicles 20:21

I recently heard a Messianic Christian from Israel teaching on the esoteric nature of the Hebrew language. He offered Hebrew courses and study guides, as well as CDs with Scripture being read in Hebrew. The idea was that there is such a mystical nature to the Hebrew language that just listening to Scripture being read in Hebrew will bring a special blessing, even if you do not understand what you are hearing. I suppose my fundamentalist background and conservative evangelical training will always keep me from crossing the line into accepting that there is such a mystical element to the Hebrew language. To speak my Savior's name as *Jesus* in English or as *Yeshua* in Hebrew makes no difference to me; His name is precious no matter how I say it.

Are Certain Words Close to God's Heart?

Still, I cannot help but wonder if certain words or phrases in the Hebrew language are closer to God's heart than others. I am not suggesting that we need to speak these words in the Hebrew itself. After all, no one really knows the correct pronunciation of the ancient Hebrew. If there are words that are dear to the heart of God, so that speaking them would result in a special response from Him, their pronunciation would not matter as much as the faith that accompanied them.

Ki le'olem chasedo (כי לעולם חסדו), *"For his mercy endureth forever,"* could be one such endearing phrase. It is found thirty-seven times in the Old Testament—twenty-six times in Psalm 136 alone. In 2 Chronicles 20:21, King Jehoshaphat used this phrase as a battle cry against the three kings who were marching against the kingdom of Judah. I believe it is safe to say that these words had far greater impact than if he had used "Your mother wears combat boots!" as his battle cry.

Jehoshaphat was a godly king in Judah. He ended prostitution, did not seek the idols of Baal, and sent Levitical teams throughout the nation to teach the law to the people and to admonish them to obey God's commandments. As a result, the nation enjoyed a period of unprecedented peace and prosperity. (See 2 Kings 22:46; 2 Chronicles 17:1–10.) In 2 Chronicles 20, we learn that three kings from Moab and Ammon had formed a strong confederacy and had begun to march against Judah. Things looked pretty hopeless, but Jehoshaphat did the right thing. He gathered the people together and sought the face of God. He cried out to the Lord, admitting that they faced impossible odds and that only He could deliver them.

God heard their cry, and He gave a prophetic word through a Levite named Jahaziel. It was only fitting that God would use Jahaziel because he was a direct descendant of Asaph, who was the chief musician in the temple during the time of David. The means that the Lord would use to defeat the three kings would not be an army but a choir! Under the anointing of God, Jahaziel predicted that the Lord would destroy the armies of the three kings without a sword being raised by Judah.

I like what happened next. Rather than declaring Jahaziel insane for making such an outlandish and impossible prediction,

Jehoshaphat fell on his face before God, praising and thanking Him for the deliverance. Jahaziel either had a proven track record for prophecy, had a solid reputation for not being a fruitcake, or bore witness to Jehoshaphat's spirit—thus confirming what Jehoshaphat already knew from God. From what I read of Jehoshaphat, I believe it to be the third option.

We read in 2 Chronicles 20:21 that Jehoshaphat consulted the people and appointed singers. The word translated *"consult"* is *ya'ats* (יעץ), which is in a niphal form and carries the idea of "deliberating" or "taking counsel." Recent research by rabbinic teachers has led them to conclude that the niphal can have a reflexive nature. Hence, Jehoshaphat took the counsel of the people unto himself. He did not just listen to the people; he took their words to heart and then appointed the singers.

An Army of Singers

Now, try to imagine this scenario. Jehoshaphat has twenty-four hours to prepare for war against an overwhelming army, and how does he equip himself? He sets up music auditions and organizes a choir. This choir is taught one song, and one song only: *Ki le'olem chasedo* (כי לעולם חסדו). They sang, *"Praise the* L*ORD; **for his mercy endureth for ever.**"*

The word rendered *"praise"* here is *hodu* (הודו), which comes from the root word *yadah* (ידה) and means "a praise of thanksgiving." So, before they even go into battle, they are thanking God. We should note that in its most primitive state, the word *yadah* (ידה) comes from the word *yad* (יד), which means "hand." They are praising and thanking God with uplifted hands.

Some rabbis dispute the vowel pointing of the Masoretes and declare that the vowel shureq* (וּ) *u* at the end of *hodu* (הודו) should really be a holem* (ֹ) *o*, thus creating the root word *hod* (הוד), which means "beauty" or "brilliance." *Hod* (הוד) is spelled hei (ה), which speaks of the presence of God, vav (ו), which tells us that God is making a connection between heaven and earth, and daleth (ד), which pictures a gateway or a portal. The people were thanking God for opening a connection between heaven and earth with His presence, and this connection opened a portal releasing brilliance, or a brilliant light, not unlike the one Paul encountered on the road to Damascus. (See Acts 9:1–19.) The letter hei (ה) is a favorite among the sages. It is the broken letter, which represents the *light* of God and a *bridge* between heaven and earth. For me, as a Christian, the hei (ה) represents Jesus Christ and His broken body on the cross.

A Gateway to God's Heart

But the real beauty of this verse is found in the word *"mercy."* This word in Hebrew is *chasad* (חסד), which is spelled chet (ח), samek (ס), daleth (ד), and means "loving-kindness" and "mercy." The spelling of *chasad* (חסד) is a sort of a built-in commentary on the word. Chet (ח), samek (ס), and daleth (ד) tell us what loving-kindness and mercy are really all about. These letters and their position in the word indicate that the loving-kindness of God is a gateway to His heart that joins our heart to His.

You see, when Jehoshaphat interviewed the potential choir members, he was not looking for those who had the best voices, but rather those who longed as he did to join their hearts with the heart of God. When a choir of people who long to know the heart of God declare, *Ki le'oelm chasedo* (כי לעולם חסדו), *"For his mercy endureth for ever,"* what they are saying is, "Our hearts are joined with His forever."

In 2 Chronicles 20:22, the Bible tells us that the instant God's people spoke those words, the Lord set an ambush against the kings of Moab and Ammon, who fought and killed each other before Judah even raised a sword. The moment the people joined their hearts with God, He moved against their enemies. Is there anything mystical in the words *Ki le'oelm chasedo* (כי לעולם חסדו), "For His mercy endures forever"? Probably just as much mysticism as the words spoken by someone who is truly repentant, saying, "Lord, be merciful to me, a sinner." (See Luke 18:13.) Such words from a sincere heart cannot help but touch the heart of God.

"Only One Thing Left to Give"

I was trying to think of a way to illustrate what happens when we say *Ki le'oelm chasedo* (כי לעולם חסדו), *"For his mercy endureth for ever,"* and I thought of a scene from a movie where a man is terminally ill in the hospital and cannot fall sleep. He asks his wife, who is resting in a cot next to him, if she will lie beside him on his hospital bed, as her presence might help him to sleep. So she lies down next to him, and he tells her, "I have only one thing left that I can give to you. I can give you my heart." She replies that she will give him her heart in return.

This is what we are saying when we declare, *Ki le'oelm chasedo* (כי לעולם חסדו), *"For his mercy endureth for ever."* We are telling God that we just cannot handle a situation, and we are asking Him, "Will You lie beside us, Lord? Your presence will comfort us." In response, He surrounds us with His presence and love. We then tell Him that we have only one thing left to give to Him—our hearts. Expressing this cannot help but touch the heart of God, for He can then give us His heart.

Study 18

It Is Vain to Serve God: *Shave' 'Ebod 'Elohim* (שוא עבד אלהים)

"Your words have been stout against me, saith the LORD. Yet ye say, What have we spoken so much against thee? Ye have said, It is vain to serve God: and what profit is it that we have kept his ordinance, and that we have walked mournfully before the LORD of hosts?"
—Malachi 3:13–14

There is an old cartoon of a man in a horse-drawn wagon with the reins to the horse in one hand and a carrot attached to a stick in the other. When he dangles the carrot in front of the horse, the horse starts walking toward it, wanting to get a bite of that tasty carrot. In this way, the wagon driver gets the horse to move the wagon; but the poor horse keeps walking toward the carrot, not realizing that he will never reach it, nor will he ever get to eat it, because it was never the intention of the driver to give him the carrot. The carrot is just a cruel deception the man uses to get the horse to do what he wants it to do.

In the above passage from Malachi, the people were essentially saying to God, "There's no use in following You, because You're just using a carrot-and-stick trick with us." The Lord's reply was, *"Your words have been stout against me." "Stout"* is translated from the Hebrew word *chazaq* (חזק), which comes from a Semitic root that means "to be stubborn." If you are *stubborn*, it means you resist any help or any attempt to change your course of action. No amount of reasoning will alter your direction.

After the people had been so stubborn against the Lord, they said, with seeming innocence, *"What have we spoken so much against thee?"* The Hebrew word rendered *"spoken"* is *devar* (דבר), meaning that these are words from the heart; and in this context, they are very significant, powerful words. They asked God, in effect, "What have we said that is so horrible?" What they had said was this: *"It is vain to serve God,"* questioning what profit there was in keeping His ordinances.

Why Do You Serve God?

Why is this such a horrible thing to say in relation to God? Let's put it into context for us today. Why do we serve God? Why do we go to church, pay our tithe, read Scripture, and behave ourselves? We are seeking God's blessing, for if we don't do these things, we will not be blessed. Yet it often seems as if, even when we do all these things, we are not blessed, anyway. In fact, it sometimes seems as if those who ignore God altogether fare better than we do.

In many Christian circles, it is commonly taught that if we pay our weekly tithe from our gross income, God will bless us with great financial reward. Yet I have encountered many Christians, as well as those who describe themselves as former Christians, who tried to follow these rules but ended up in bankruptcy court. So, they decided never to attend church again because Christianity just didn't "work." Western Christianity is littered with the dry, sun-baked bones of Christians who faithfully served God and kept His commandments and yet ended up turning against Him because they were not adequately blessed (paid?) for all their efforts.

Often, if we are not blessed, we are tempted to conclude, *"It is vain to serve God."* The Hebrew word translated *"vain"* is *shave'* (שׁוא),

which means "to make a worthless noise." Or we might say, "*What profit is it that we have kept his ordinance?*" The word translated "*profit*" is *batsa'* (בצע), which means "to plunder" or "to gain at the expense of another." If you, as a righteous person, were bidding for a job against an unrighteous person, would you not expect God to enable you to get that job since you are righteous? If you don't get the job, should you then throw your hands up and say, "So, what did all this honesty get for me, anyway?" That is essentially what the Israelites were saying. They felt that by keeping the laws of God, they should profit over those who *didn't* keep His laws.

Well, it is obvious what the prophet is saying: *the great sin that was being committed was to serve God and keep His commandments merely in order to get richly paid or blessed for doing so.* The same applies to us. But wait, there is something more to it than that. If we are really searching for the heart of God, we will realize that by saying such things to Him, we are accusing Him of deception, like the cartoon of the old boy dangling a carrot in front of the horse in order to get the horse to move, yet never intending to let the horse have the carrot. We start to think that God dangles all these promises of riches and blessings in front of us to get us to obey Him and live a good life, but then never intends to make good on any of those promises.

This is like the wife of a rich man who, upon hearing that her husband has suddenly lost his wealth, just packs up and leaves because he is no longer able to buy her the things she wants. Her husband is shattered and heartbroken, realizing that his wife never loved him to begin with, but married him only for his money. (I recently read about a twenty-nine-year-old fashion model who married an eighty-five-year-old man. The man is worth half a billion dollars. Of course, I am sure his money had nothing to do with her decision to marry him.)

This is why it is so horrible to say, "'*It is vain to serve God*'; what profit is there in keeping His laws?" I see so many Christians whose attitude as the bride of Christ is nothing more than that of a Christian gold digger. They marry God for His money.

We should ask ourselves what we are really saying when we tell God, "I love You." Are we saying, "God, I will love You as long as You pay me, but if the paychecks ever stop coming in, then I will just find myself another god who knows how to take care of me"? Can we honestly say, "God, if You seem to go broke tomorrow, so that You no longer appear to be the great Provider, I will still trust in You, just as Job did"? (See Job 13:15.) Some of us may have to face that test just to be sure of why we love Him.

There is a scene in the movie *Fiddler on the Roof* where Tevye is reflecting on the marriage of his daughter Tzeitel to the tailor Motel, and he sighs, "They are as poor as church mice, yet they are so happy they don't know how miserable they are." If we are truly the loving bride of Christ, then God does not need to dangle a carrot in front of us to get us moving—we move ahead simply because we love Him "for better or worse, for richer or poorer, in sickness and in health." And if He chooses to allow sickness, poverty, or "worse" to come into our lives, we will still be so happy in Him that we won't know just how miserable we are, because we will be blinded by His love for us and our love for Him.

Study 19

Hedge: *Gadar* (גדר)

"And I sought for a man among them, that should make up the hedge, and stand in the gap before me for the land, that I should not destroy it: but I found none."
—Ezekiel 22:30

Most of the time, I hear the above verse quoted in reference to intercessory prayer. Let's take a closer look at its meaning. The context is that God is about to destroy the land, and He declares that He is looking for a man, just one man, who will stand as a *"hedge."* What is a *"hedge"*? If you check your dictionary or lexicon, it will tell you that it is a wall or a fence. So, the question remains, "What are the requirements or qualifications to be a *'hedge'* for God?"

Qualifications to Be a Hedge

We must first look at the role of a *"hedge."* The analogy of "standing in the gap" gives a picture of a warrior who positions himself at a breach in the wall of a city or at its entrance, ensuring that no enemies will get in, and who is ready to defend should there be an invasion. It seems extreme that one man would be able to fend off an invading army; such a person would have to be a superhero.

The word in Hebrew for *"hedge"* is *gadar* (גדר), which is spelled gimmel (ג), daleth (ד), resh (ר). By examining the meanings of these three letters, we can learn the qualifications of a *"hedge."* Since this *"hedge"* does appear to be some sort of superhero, I asked Nikko, my study partner's twelve-year-old nephew and an expert in the field of superheroes, to help me decipher these meanings and to share his insights into the Hebrew letters that spell out the word *gadar* (גדר).

First, we know that this *"hedge"* is a guardian, or protector, of the city. But the guardian must first be a gimmel (ג), which is one who does loving deeds for others. He doesn't just say to someone without a coat, "Be warm"—he gives him his coat, as well. (See James 2:14–16.) He is self-sacrificing, one who lays down his life for others, like the Good Shepherd.

The next letter, or qualification, for a *gadar* (גדר), or *"hedge,"* is the *daleth* (ד). This guardian knows whom to keep in the city and whom to let out. He has great spiritual discernment and is able to look beneath the surface or the outward appearance to know who is a friend of the city that he is protecting and who is its enemy. He is able to see beyond the person's appearance and speech and read his heart.

The third letter tells us that this guardian must also have the attributes of the resh (ר). He must continually examine his own life and motives, be quick to repent when he is wrong, and not be offensive to God.

So, we learn from the Hebrew word for *"hedge"* that to be a guardian, one must show the attributes of the letters for *gadar* (גדר), spelled gimmel (ג)—self-sacrificing; daleth (ד)—able to open the doorway, or blockage, to the hearts of others; and resh (ר)—always ready for self-examination and willing to repent when he is wrong.

The Guardian's Weapons

Remember that this guardian, or protector, is to stand in the gap to protect any entrance to the city. But how does he protect it? What are his weapons? The word *"gap"* in the Hebrew is *paras* (פרץ), which is spelled pe (פ), resh (ר), sade (ץ). (The word *paras* (פרץ) uses the final form of the letter sade.) This protector's first weapon is the pe (פ), which represents his mouth, his words, his entire communication.

He speaks the words of God from his heart out of true compassion for the people he is protecting. He is one who expresses gratitude, appreciates what he has, doesn't gossip, and knows how to keep a secret.

His next weapon is the resh (ר), which represents the head, or the leader. He does not abuse his power as a leader; he depends on God and not his own abilities. If he makes a bad decision, he repents, turns away from it, and never looks back.

His third weapon is the (final) sade (ץ), which represents righteousness. He is always seeking to do what is right, even at the cost of his life; he is trustworthy and keeps his word. His good works are done in secret and not for man's applause.

In other words, a "*hedge,*" or protector, who can stand in the gap is like one of Nikko's favorite comic book heroes. No wonder God never found a man who could be a hedge and stand in the gap! To qualify, such a person must have the heart of a superhero, and only God has a heart like that. Then again, through the power of Jesus Christ, God the Father, and the Holy Spirit, perhaps we might come to understand God's heart, and then our hearts and His could become one. If that were to occur, we would have the heart of a spiritual superhero and be the hedge that stands in the gap.

(By the way, if a twelve-year-old can come to a deeper understanding of a Hebrew word by studying the meaning behind its Hebrew letters, just how much more could you accomplish?)

Study 20

Cure: *Rapha'* (רפא)

"Behold, I will bring it health and cure, and I will cure them, and will reveal unto them the abundance of peace and truth."
—Jeremiah 33:6

The Hebrew word for *"cure"* in the above verse is *rapha'* (רפא), which is often translated as "cure," "heal," "restore," "prosperity," "repair," "forgive," "pardon," "render whole," and other such ideas. The word translated *"health"* is *'arak* (ארך), which also means "health," "restore," and "cure," but in the sense of creating longevity.

What Type of Healing?

Many Christians know the word *rapha'* (רפא), particularly as a name of God—*Jehovah Rapha* (רפא יהוה), meaning "God is our healer." (See Exodus 15:26.) Isaiah 53:4–5 tells us that by Jesus' stripes we are healed, and there is great debate over whether this refers to the healing of our sins or to physical healing. When you consider the wide range of usages for the word *rapha'* (רפא), it would be safe to say that it means both. However, considering the context and the proper use of biblical exegesis, I would say the argument leans toward this being a reference to sin and not to physical healing. But then, as a student of Hebrew, I strongly question whether we should use the same method of exegesis with the Hebrew that we do with the Greek. When we consider the ambiguity of the Hebrew language and the various secondary meanings of many of its words, I find that the context is only a wrapper over the real treasure of a particular word. We generally eat the candy bar, not the wrapper it comes in, although in some rare cases, there are times when we do eat the wrapper, too.

"Fixing Something Up"

Let's take a closer look at this word *rapha'* (רפא), which has created so much debate. *Rapha'* (רפא) is spelled resh (ר), pe (פ), aleph (א). I already told you what lexicographers* believe the word means, but they are not the final word. Nor do I for a moment consider their work to be under the inspiration of God. We need to look at this word from the standpoint of a linguist and consider its etymology.

Perhaps you have read a magazine article or seen a TV documentary that describes the method used by Middle Eastern weavers to repair a garment. They hang the garment on a pole and attach rocks to the bottom of the clothing in order to stretch it. Then they put a stick between the threads of the garment to separate them. After this, they pull out the old, damaged, or worn threads, insert new threads, and then pull the stick down a little further to tighten the threads in place. They develop a sort of rhythm as they work the garment by pulling out threads, putting in new ones, and pulling down on the stick. As they do this, the rocks stretching the garment strike one another and make a noise that sounds like "rapha, rapha." This is where the word used for healing, *rapha'* (רפא), is derived. As you can see, it also has the idea of "repair," "restore," "sew," "weave," and similar words. In its Semitic root, it contains the idea of *fixing something up, not creating something new.* There is a difference between *bara'* (ברא), meaning "to create," and *rapha'* (רפא). In the first instance, something new is made; in the second, something new has been added to the old.

One of my students once asked me if "*cure*" could also mean "medicine." Understanding that she was referencing the word *rapha'* (רפא), I responded that it depends upon the definition of *medicine.* A physician practicing medicine is practicing the art of offering cures, which would fit the word *rapha'* (רפא). But I would be hard-pressed to say that *rapha'* (רפא) could represent pills, injections, or one of those awful concoctions patients are given before certain medical tests. *Rapha'* (רפא) is more the *act* of being healed than the tools used in healing.

How Are We Healed?

Okay, that is about as far as I can go with my training from Christian teachers. Now let's go to my training from rabbis, which brings us to a letter-by-letter examination of *rapha'* (רפא). These letters are sort of a built-in commentary telling us *how* we are healed. We are healed by the resh (ר), the pe (פ), and the aleph (א).

The aleph (א) represents God Jehovah. All healing comes from Him. The pe (פ) represents the mouth, or powerful speech. Remember that the world was created by speech. God first imagined creation and then spoke it into being. He has given us similar authority to imagine and then speak. James 4:2 tells us that we *"have not, because* [we] *ask not."* So, healing involves speech or prayer.

Finally, we come to the first letter of the word, resh (ר), which represents repentance. I purposely started with the last letter and ended with the first, because this first letter is often overlooked in the healing process.

There is an old Jewish story of a rabbi who was called to the bedside of a dying man who was in a coma, because the doctor could do nothing for him. As the family stood around reading the Psalms, the rabbi closed his eyes. When he opened his eyes again, he ordered the family to bring the dying man food. The man awoke from his coma and ate a full meal. In just a few minutes, he was sitting up in bed, totally healed. As the rabbi was leaving the home, the doctor ran to him and asked what he had done. The rabbi said that his spirit had spoken with the spirit of the dying man and told him he must repent of his sins and follow Torah. If he would, he promised that he would be healed. The man repented and agreed to spend the rest of his life following Torah. The rabbi then said, "Once the spiritual part of the man was healed, the physical healing was easy."

So, we are back to the old argument: Does *rapha'* (רפא) mean a spiritual healing or a physical healing? Again, I would say both, but let's not get so focused on the physical healing that we neglect the spiritual healing.

Study 21

Antimony: *Pavak* (פוך)

"O thou afflicted, tossed with tempest, and not comforted, behold, I will lay thy stones with fair colours, and lay thy foundations with sapphires."
—Isaiah 54:11

Throughout these Hebrew word studies, we need to keep in mind that Classical Hebrew is constantly drawing a picture for us. In the above verse, the nation of Israel is pictured as a people being tossed around in the sea. My study partner mentioned how stones or gems are polished. They are placed together in a container with water, and then the container is tossed around. This allows the stones to bounce against each other, thus smoothing and polishing them. That picture really seems to fit this verse.

Polished and Presented

The Hebrew word used for *"stones," 'even* (אבן), is the same word David used when he referred to the five smooth stones he picked up that had been beaten and smoothed by the water. (See 1 Samuel 17:40.) The King James translation of the Hebrew word for *pavak* (פוך) is *"fair colours,"* but *pavak* (פוך) actually means "antimony." In its Semitic root, *pavak* (פוך) means "eyeline." Its origins lie with the

Egyptians, who used antimony as makeup around their eyes. The stone that has been polished is now placed in antimony, something to enhance its beauty and show it off, like a setting for a necklace or a ring.

Prepared for Rest and Healing

This meaning expresses something very important to anyone who has been tossed around by the storms of life. In our study text, we are pictured as stones tossed around, resulting in our being polished and then placed in a setting. The Hebrew word translated "*lay the foundations*" is *yasadithike* (יסדתיך), which is in a hiphil (causative) participle form. As a hiphil participle, it has the idea of *laying to rest.* So, even as the storms toss you around, God is polishing you and preparing you for a rest.

Then God will *lay your foundations.* The root word for the term translated as "*foundations*" is *yasad* (יסד), which is the same word that is used for *intimacy* or *intercourse.* The King James Version says that this intimacy will be built upon "*sapphires.*" The Hebrew word for "*sapphires*" is *saphir* (ספר) and actually refers to lapis lazuli, a deep, rich, blue stone. Ancients used to grind up lapis lazuli and mix it with milk to be used as an aphrodisiac and also to heal an open wound, such as an ulcer. Thus, this foundation, or intimacy, will be built upon a healing ointment.

What is being pictured in this verse is that as we face the storms of life and are battered by them, God is polishing us as gemstones—smoothing all our rough edges and eliminating our impurities. He then places us in a beautiful setting, or an antimony, to be shown off by Him. Although we may still carry a lot of the pain and heartbreak from the storms, God will build a foundation of intimacy upon which we will find a balm of healing.

Study 22

Wrestle: *'Aveq* (אבק)

"And Jacob was left alone; and there wrestled a man with him until the breaking of the day."
—Genesis 32:24

Jacob was probably about seventy years old when he took on an angel in an all-night wrestling match. We learn in Genesis 32:25 that this angel could not beat him after hours of wrestling. Can you imagine an angel wrestling with a seventy-year old man and being unable to pin him? I have always said that the way my luck runs, that is probably my guardian angel.

An angel's inability to strong-arm a seventy-year-old man is not the only unusual thing about this passage. In our study verse, we learn that Jacob was *"alone,"* but that he *"wrestled a man."* The Hebrew word translated *"alone"* is *badad* (בדד), which means "solitary," "separated," or "alone." Not only that, but the word is in a *piel*, or intensive, form, meaning that he was *entirely* alone. Yet the Bible says that a *"man"*—the Hebrew word *'ish* (איש)—was also there.

Wrestling with Himself

The word translated *"wrestled"* is *'aveq* (אבק). As a verb, it means "to get dusty," and in noun form, it means "dust." In our study verse, the word is found in a niphal form, which some Hebrew scholars believe gives it a reflexive nature. In other words, you would render this word as *he wrestled with himself* before a presence that was with him. The Hebrew word *'ish* (איש), which is often rendered as "man," as in Genesis 32:24, could mean a spiritual man or a spiritual presence. Jacob was indeed alone with no other corporal being around—but there was a spiritual presence there.

Now let's take a closer look at this word *'aveq* (אבק), or *"wrestled."* The thing to keep in mind is that wrestling as a sport did not come into being until the time of the Greeks and the Romans. But Bible translators figured that our modern term *wrestle* fit this situation well, because what would two people be doing in such a situation, getting each other dusty, if they were not wrestling? Recent insight into the Hebrew language, thanks in part to the Dead Sea Scrolls and the teachings of many Hebrew scholars, gives credibility to translating this word *'aveq* (אבק)—which is in a niphal form as reflexive—as *"wrestled."* If this is correct, Jacob was rolling on the ground, getting himself dusty before a spiritual being who stood watching the whole thing. This "being" could very well have been the preincarnate Jesus.

What could this "rolling" signify? We commonly speak of "walking in someone else's footsteps." The origin of this saying comes from an ancient belief that when a person walks, a part of his wisdom and intelligence passes through the soles of his feet into the dust. This belief was so strong that disciples of a teacher would actually roll in the dust their master kicked up while walking, hoping to pick up traces of his wisdom.

Struggling to Submit to God's Will

Now let's look at the context and timetable of Genesis 32:24. Jacob was on his way to meet his brother, Esau. When we last saw Esau and Jacob together, Esau was out to kill Jacob for stealing his birthright and his blessing. But God is leading Jacob back to his homeland to look up his brother and to make peace with him, even if it means returning the inheritance he stole from him. I would say that Jacob had a real problem with all this and was hoping that God would call the whole thing off before someone got hurt—most likely Jacob.

Thus, I believe this so-called wrestling match was not a physical match with an angel but a mental match. This would be no different from what you or I might do when facing an extremely difficult decision: we might roll around in bed or rock back and forth in a chair, agonizing over the decision while weighing the pros and cons. Is that not like rolling in the dust? Maybe half our battle in making such a decision is in determining God's will. Perhaps Jacob was rolling in the dust, hoping to absorb some of God's wisdom in order to know His perfect will. Yet more than likely, he knew what God's will was, or knew God's heart, but was not ready to accept it, so he spent the entire night wrestling with the decision to submit to that perfect will.

Most of my own "wrestling matches" are not with God or even with an angel but with myself. On my journey to discover God's heart, I do catch glimpses of it, and there are many times when I am not sure I want to submit to His desires. Then I find that, like Jacob, I enter into a wrestling match with my own spirit until God prevails.

Study 23

Curse: *'Arar* (ארר)

"Thus saith the Lord*; Cursed be the man that trusteth in man, and maketh flesh his arm, and whose heart departeth* {turns away} *from the* Lord*."*
—Jeremiah 17:5

The prophet Jeremiah lived at the same time as the prophet Nahum. Nahum dealt with the coming destruction of the nations that opposed Judah, whereas Jeremiah dealt with the sins of Judah and its future destruction. Jeremiah focused on the fact that although King Josiah was purging the nation of idolatrous practices, idolatry still remained in the hearts of the people. He continued to prophesy for twenty-three years after the death of King Josiah, up to the point of the Babylonian captivity. Yet during all that time, the people refused to believe that destruction was at hand. They looked around at their prosperity, at the magnificent temple, and at their religious life and could not believe that it would all end. They were, after all, God's people, and surely God would not bring down His temple!

Trusting in Human Reason and Resources

The people's beliefs had been corrupted because they were following the system of the world. Jeremiah prophesied, *"Cursed be the man that trusteth in man….*" The Hebrew word translated *"cursed"* is *'arar* (ארר), which means "to be without protection." In this context, it means to be without the protection of God. The word rendered *"man,"* the first time the term occurs in the verse, is a curious choice; it is *gavar* (גבר), which specifically speaks of a mighty man—a governmental, religious, and/or family leader. The word translated *"trusteth"* is *batach* (בטח), which means "to cling or adhere to something." In this case, that "something" is *'adam* (אדם), the second Hebrew word in the verse translated as *"man."*

This second *"man"* is the one in whom the great man puts his trust, and the word *'adam* (אדם) indicates this is the earthly, or fleshly, man. *'Adam* (אדם) is also used to express earthly wisdom and reasoning. Thus, this curse is upon a leader or another person of power who clings to human reason, power, influence, and/or resources, forfeiting his protection from God.

Such a leader *"maketh flesh his arm."* The word in Hebrew for *"flesh"* is *basar* (בשׂר), which is often rendered as the good news or counsel of man. The word *"arm"* is *zarar* (זרר), which represents the primary source of nourishment or financial security. The word for *"heart"* is *lev* (לב), which is defined as the source of all passions. The word rendered *"departeth,"* which I translate as "turns away," is *yasar* (יסר), meaning "to withdraw" or "to pervert." A leader whose passion withdraws from God or who perverts His teachings will lose all hope in God.

Thus, this study's verse teaches that the leader who clings to the wisdom and power of man and makes man's counsel, power, or influence his source of security, withdrawing from God or perverting His message, will be without the power and protection of almighty God. I think of the many times I have been in a Bible study when a question comes up and everyone has an opinion about it; they say things like the following: "I think…." "My opinion is…." "Well, Dr. So-and-So said…." Rarely do I hear, "The Bible says…." That was one of Billy Graham's most famous expressions, and we know how mightily God used him. True security and protection are found in God's Word, not in man's words.

Trusting in False Gods

On the surface, it looked as if revival had come to Judah under King Josiah, yet secretly the people still paid tribute to the "queen of heaven," the false goddess Asherah, whom they saw as their source of security in hard times. They also still worshipped Baal, which included the god Moloch, associated with the practice of "passing children through the fire," or sacrificing them as burnt offerings. (See, for example, 2 Kings 23:10.) Archaeological discoveries have shown that these children were newborn babies who were offered by their parents, many of whom did not want the responsibility of parenting and used the practice as a legal way to resolve the problem. Many have likened this practice to abortion. Child sacrifice was also performed by people who were desperate for a miracle.

Additionally, archaeological findings have revealed that these altars to Moloch had a drum and bugle section where musicians would play loudly to drown out the agonized cries of the babies as they were being burned. It is not that these people were all so heartless and cruel as to allow little babies to be burned to death. Yet many of them were so desperate to receive a miracle that they would resort to even such barbaric practices.

We, of course, do not go to such extremes today to try to bribe a miracle out of God, but I have seen people do some pretty desperate things in hopes that God would be pleased enough to grant them a miracle.

How to Move in God's Power and Protection

Jeremiah described the fourfold judgment that would fall upon the nation of Judah over a twenty-year period. First, there would be economic collapse, resulting in famine and starvation. People would suffer weakened immune systems from their poor diets and hunger. Next, violence would break out; people would be forced to hide in their homes while hungry marauders fought each other over a morsel of bread. On top of that, a plague would come. Finally, the Babylonian army, seeing Judah's weakened state, would invade the land and take many of the surviving people captive.

Yet those who put their trust in God rather than in their own abilities, or in other people's, moved in His power and protection. This included Jeremiah, who was treated with respect and honor by the invading Babylonians (mainly because he encouraged Judah to surrender to them). Also, those who did not seek the "arm of flesh"—like Daniel, Shadrach, Meshach, and Abednego—were well-treated. The nation may have fallen on hard times, but those who made God their only Source prospered. Their situation may not fit your definition of prosperity, but these people were blessed nonetheless.

The lesson clearly stands for us today. Will we trust in God alone, or will we, like Judah, claim to trust in God but secretly trust in the arm of flesh? If we are trusting in the latter, we may have an *'arar* (ארר), or a curse, upon us. We may be *without God's protection*.

Study 24

Pure: *Tsaraph* (צרף)

"Every word of God is pure:
he is a shield unto them that put their trust in him."
—Proverbs 30:5

I am often asked what the literal rendering of a verse would be. In other words, what is the direct, word-for-word translation? In many cases, a word-for-word translation often makes little sense. Accordingly, a Bible translator knows that he or she will not be able to express the true intent of a passage without paraphrasing it. That is the case with Proverbs 30:5.

Literally, this verse reads, "God is the refiner of every saying." Refining is the act of separating impurities from a metal. Thus, this statement is a metaphor telling us that the words of God go through a refining process. Why does God's Word undergo such a process? If He is perfect, then His words are perfect and pure. To take this verse literally would be to suggest that God's words carry some impurities. Hence, the translators simply paraphrase this metaphor and say that God's words are pure.

A Revelation of God's Nature

But if we are talking literalness, let's be literal. The word for *"pure,"* or "refine," is *tsaraph* (צרף), which is in an imperative* (command) form and has a paragogic* (intensive) hei (ה). It is also used as a participle. Frankly, I don't know how to express it in English. The best I can do is to speak about it in relation to those who feel they have received a word from the Lord in some manner.

The Hebrew term translated *"word"* is *'amar* (אמר). When used as *a word from God*, it conveys the idea of God making a revelation about His nature. Perhaps you have received a word from God, either in a dream, as a witness in your own spirit, or from someone you trust who hears from God. In whatever way you received this word, you may have clung to it for years, waiting for God to fulfill His promise.

God's Word Refines Us

Now, if you were to put the word you have received from God into an imperative* (command) with a paragogic* (intensive) hei (ה), you would not have the idea that God refines His word before giving it to you, but rather that once He gives it to you, He orders that word to start *refining itself in you*. For example, if God were to give you a word that you were going to receive a candy-apple-red Porsche, you might shout, "Yippee!" But God is commanding that promise to burn itself in you and to refine you of all your trust in yourself, so that your trust is in Him alone. Maybe what you see is a new Porsche, but God sees a fifteen-year-old Ford Focus whose lack of ability to run will keep you trusting in Him. He sees a believer who finds his shield in God and puts his trust in Him.

The Hebrew word translated *"shield"* is *magan* (מגן) and is really a play on the word *magen* (מגן), which is the term for *gardener*. The word that God plants in you is commanded to be a refining process within you; and as you go through this refining process, He carefully tends His word in you, just as a gardener tends to the seeds he has planted.

Maybe the result *will* be the gift of a candy-apple-red Porsche—or maybe not. But through this refining process, you will see the word for what it really is: a means of bringing you into complete trust in

God. The Hebrew word translated *"trust"* is *chasah* (חסה), which is a word for *shelter, a place of protection.*

Thus, whatever promise or word you receive from God, expect Him to refine it and nurture it in you. And when it fully matures, you may find that it is not the candy-apple-red Porsche you once thought He promised. Instead, it may be the peace, the security, and the assurance of His care for you that you really desired from the idea of owning a Porsche. All the self-centered desires you thought that word or promise from God was going to fulfill will be refined away, and what will remain will be the true and pure word from Him.

Seeing Clearly What Is in God's Heart

I remember hearing a minister tell how he was sent out on an internship during his final year of seminary. He felt he had received a word from God that he would be assigned to work with a loving, God-fearing, deeply spiritual pastor who would encourage him to go deeper in his walk with God. As the Lord refined this word in him, however, he found he was placed with a man who was not only the most liberal pastor in the whole denomination but also the coldest and most self-centered. Yet God's word was fulfilled, because being with this liberal pastor forced the man to reevaluate his walk with God, causing him to go deeper in his relationship with His heavenly Father. The loving, caring pastor he had thought the Lord would send was just his own interpretation of God's word to him. God had to refine that idea out of him and leave the true, pure word, which called this minister to move into a deeper walk with Him.

You see, in this refining process, God purges all the deceit in our hearts so we can clearly see what is in His heart.

Study 25

Dream: *Chalam* (חלם)

"In a dream, in a vision of the night, when deep sleep falleth upon men, in slumberings upon the bed; then he openeth the ears of men, and sealeth their instruction."
—Job 33:15–16

If you were to look up these verses from Job in various translations, you would find many different renderings. But if you checked some Bible commentaries, you would find that they all seem to agree on the idea of *sealed instruction* being the "*instruction*" we receive in dreams that are meant for us personally.

However, when I study the above verses in the Hebrew, I wonder if this is correct. The King James Version says that God *"openeth the ears of men."* The Hebrew word translated *"openeth"* is *galah* (גלה), which means "to lay bare," "to reveal," "to be intimate with," or "to have intercourse." The Masoretes pointed up this word in Hebrew as a simple *qal** verbal form,** but just a little change in the vowel's pointing would put this into a *piel* intensive form, and thus it would more specifically mean "to have intercourse." My point is that dreams that come from God may have a purpose beyond just the prophetic. In fact, many rabbis see the Hebrew verb for *"openeth"* as a *piel* (meaning intimacy) and thus would conclude that dreams are a way in which God shares His intimate secrets with us.

Seeing What God Sees

The sages taught that during sleep, your soul is active and not influenced by the physical body. It is during this time that God can become intimate with your soul. In such intimacy, you will see what God sees. God sees the past, the present, and the future. Thus, a by-product of this intimate time with God is that we get to see what He sees, including the future.

The sages go on to teach that if we were really to see exactly as God sees, we would not be able to endure it, especially in terms of the future. Therefore, He wraps our dreams in symbols so that we will not be too startled by what we see. In many cases, He will not allow us to remember a dream because the knowledge of our intimacy with Him would be too shocking for us to endure. Hence, this verse would be rendered, as it seems to be in the King James Version, that God will "seal" our instruction. He will give us a dream, have an intimate moment with us, and then bury what He has shared in symbolism or cause us to forget it completely.

The verse that follows our study passage even gives a reason why we may be caused to forget—because we could become proud. (See Job 33:17.) Or it might be because we've had a dream about the future, and we are not yet ready to accept what is in store for us. How many times have we passed through the fires of life grateful that God did not reveal to us earlier what was going to happen?

Life and Health Found in Dreams?

I know that my next comments might make it seem as if I have "left the reservation," but consider the fact that God created us as beings who need to spend literally one third of our lives in a "nonproductive" state of sleep. God could easily have created us not to require sleep. Therefore, to me, there must be some spiritual reason why He created us to spend a third of our lives in an unconscious state.

The Hebrew word for *"dream"* might provide a clue. It is *chalam* (חלם), which is spelled chet (ח), lamed (ל), mem (מ) (with mem written in its final form); it comes from a Semitic root word meaning "the yolk of an egg," where life is formed. It also means "to restore to health." This word *chalam* (חלם) is telling us that we find our life in our dreams, and it is our dreams that can restore us to health. This is possible if our dream state is indeed an intimate time with God. Our bodies may be unconscious, but our souls are very much awake. With the body at rest and not interfering, God can use that time to share His heart with us.

Looking further at this word for "*dream,*" I find that the chet (ח) represents bonding and binding with God, the lamed (ל) represents instruction from heaven, and the mem (מ) represents the hidden mysteries of God. It is in our dreams that we bind ourselves to God as He reveals His hidden mysteries to us.

Discerning Our Dreams

But not all dreams create a warm, fuzzy feeling inside us. There are such things as nightmares. We must realize that sometimes dreams are nothing more than the imaginings of our own subconscious, while other times they are the expressions of intimate times with God. Furthermore, we must understand that the enemy can also enter our dreams. Perhaps some nightmares are the result of our soul conversing with the enemy. Consider this question for a moment: Before you go to sleep, what do you fill your soul with? Do you reflect on all the day's problems? Do you read some novel about vampires or watch a movie about zombies? At night, your body may be asleep, but your soul continues to remain awake. What did you give it to dwell on?

First Corinthians 14:32 tells us that the prophet is in control of his spirit. Let me suggest an experiment. Before you go to sleep, command your spirit to praise God. You can do this by meditating on the Word or by singing songs of praise to Him. You might find yourself waking up in the middle of the night, worshipping and praising God. And God might even share His secrets with you through a dream.

Study 26

Snow: *Shaleg* (שׁלג)

*"Hast thou entered into the treasures of the snow?
Or hast thou seen the treasures of the hail,
which I have reserved against the time of trouble,
against the day of battle and war?"*
—Job 38:22–23

The Hebrew word rendered *"snow"* is *shaleg* (שׁלג), which your lexicon will tell you means "snow" or "to be white *as snow.*" In our study passage, the phrase *"treasures of the snow"* is a metaphor, but Joshua 10:11 tells us that God did stop Israel's enemies with snow and hail, which made snow a literal treasure to Joshua and his army.

God Desires to Give Us a Pure Heart

The beauty of the Old Testament and its poetry is that you can drill down below its literal meaning and discover hidden treasures. For instance, hail was often viewed as seeds falling from heaven and replanting the earth. And snow carries a very powerful symbolic meaning for the Jews. Jewish literature represents snow as the purist form of white, hence signifying the purity of God and His wisdom. The idea of "trouble," particularly for old Job, is the loss or potential loss of something of value; the idea of "battle and war" likewise reflects the loss of something of value. Yet God is asking, in effect, "Have you seen the treasure house filled with hail, or seeds, to replant what you have lost, and have you entered into the purity of the wisdom of God?" In the midst of trouble, we can look at the purity of God and know that all we will lose in our difficulty is what keeps us from the purity of God—which is a doorway to His heart. Thus, the image of snow indicates God's desire to give us a pure heart.

Bible dictionaries and lexicons do not help us much to further understand the meaning of *shaleg* (שלג), because they merely tell us that the word means "snow." But let's look at this word from a different perspective. If we translate it letter by letter—that is, if we look at the built-in commentary of *shaleg*—we find that it is spelled shin (ש), which refers to God's love and passion; lamed (ל), which indicates a teaching from heaven; and gimmel (ג), which whispers to us about God's loving-kindness. Hence, "snow" is one method used by God to teach us something about His passion and His loving-kindness. By using the numbering method of Gematria,* we find that *shaleg* (שלג) combines shin (ש), or 300; lamed (ל), or 30; and gimmel (ג), or 3, for a total numerical value** of 333. The number 3 represents God, and 333 could designate the Godhead—Father, Son, and Holy Spirit. In this way, the whiteness of snow would remind us of the purity of the Godhead. The Hebrew word *shikachah* (שכחה), which means "forgetfulness," also has a numerical value of 333. Snow helps us to forget, because it covers all the filth and dirt. This passage would then be asking the question, "Have you entered the storehouse of forgetfulness?"

After a snowstorm, I have walked or driven through some of the most rundown areas in the city of Chicago, and the newly fallen snow makes these areas look beautiful; it makes you forget all the clutter and the trash that covers them. In the midst of your own trouble, have you entered God's storehouse of snow, which will help you to forget all the horrible things cluttering your life?

God's Storehouse of Snow

When we come to the treasury of God's storehouse of snow, we enter a wonderland of all the things that God has prepared for us, beyond what we can even imagine. (See 1 Corinthians 2:9.) No wonder God told Job, as he was sitting in misery, "Job, all you see is your trouble. Rather than look at that, *enter* My storehouse of snow and see My purity and My beauty." The Hebrew word translated *"entered"* is *bo'* (בוא), which contains the idea of *coming into*, *being a part of*, or *having intercourse with*. This passage in Job is reminding us that in the midst of our trouble, we need to learn not to dwell on our difficulty but to walk into all the beautiful things God has prepared for us, and to surround ourselves with them.

During the winter months, many of us who live in colder climates wake up to newly fallen snow. We go outside and see a little mountain of white and realize that it is actually our car, which we need to dig out so we can then slip and slide our way to work. At those times, we can think of what is on God's heart, and say, "Let it *snow*!"

Study 27

Sticks: *'Atsah* (עצה)

"And she said, As the Lord thy God liveth, I have not a cake, but an handful of meal in a barrel, and a little oil in a cruse: and, behold, I am gathering two sticks, that I may go in and dress it for me and my son, that we may eat it, and die."
—1 Kings 17:12

The word for *"sticks"* in Hebrew is *'atsah* (עצה). This word has a wide range of meanings and could signify anything from a twig, to a stick, a branch, an entire tree trunk, or a tree. Because there are only about 7,500 words in Classical (biblical) Hebrew, one word is often used to mean many and various things. Hence, Classical Hebrew tends to be more contextual than definitive. That is, rather than go to a dictionary alone to see what a word means, you must also examine the context. This is why I generally do a word study in conjunction with a Scripture verse. Our study text provides an excellent example of how knowing the context can help to define a word.

Reading the above verse, we automatically assume that this widow is collecting sticks to make a fire so she can bake bread with her remaining grain and make a final meal for herself and her son. Yet why does Scripture say she was collecting only two sticks, which certainly would not be enough to build a fire to bake bread?

Faith in God's Provision

As I mentioned, the Hebrew word for *"sticks"* could mean a twig, a stick, a branch, an entire tree trunk, or a tree. The only way you can know how to render this word correctly is from its context. And the only way to know the context is to understand the culture in which this woman lived.

The people of the northern kingdom of Israel were separated from Jerusalem and were not allowed to worship at the temple there. Consequently, those who had a sincere heart toward God sort of adapted temple rituals to fit their particular environment. One of these ancient rituals may have been related to the showbread in the temple. The ritual was for a family to tie a cloth to two sticks, forming a kind of stretcher. They would put two pieces of bread on the cloth, and then the husband and wife would carry it to an altar. There they would ritually eat the bread before the presence of God. This act was reminiscent of the priests eating the temple showbread after it had been replaced by new loaves on the table of showbread in the Holy Place.

This widow and her son were godly people who believed that the Lord would provide for them. They had waited to the point of starvation for the fulfillment of God's promise that He would provide. It was now the eleventh hour, but He had not provided any food. So, in an act of desperation, they were going to carry out a final ritual and eat their bread before God as a demonstration of their faith in His provision and in worship to Him.

Giving and Receiving

Note that the widow says, *"That we may eat it, and die."* The word for *"die"* is *matanu* (מתנו), which is a strange Hebraic form of the word *moth* (מות), or "death." As I wrote previously, there were originally no vowel pointings in Hebrew. Hence, without the indication of vowels, we cannot be certain if the root word was *moth* (מות), for "death," or *nathan* (נתן), which means "to give." I suggest that in this context, the root word should be *nathan* (נתן), which is spelled with a final nun and means "to give" or "to receive so you can give again." The sages point out that this word is spelled the same way backward and forward, giving it a sense of repetition.

If the root word is *nathan* (נתן), what this godly woman would be saying is, "I am about to offer my final meal to God. May He show us mercy and return the meal so we can live, for if He does not, we will die." The woman's faith had reached its limits. As one last act of trust, she and her son would eat what could be their last meal in worship to the God they loved. Then, at the moment the widow began looking for the two *'atsahs* (עצה), or sticks, that she and her son (in the place of his father who had died) would use to carry the final bread to be offered to God, who should suddenly appear but the prophet Elijah, ready to fulfill God's promise.

It Is God Who Delivers

Do you ever feel like you've reached the limits of your faith and just can't go any farther? Most people starving in the little village where the widow lived probably cursed God and then died. But this woman worshipped God and lived. She and her son held to the promise and continued to worship Him even when their circumstances appeared hopeless.

Sometimes, it seems that God waits until the eleventh hour—until you've exhausted all your resources, trying everything you could in the natural. And then one day, when your furniture has been loaded onto a truck to be repossessed, God says to the truck driver, "Okay, you can put it back." I mean, that's hard on your heart. But I will tell you one thing: you will know it was God who delivered you and not your own cleverness.

Study 28

Strong Donkey: *Chamor Garem* (חמר גרם)

"Issachar is a strong {donkey, crouched} *down between two burdens."*
—Genesis 49:14

As with all Semitic languages, Hebrew is filled with many strange idioms.* *Chamor garem* (חמר גרם), or "strong donkey," is one such idiomatic expression that is used to denote *a bitter medicine that cures through cleansing the body.*

Cleansing Through Affliction

There is a sort of play on words here. The name *'Issachar* (יִשָּׂשכָר) comes from the root word *shacar* (שׂכר), which means "reward," "gift," or "intoxication." The Hebrew word for "donkey" is *chamor* (חמר), which is also the word used for fermenting and foaming. There are a number of words in Hebrew that can be rendered as "strong," but the word used here is *garam* (גרם), which signifies *to gnaw at a bone and lick it clean*. It carries the idea of *cleansing through affliction*. In fact, the word *garam* (גרם) has a numerical value of 243, which is the same numerical value as the word *ragam* (רגם). *Ragam* has exactly the same letters as *garam*, but they are placed in a different order. *Ragam* means "to cleanse through stoning." It follows the ancient belief that putting someone to death for their crime purifies them of their guilt. Thus, *ragam* (רגם) has the idea of cleansing through rather painful and extreme measures.

A Gift in Disguise

Accordingly, the term "strong donkey" is really a play on words expressing the idea of drinking a medicine that is very bitter to the taste yet will cleanse the body of whatever is causing it to be afflicted. Today, we say things like, "It will cure what ails you," or "The cure is almost worse than the sickness." An invasive operation, a round of chemotherapy, or even an injection would be an example of a *chamor garem* (חמר גרם), or a "strong donkey." Remember that *'Issachar* (יִשָּׂשכָר) basically means "gift," "reward," or "intoxication." The "reward" or "gift" of drinking wine can be intoxication. I have never been intoxicated, but I've been told by some who have been that it can be a good, warm feeling. Additionally, we often use the word *intoxicated* in relation to being in love, or just as an expression of joy.

The picture here is that Issachar may represent a "strong donkey," or a bitter healing agent, but it is really a gift in disguise that will bring great joy. The expression "{crouched} *down between two burdens*" is encouragement for the one who is drinking this bitter agent. The Hebrew word for *"two burdens"* is *hamishepethaim* (המשׁפתים). This term refers to an enclosure for cattle or an animal stall. The stall is used to keep the cattle from wandering away and to protect them from predators. It is sort of like a hospital where you are surrounded by nurses, doctors, and security personnel dedicated to protecting you while you recover.

So, what is your Issachar today? What is the "strong donkey" that God is using to cleanse you? Is it that coworker who drives you nuts, or your demanding, never-satisfied boss? Is it that crazy driver who cuts you off in rush-hour traffic? Is it that unpaid bill, that car problem, that troubled relationship? Is it something else? What you are experiencing may be a strong donkey, or a cleansing agent of God, that is in reality an Issachar—a gift. While you receive this gift of cleansing, God will place you between two "burdens," or a *hamishepethaim* (המשפתים)—a protective "hospital" where you have nothing to do but heal as He closely watches over you, like a member of a skilled medical staff, as you go through your period of cleansing.

Study 29

Thirst: *Yisemah* (יצמא)

"And the people thirsted there for water; and the people murmured against Moses."
—Exodus 17:3

The above verse is found in the story of the Israelites crossing through the desert on their way to the Promised Land. In Exodus 17:1, God had commanded the children of Israel to stop and make camp at Raphidim. It is a wonder that God asked them to camp in this area. Not only was there no water there, but they were later attacked by the Amalekites at Raphidim. According to human reasoning, this was not the place to set up camp!

A Place Without Water

However, note that the Bible does not say the Israelites were without water; it merely says there was no water at Raphidim. Obviously, they carried water with them, and one reason to stop and set up camp somewhere would be to replenish your water supply. But here God had instructed them to camp at a place where there was no water, and they were to stay there until God said it was all right to move on. When the pillar of cloud started to move, they were to move. But the cloud did not move. And as each day passed, the water they had brought into camp with them was slowly being used up.

Exodus 17:3 says, *"The people thirsted there."* The Hebrew word translated *"thirsted"* is *yisemah* (יצמא), which comes from the root word *tsamah* (צמא), meaning "thirsty." In Jewish literature, I have found that the sages and rabbis sometimes use this word to describe *an overwhelming desire for something*, either for something in the natural world or for the hidden knowledge of God.

Here is what caught my attention—every English translation indicates that the people *were* thirsty. The translators automatically put *yisemah* (יצמא) into the past tense. One Bible version (NLT) even says they were *"tormented by thirst."* But that little yod in front of the word *yisemah* (יצמא)—that "tittle" (see, for example, Matthew 5:18), the smallest letter in the Hebrew alphabet—gives some very important insight into this story. The yod puts this word into a simple *qal* imperfect form, not a *piel* (intensive) form. They were not tormented by thirst; they were not dying of thirst; and in fact they were not thirsty at all. But they were filled with fleshly desire. The use of the imperfect, or future, tense suggests that they were *going* to be thirsty. The question is, what were they going to be thirsty for? They had enough water for the day, and maybe for the next day or even longer. They were not thirsty yet; they had not reached the crisis stage yet; but it was looming out there in front of them. I can imagine them sitting around the campfire at night, bellyaching:

"That crazy Moses, why does he make us camp at a place where there is no water? If we don't leave now, we will never have enough water to make it to the next oasis."

"Not only that, but Moses will probably make us stay here until the water is gone, and we will die of thirst right here!"

What Do You Thirst For?

Moses was not worried about water. Oh, he could get thirsty, just like the rest of the Israelites. But he also had a deep spiritual thirst for the hidden knowledge of God, whereas the others thirsted only for natural things—like satisfaction for their own fleshly gizzards. Moses was focused solely on obedience to God. If God wanted them to camp at Raphidim, then they would camp at Raphidim—water or no water. But the people were focused on the natural world and not on eternal things, and they began to murmur out of fear.

Are you camped at Raphidim? Maybe you just received a layoff notice, an unexpected bill, or a troubling medical report. Maybe an important relationship suddenly hit a rocky stretch. Are you like the Israelites, fretting for fear that your funds will dry up, your health will fail, or your relationship will fall apart, even before anything has happened? Are you fretting over a lack of water, even before you become thirsty? Yet you *are* thirsty, in the sense of *yisemah* (יצמא)—you are filled with desire. The question is, what do you thirst for? Are you *yisemah* (יצמא)—thirsting, desiring—natural security? Or do you seek to use this experience for the flip side of *yisemah* (יצמא), which is a thirst to discover the hidden secrets of the God you love?

Study 30

Trouble: *Ra'ah* (רעה)

"For in the time of trouble he shall hide me in his pavilion:
in the secret of his tabernacle shall he hide me;
he shall set me up upon a rock."
—Psalm 27:5

Sometimes I will simply open my Hebrew Bible and start reading, and a passage will explode in my face. I will wonder why I never really noticed it before, so I will turn to my English Bible, where I usually discover the reason. As I have noted previously, the English translations tend to narrow the picture that the Hebrew gives. The above verse is a good example of this.

In the Time of Rejection and Betrayal

Every English translation renders the word *ra'ah* (רעה) in Psalm 27:5 as *"trouble."* This is a correct translation, depending upon how one views the English word *trouble*. To me, it suggests a time of real stress. We often hear people talk about "these troubled times," indicating that the problems we face are greater than ever before. Yet the word *ra'ah* (רעה) is probably the mildest of the *ra* (רע) words. In fact, it was used by David in Psalm 23:1, where he said, "*The Lord is my shepherd* [*ra'ah*]." David used the very same word for *"shepherd"* in Psalm 23 that he used for *"trouble"* in our study verse. Moreover, *ra'ah* (רעה) can also mean "friend."

How can one word in the Hebrew mean "trouble," "shepherd," and "friend"? In its Semitic root, the word means "to consume." In today's terms, we might say it means "to focus." A shepherd is totally focused on his sheep; he would even lay down his life for them. When used to refer to a friend, *ra'ah* (רעה) means one with whom we have a deep friendship. I recently read of a Navy Seal in Afghanistan who died when he threw himself on a grenade to save his friends. That is the time when you would use the word *ra'ah* (רעה) for "friend"—one so focused on his friends that he would lay down his life for them.

Yet *ra'ah* (רעה) can also have a shadow, or negative, connotation connected with it. The shadow aspect of *ra'ah* (רעה) is when you rely on a trusted leader or a friend, but they let you down. The spelling of *ra'ah* (רעה)—resh (ר), ayin (ע), hei (ה)—expresses the idea of an emotional brokenness you experience when a leader or a close friend abuses his position to take advantage of you.

This is the trouble that David was referring to. He knew rejection. He knew what it was like to have his best friend stab him in the back. In those times when David was emotionally broken by a natural relationship, the Lord hid him in His *sukkah* (סכה), or His *"pavilion."* The Hebrew word translated *"hide"* is *satar* (סתר). This is a hiding that someone else provides for you. It is a hiding at a time when you are wounded, and someone makes sure you are protected and tends to your wounds. It is a hiding where you are totally dependent upon that other person for your safety. Five verses later, in Psalm 27:10, David expressed a similar thought: *"When my father and my mother forsake me, then the LORD will take me up."* When everyone whom we trusted in and depended upon is unable to help us, God will *satar* (סתר), or hide, us in His *sukkah* (סכה), or His covering of protection.

Treasured by God as We Rest in Him

Psalm 27:5 also says that God will *"hide"* us in His *"tabernacle."* This second instance of the word *"hide"* in our study verse is translated from a different Hebrew term, *tsaphan* (צפן). My discovery of this difference is what drove me to see how our English translation handled it, because what I had read in the Hebrew was the word *treasure*. True, *tsaphan* (צפן) does mean "to hide," but it refers to the hiding of a treasure or of precious gems. Thus, God not only protects us in His hiding place, but He also treasures us as we rest in His tabernacle.

The Masoretic text puts the possessive of this word *"tabernacle"* in the third person—"His tabernacle." The scribes had to do this, because God surely does not treasure us in *our* tabernacle. Or does He? The Hebrew word rendered *"tabernacle"* is *'ahal* (אהל). The sages teach that *'ahal* (אהל) simply means "tent" but is also used to donate "tabernacle." But when it is used for tabernacle, an assumption is made that you are referring to a tabernacle as a place of worship and praise, so you could easily render this word as "a praise to God" rather than as merely "tent" or "tabernacle." Thus, we can easily keep this in the first person by saying, "He treasures me in my praise to Him."

Finally, David says that God sets him *"upon a rock."* After all this hiding and secreting, the Lord sets him on a rock for all his enemies to see him? This is actually a good thing. The Hebrew word for *"rock"* is *basur* (בצור). The Septuagint translates this word into the Greek as *petras*, the same word used in 1 Corinthians 10:4, where Paul says, *"Christos ho en oe petra,"* which I render as, "And yet the Messiah [Jesus] was the Rock." When the world sees that we are resting on the *basur* (בצור), the Rock, no one will touch us.

Study 31

Understanding: *Levav* (לבב)

"But I have understanding as well as you; I am not inferior to you: yea, who knoweth not such things as these?"
—Job 12:3

I was quite fascinated when I read this verse in my Hebrew Bible, because the word translated as *"understanding"* is *levav* (לבב), which means "heart." In its literal form, what Job is saying is, "I have a *heart* just like yours." I have read in Jewish literature that when you find the word *heart* with a double beth (בב) after the lamed (ל), it indicates *your heart and God's heart joined together.* In the majority of the cases where this word is used, it only has one beth (ב). So, Job is also essentially saying, "I understand God's heart as well as you do." To be sure, each word in Hebrew can have a wide range of meanings, and *levav* (לבב) is often used to express the idea of "understanding," "thought," "reasoning," or "judgment." But let's be real here—all these things stem from the *heart.*

Job's Understanding of God's Word

Our study verse would suggest that Job is getting really annoyed with his friends. It appears he is saying to them, "Tell me something I don't already know." I have no doubt that this is what Job is saying, but I think he is also saying much more. As I indicated above, the sages used to teach that when two beths (בב) were used, it indicated man's heart and God's heart joined together. Hence, Job is further saying, "My heart is joined with the heart of God, just as yours is, and yet we disagree."

The Hebrew word translated as *"inferior"* is *naphal* (נפל), which means "to fall" but signifies *to fall in surrender* or *to just give up*. A literal translation of Job 12:3 would therefore be, "My heart is joined with God's heart, just as yours is, yet I am not surrendering because of what you are saying to me."

Job's Understanding of His Own Heart

Next, the phrase rendered in English as *"who knoweth not such things as these"* could be rendered in a different way. The Hebrew word for *"these"* is *'alah* (אלה)—again, not to be confused with the Arabic *Allah*. With just the pure consonants, *'alah* could be used in a wide variety of ways. It could denote "these," or it could mean "to worship and adore." Additionally, it could mean "to swear"—or, as my study partner pointed out, "to curse," as in *to curse one's soul*. Another meaning is "to be fat," or "stout." Finally, as shown in a previous study, it could mean "to be without God." You might ask, "Which meaning should we use?" The answer, once again, is that it depends upon the context.

To fit the context of my translation so far, I would have to translate *'alah* (אלה) as "curse one's soul." Hence, I would render this passage as, "I have a heart just like yours, but it is not surrendering because of what you are saying to me. My heart does not curse my soul, as you are doing." Job is not rejecting his friends' advice simply because he doesn't like it. Rather, he is rejecting it because he knows his own heart, and he knows that his heart is one with God's; and what his friends are telling him does not bear witness in his own heart.

I have had many people prophecy over me, but often what they say does not bear witness in my own heart. At such times, if I believe my heart to be one with God's heart, I could say, like Job, "Look, my heart is one with God's heart, just as you claim your heart is one with God's heart when you are speaking to me. Yet what you say does not bear witness with my own heart. I have made every effort to join my heart with God's, and what you say sounds really good (or bad), but I'm sorry—in this case, I must claim Colossians 3:15: '*Let the peace of God rule* [Greek, *brabeue*, meaning "to umpire," or "to arbitrate"] *in your* [own] *hearts.*'"

Study 32

Beloved: *Yadiyad* (ידיד)

"My beloved spake, and said unto me, Rise up, my love, my fair one, and come away {with me}."
—Song of Solomon 2:10

I know that Song of Solomon may get a little mushy for some of us, but most of us will agree that this book of the Bible is a representation of our relationship with God. More than that, it is a picture of God's heart—and, as we have seen in previous studies, we must come to truly understand His heart toward us, lest we offend it.

The very first word in our study verse sets the groundwork for entering into the heart of God, because unless we can call Him *Beloved*, we have no right to enter. The Hebrew word translated *"beloved,"* is *dodi* (דודי), from which the name *David* comes, as well as the word *yadiyad* (ידיד). *Dodi* (דודי) comes from a Semitic root that means "to boil"; it is also a word used for *love*. But this is not a "Hey dude, love ya" type of love. It is the real thing. The "boiling" expresses this love not only as passionate and overflowing, but also as active—always doing something and always seeking a way to express itself.

When the young woman speaking in Song of Solomon 2:10 essentially calls Solomon her *dodi* (דודי), she is saying that she is completing him in love. Jewish literature teaches that a man is not complete until he has a mate. The idea is that love is not complete until it is shared. We will return to this theme later in this study. Jewish literature further teaches that the highest form of prayer fills a lack in the *Shekinah* (שׁכינה), which is traditionally an expression of the feminine aspect of God. The highest form of prayer is when we take on the role of a "husband" to God; God is a "wife" to us in the sense of one who desires the love and attention of her husband.

Hand in Hand, Heart in Heart

You enter the heart of God the way a man enters the heart of a woman. He looks at her and says, "You are my beloved. There is no one else but you." The word *yadiyad* (ידיד) is formed from the word *yad* (יד), which means "hand." Note that *yad* (יד) is repeated in *yadiyad* (ידיד), thus meaning "hand in hand." The other day, when I was walking in the Chicago Loop (the main business district along the Chicago River), I saw a man and a woman walking together. He was short, and she was tall; he was not that attractive, and she was very attractive. Just looking at them, I never would have put the two of them together romantically—but there they were, holding hands. Their action immediately declared that they were either lovers or shared a special relationship.

Jesus may be your Savior, your Master, and your Friend, but is He also your *yadiyad* (ידיד)? When you and Jesus walk down the street, do people see a boss and an employee? A master and a servant? Or do they see *yadiyad* (ידיד)—beloved friends, hand in hand? Many ancients believed the heart was in the palm of the right hand, so when people joined their right hands together, it was a symbol of sharing each other's hearts. Thus, a handshake in those days bore greater significance than it does today. Beloved friends are *heart in heart*; they share each other's hearts.

A Consuming Passion

What does Jesus, our *yadiyad* (ידיד), or Beloved, say to us? He says, *"Rise up, my love."* As noted in an earlier study, it is interesting that the Hebrew word for *"my love"* is *ra'ah* (רעה), which can mean "shepherd" or "friend." Neither term may sound as romantic as *"my love"* until you consider the broader implications of the word *ra'ah* (רעה)—it is sometimes used for "evil." This particular meaning of "evil" is *an evil of consumption* and describes *a consuming passion*, one that takes priority over more important things. For example, someone may have a consuming passion to make money; that passion becomes evil when the person sacrifices his family and friends for the sake of accumulating wealth. But a consuming passion does not have to be evil. In the case of our study verse, Solomon is not just calling his beloved his love; he is saying that she is his *consuming passion*.

As we saw previously, *ra'ah* (רעה) also expresses a relationship in which a person loves so much that he makes himself completely vulnerable to the object of his love, thus opening himself up to heartbreak if that love is betrayed. When Jesus calls us His *ra'ah* (רעה), He is saying, "I have opened My heart to you. I am, by choice, by an act of My will, making Myself vulnerable to you. You now have the ability to break My heart or to do evil to My heart. But I love you so much that I am willing to take the risk."

I have heard Christians pleading with God, telling Him that they want to know Him and be intimate with Him—and yet they have other "gods," or idols, in their lives. Just as a woman will not share her innermost heart with a man if she knows he will be unfaithful to her, God may not reveal His secrets to us if He knows we carry unfaithfulness in our hearts.

A Completed Love

After saying *"Rise up, my love,"* God calls us His *"fair one."* The Hebrew word for this term is *yapath* (יפת), which means "complete" or "fullness." He is calling us His *complete one*, or *the one who will complete His circle of love*. As I emphasized earlier, you can love someone from a distance, but it is not until that love is returned that you feel the elation and joy of being loved. Love needs to be returned to be complete.

I don't really read the last phrase as "come *away* with me." In the Hebrew, there is a lamed (ל) before the pronoun* me. Traditionally, when used as a preposition, as in this case, the lamed (ל) is generally rendered as "to" or "unto." Thus, we would render this passage as God simply saying, "Come to Me."

Come as Far as You Can

The Talmud tells a story about about a king who had a disagreement with his son. As a result of this falling out, the son left home to live in another kingdom. After some time, the father sent a messenger to his son, asking him to come home. The son replied, "It is too far for me to come." So, the father sent the messenger back with this response: "Then come as far as you can, and I will meet you."

Can you call Jesus *yadiyad* (ידיד), Beloved? If not, He is still saying to you, "Come to Me. Come as far as you can, and I will meet you." Once you meet Jesus, you can be *yadiyad* (ידיד) with Him, hand in hand, and heart in heart.

Study 33

Wait: *Chakah* (חכה)

"Therefore will the L*ORD wait, that he may be gracious unto you, and therefore will he be exalted, that he may have mercy upon you: for the* L*ORD is a God of* {justice}: *blessed are all they that wait for him."*
—Isaiah 30:18

The above verse seems pretty clear-cut. The Lord will wait so that He may be gracious, and all those who wait for Him are blessed. But it does sound like an awful lot of waiting. In the Hebrew, the word used for the waiting that the Lord is doing in order to be gracious—*chakah* (חכה)—is the same word used for the waiting that we are doing to be blessed. We should keep in mind that this is not the word for "*wait*" that Isaiah uses later in chapter 40, verse 31, in the familiar passage that says, "*They that wait upon the* L*ORD shall renew their strength.*" That word for "*wait*" is *qavah* (קוה), which is also the term used for making rope. It denotes a binding process—those who *bind themselves* to God will have their strength renewed.

Chakah (חכה), however, refers to what we generally think of in regard to the word *wait.* It means "to wait," "to be patient," or "to hold back." It is interesting that the first use of the word *chakah* (חכה) in this verse is in relation to God waiting so that He can be gracious.

The Hebrew word translated *"gracious"* is *chanan* (חנן), which carries the idea of compassion and favor. Why does God wait to bestow His favor? Why does He hold back on it? The answer that we are given is so that He can be exalted.

Waiting Until the Eleventh Hour

There is one additional twist to this word *chakah* (חכה). It is in a *piel* imperfect form, which implies a waiting until the last minute or even the last possible second. Sometimes, it does seem that God operates in that manner in our lives. For example, suppose we have applied to work at a certain company. God may wait until our last unemployment check has run out before telling the human resources manager at that company, "Okay, you can give the old boy a call and tell him he starts on Monday." It is not always that way, but God does seem to have established a pattern of intervening at the last moment. Sarah did not have a child until it seemed too late for her to be a mother. (See, for example Hebrews 11:11.) King Saul gave in to the temptation to perform the sacrifice before a battle because the prophet Samuel, who was supposed to perform it, was running late. (See 1 Samuel 13:5–14.) Jericho did not fall until the seventh day, and even then the walls didn't fall until the Israelites marched around them a full seven times, as God had instructed them. (See Joshua 6.)

Perhaps one clue as to why God waits until the eleventh hour to tell the executioner not to pull the switch lies in the last part of Isaiah 30:18, where the word *"wait"* is used a second time. This time, it is we who are doing the waiting, not God. We are supposed to be blessed when we wait. I was surprised to find that the word translated *"blessed"* here is not *barak* (ברך), as I had assumed. It is *'ashar* (אשר), which doesn't just mean happiness but rather "moving in the direction of peace and happiness." The word for *"wait," chakah* (חכה), is in a *qal* participle form, giving the idea of a present tense. Hence, we are patiently, contentedly waiting for Him to act and to show us His favor. The roof may be about to collapse, the floor may be about to give way, but we just sit patiently, knowing that God will come through. How can we sit by joyfully and wait contentedly? Because we know that He will have mercy and compassion on us, and that He is a God of justice.

When We Wait, God Alone Is Exalted

There is one final piece to this puzzle. Just how is God exalted by waiting until the last minute? Think about when that last minute, or that eleventh hour, usually comes. It is when we have exhausted the last of our own resources, and the whole situation seems hopeless and impossible. Recall the story of when God reduced Gideon's army to just three hundred men to go against an enemy army of one hundred and ten thousand Midianites. God knew that even if Gideon had a ten-thousand-man army, he might still have said, "Hey, look at what I've done (by the grace of God, of course)." But with merely three hundred men, Gideon could only say, in effect, "That had to be God's doing, and His alone." (See Judges 7.) At the eleventh hour, God can step in; and when He does, we know that it is He—and not we—who has brought the deliverance. Then He alone is exalted.

Study 34

Discouraged: *Qatsar* (קצר)

"And the soul of the people was much discouraged because of the way."
—Numbers 21:4

Some years ago, there was the story of a college president who one day just walked away from his job and his family, boarded an airplane, and left it all behind. Perhaps, when things get tough, all of us occasionally fantasize about leaving our lives behind and making a new start.

I grew up hearing stories from people who testified how they had walked a tough road, but God had sent miracle after miracle to deliver them. They waxed lyrical about how God had supported them and carried them through various dangers on their life's journey. Yet many of us have no such testimonies. We continue on the journey and grow weary of our travels and of being a "good soldier." As David said in Psalm 55:6, we long for the wings of a dove so we can fly away and be at rest. I suppose that after David became king, he sometimes contemplated writing a simple note that read, "I'm out of here," sneaking out, finding a flock of sheep, and going back to being a shepherd.

"I'm Out of Here!"

In Numbers 21, we learn that during the Israelites' journey, the Canaanites attacked them and took some of the people prisoner. In verse 3, we find that they cried out to God, and He gave them a great victory. Yet the very next verse says that *"the soul of the people was much discouraged because of the way."* They, too, probably wanted to say, "I'm out of here!" We often criticize the Israelites when we read about their complaints and their disobedience as they wandered in the wilderness, and we marvel at God's patience with them. But are we in danger of acting like they did?

The Hebrew word translated *"discouraged," qatsar* (קצר), is in a *qal* imperfect (future) form, and can mean "impatient," "discouraged," "to cut down," "to reap," "grieved," "unable," "short," "deficient," or "passionate." A *qal* imperfect form means that this is a simple verb for speaking about an event that is occurring and continues to occur. Our modern translations usually render *qatsar* (קצר) in one of three ways: "impatient," "weary," or "discouraged." Young's Literal Translation renders the word as "short." In modern English, these words carry very different meanings. But for those of us who feel that we are wandering in a "wilderness," it is very important that we understand just what the Hebrew people were feeling, because we need to know if we are making the same mistakes and falling into the same sins. If we are just *discouraged*, perhaps God will understand. If we are *weary*, well, that is also understandable. But if we are *impatient*, that does not sound very good.

I would have to rule out "impatient," "passionate," "grieved," "reap," "short," and "indifferent," as they do not fit the context as well as other definitions—leaving us with "discouraged," "to cut down," and "unable." For me, "discouraged" embodies the idea of being "cut down" or "unable." Thus, I would consider the best rendering, as found in our study verse, to be "discouraged."

Discouragement as Self-Righteousness

The word *qatsar* (קצר) is spelled qof (ק), sade (צ), resh (ר). At various times, the ancient sages have associated each of these three letters with self-righteousness. Discouragement tends to carry an idea of self-righteousness. The text says that Israel was growing discouraged "*because of the way.*" The Hebrew word translated "*way*" is *derek* (דרך), which means "a journey," either spiritual or physical.

Perhaps you, too, have become *qatsar* (קצר), or "*discouraged,*" in your life journey for the same reason the Israelites did: you have become self-righteous. Maybe you have experienced miracles and deliverances from God, but now the journey is really rough, and you feel disheartened because God has not delivered you as He has in the past. Like Israel, you have been faithful, you have left Egypt, and you have worshipped and praised God. But now you have begun to think, *I have known His miracles. That makes me special, like Israel. I am one of God's people, and I deserve better than this.* So, you become self-righteous, thinking you deserve better treatment than the next person simply because you have done many little "favors" for God. You have the King's ear, and you are His child and friend; therefore, you should receive special consideration.

Yes, indeed, you do get special attention, but it may be different from what you anticipated. Like Paul, you can share in the sufferings of Jesus. You can understand the suffering that is going on around you. A rabbi once told me how he loves to enter into silence, for in silence he can hear the world cry.

Feeling God's Heart

I remember one time when I was sitting in a library, quietly crying out to God to speak to me—to show Himself to me. I heard nothing. I told God that all I ever wanted was to know His heart. He said nothing. But then, I did hear something. Not audibly, but deep in my heart. I looked at a person sitting nearby, and in my heart, I heard her weeping. Then I saw a man at a computer looking for a job online, and in my heart, I felt his despair. I also saw another man, obviously homeless, sitting in the library, probably just to keep warm, and suddenly I felt his loneliness. I soon realized I was not feeling the despair and loneliness from *them*—I was feeling it from *God's heart*, which was feeling it from them. It wasn't the people's weeping I heard; it was God's weeping.

I felt that I heard Jesus saying, "I have given you special attention. I have given you the best. I have allowed you to enter My heart. You wanted to enter into My heart, and now you have. Now you feel what I feel as I look upon those whom I love as much as I love you. There are many rooms in My heart. You have enjoyed some of My more joyful rooms, but now I am letting you share a very special and private room with Me. It is My weeping room, the room where I go to weep over the suffering in this world. Will you weep with Me? Is that acceptable to you? Do you still want to enter My heart?"

Perhaps God is whispering the same thing to you. Do you still wish to enter His heart?

Study 35

Fast: *Tsum* (צום)

"So we fasted and besought our God for this: and he was intreated of us."
—Ezra 8:23

Ezra was about to lead the Israelite captives back to their homeland from exile. Before their journey, he proclaimed a fast for safety. But Ezra faced a little problem: the Persian king had sanctioned this move back to Israel, offering to provide military troops to ride with the Israelites as protection on their trip. Ezra, however, had told the king, in effect, "Naw, we don't need your troops. God will protect us."

Ezra had refused the offer of protection because he wanted to make sure the king understood that this return was of God and not of man. But when he faced the realities of the journey, he realized why the king had offered to send troops to protect the people, and he began to think, *What have I done?* At least, that is how it appeared to me when I first read this passage in Ezra. But when I took a closer look at it and read it in the Hebrew, I got a different picture.

The Working of God, and Not of Man

The so-called "Ezra Fast" that is described in Ezra 8 is considered a fast to resolve problems. Yet it would seem that Ezra called for a fast not so much to resolve problems as to confirm that this was God's journey they were making, and they wanted Him to affirm that He was a part of it. Thus, the way I read our study text, Ezra's concern does not appear to be so much about safety, because his faith seemed to be intact. Rather, his concern was to make sure that everyone understood that this move was of God, and not of man.

The word used for "*fast*" here is *tsum* (צום), which basically means "to put a cover over your mouth." In other words, this was a food fast. *Tsum* (צום) is spelled sade (צ), vav (ו), mem (ם), with the mem written in a final form. These specific letters may actually give us the reason for this type of fast. The sade (צ) represents humility, the vav (ו) represents a connection from earth to heaven, and the (final) mem (ם) represents things that are hidden. There was so much human effort involved in the preparations that the people making the journey had almost forgotten that God was behind their move. So, the fasting was an act of humility and an outward recognition and confirmation that this whole operation was the working of God.

Worship Before Undertaking the Journey

Ezra says that they "*besought*" God on this matter. It stands to reason that if God was really behind their move, they did not need to pray for "traveling mercies," as that would be assured. Again, they sought the Lord to confirm that they were only following His direction. The Hebrew word translated "*besought*" is *baqash* (בקש). This term means "to seek" or "to ask," but when it is used in relation to God, it is an act of worship. Note, too, that this is in a *piel* (intensive) form with a paragogic (intensive) hei (ה). This is a grammatical device that indicates a high level of intensity. So, the people did not simply join hands and ask for a safe journey—they went into serious worship before God.

What is really interesting here is that merely asking or petitioning God is a form of worship. It would seem that even if we go to God with nothing but petitions, at least we are communicating with Him, and that can be worship. Worship does not have to take the form of a well-orchestrated, rehearsed ceremony with flowery words, and it does not need to include a worship team of skilled musicians and singers. Worship can simply be going to God in humility and acknowledging Him in all things.

God Journeys with His People

That is what Ezra 8:23 is all about. The people turned their preparations and anticipation for their journey into a time of worship, and God responded by being *"intreated"* of them. Some translations render this phrase as "He listened" to them or "He answered" them. The Hebrew word translated *"intreated"* is *'atar* (עתר), which carries the idea of "becoming favorable." It is in a niphal form, which makes it reflexive, meaning that God would make Himself accommodating. In other words, God would fit naturally and perfectly into the journey with His people. To have foreign soldiers protecting them on such a trip would be insulting to Him, since He would be such a vital part of their journey. If an enemy were to attack them, it would be attacking God, as well.

As we begin each day and perform the duties entrusted to us, we need to approach our ongoing life journey as Ezra and the Israelites did. They began their journey to their homeland in a state of *baqash* (בקש), or *worshipful petition*, to which God responded in *'atar* (עתר)—He became a favorable part of the journey. No matter what our daily activity may be, if we do it as unto God and allow Him to *'atar* (עתר), or to become a favorable part of our activity, we will spend the day in worship; accordingly, we will, as Paul says, *"pray without ceasing"* (1 Thessalonians 5:17).

Study 36

Breath: *Neshimah* (נשמה)

"Let every thing that hath breath {a soul}
praise the Lord. {Hallelujah}."
—Psalm 150:6

In the last study, I mentioned *praying without ceasing.* I would like to examine this idea more closely. Hebrew tradition teaches that the Hebrew words for "soul," *neshamah* (נשמה), and *"breath," neshimah* (נשמה), are related. The soul fills the entire body, and when a person sleeps, it "rises" to draw down life from above. Similarly, with each and every breath that a person takes—as his breath leaves him from below and returns to him from above—he should praise God, because God renews our breath every minute, not just when we are asleep.

Offering Constant, Humble Praise to God

First Thessalonians 5:17–18 says, *"Pray without ceasing. In every thing give thanks: for this is the will of God in Christ Jesus concerning you."* The Greek word translated *"pray"* is *proseuchomai,* which is used eighty-seven times in the New Testament for prayer. However, there are many types of prayer, and the word *proseuchomai* doesn't give us much insight into how we should pray. Let us therefore explore some Hebrew words for prayer and their meanings: *harim* (הרם) means "to extol"; *berek* (ברך) means "to bless"; *gil* (גול) signifies "to rejoice"; *hagah* (הגה) denotes "to meditate"; *histahawah* (הצהוה) means "to adore" or "to lay prostrate"; *'anah* (אנה) communicates "to sigh," or "to express deep feelings"; and, of course, *halah* (הלה) means "praise," from which we get the word *hallelujah*, meaning "praise the Lord."

There is one other Hebrew word, *palal* (פלל), which is often translated as "to pray" but specifically means "to offer supplication to God" or "to offer humble praise to God." The Septuagint uses the Greek word *proseunchomai* for *palal* (פלל). Thus, when Paul said we should pray without ceasing, he meant that we should offer constant, humble praise to God. Paul didn't throw that verse into his first letter to the Thessalonians to take up space, to sound pious, or to make people buy his books. This is a command from God; this is His Word.

With Every Breath, We Speak God's Name

But the question we will look into further is this: how can we praise God without ceasing—whether we are awake or asleep? Perhaps Hebrew tradition was on to something in this regard. In Exodus 4:10, we learn that Moses confessed to having a speech problem. The Talmud teachers say he was "thick of tongue." The ancient Hebrew sages taught that this problem made it impossible for him to correctly speak the name of God, for pronouncing all the names of God required the use of the tongue. So God gave Moses a name for Himself that did not require the use of the tongue but only the breath: *YHWY* (יהוה). We speak that name with our *neshimah* (נשמה), our breath; or with our *neshamah* (נשמה), our soul. Perhaps this is part of what Paul had in mind when he spoke about praying without ceasing. With every breath that we take and release, we speak the name of God. Thus, even in our sleep, we speak His name.

Let me give you an illustration of what I mean by praising God with our breath. Let's say I am scrolling down the phone numbers on my cell phone looking for a fellow named Paul. I am muttering to myself, "Paul, Paul, Paul…," and next to me happens to be a person named Paul. That Paul looks at me and says, "Yes?" I respond, "Sorry, I wasn't talking to you. I was just muttering to myself." So, too, with every breath we take, we are saying, "*Yah-weh, Yah-weh.*" God says, "Yes?" And we respond, "No, I was just muttering. I was just pondering my problem, fretting over this bill, worrying about this relationship." Or we say, "No, I was just watching this movie, reading this book, playing this game." We can get so busy and distracted in life that we are not conscious of God's presence. I believe it was for this reason that in Psalm 103:1, David grabbed hold of his *neshamah* (נשמה), his *"soul,"* and *commanded* it to bless the Lord, saying, in effect, "Soul, when I call out to God, you bless Him!" We need to do what David did and consciously remind our soul to praise God. We sometimes have to grab hold of our soul by the collar, slam it against the wall, and command it to bless the Lord.

You might also want to try this: Before you go to sleep at night or enter into any activity that will distract you from the presence of God, command your soul to bless and praise the Lord. Then, every breath you take will be in praise to God, and you may discover what Paul meant when he said, *"Pray without ceasing."* Everything you do and say will be as unto God. You will find that once you enter God's heart, you can remain there even while working at your job, cleaning the house, taking an exam, or doing any other activity where you would not normally think about Him. If you command your soul to praise the Lord during that activity, your soul will praise Him even when you are not consciously thinking about Him.

May every breath, or *neshimah* (נשמה), that you take today be in praise to God.

Study 37

From the Hidden: *Miktam* (מכתם)

"Michtam of David. Keep me, O God; for I have taken refuge in Thee. I have said unto the LORD: 'Thou art my LORD; I have no good but in Thee.'"
—Psalm 16:1–2 (JPS Tanakh 1917)

The word *"michtam,"* or *miktam* (מכתם), is a transliteration from the Hebrew that literally means "from gold" or "from the hidden." Many commentators simply interpret the term to mean "Poem of Gold" and ignore the *hidden* idea. Indeed, "Poem of Gold" is a good translation, as gold is a symbol of the glory of God. Still, there is a secondary meaning that is worth exploring. The root word of *miktam* is *ketam* (כתם), which means "hidden" and is spelled kap (כ), taw (ת), mem (ם), with the mem written in the final form. The kap (כ) tells us that our hearts are filled with God's thoughts, the taw (ת) represents truth, and the (final) mem (ם) speaks of the hidden knowledge of God. I personally translate *"Michtam of David"* as "a spiritual secret of David." More so, David is sharing his heart with us in this poem, which is what a poet does when he writes his verse. David, a man whose heart was joined with God's—he was "a man after God's own heart" (see Acts 13:22)—would have a lot to communicate when he shared his heart, because he would also be sharing the heart of God.

"Keep Me, O God"

So, what is this secret from David's heart, a heart that is joined with God's heart? David is able to command God to *"keep"* him. The Hebrew word translated "keep" is *shamereni* (שמרן) and is from the root word *shamar* (שמר), which means "to watch closely, to observe, and to never lose sight of." This word is in an imperative, or command, form. David is not asking God; he is commanding Him. But it is also in a *qal* form, so it is a mild command—more like a supplication. It is not David's usual style to use the *qal* form in his poetry, and the *qal* is not as strong emotionally as the other verbal forms. Thus, this verse would be rendered more like this: "You promised me. Now keep Your promise."

The promise is for God to watch over David's every move and to make him aware when he is slipping and falling into sin. The enemy's deceitfulness is so subtle, and David (who once committed adultery and then murder to cover it up) knows that all too well and does not trust himself, so he is calling on God to be on guard on his behalf. By what right does he make such a demand upon the Master of the universe? By the right he claims when he takes refuge in Him. You see, the refuge he is seeking here is to escape from the enemy who seeks his soul, the enemy who will cause him to sin. The word in the Hebrew for *"refuge"* is *chasithi* (חסת) and is spelled chet (ח), samek (ס), taw (ת). By finding refuge in God, David will find a chet (ח), or a bonding with God, such that he is a samek (ס), or one who is protected. This protection comes in knowing the taw (ת), which is truth.

There are many times in our walk with God when we do not know what is right and what is wrong. Sometimes, according to our limited human understanding, we believe that what we are doing is right and is truly of God, only to find out down the road that we missed it completely. Even if we were to stand on a street corner preaching the gospel, it is possible that our actions could be wrong. To preach the gospel in this way may seem right and noble, so how could it not be of God? But then, how do we know it is not a trick of the enemy to distract us from the perfect will of God, who may have something different for us to do? Like David, we need to find *chasithi* (חסת), or *"refuge,"* in God so that He can *shamereni* (שמרן), or "keep us" from straying from His will and sinning.

We don't know the complete story of David and Bathsheba. The Bible tells us that David's heart lusted after her. But on the surface, perhaps David convinced himself that he was only ministering to a lonely, frightened woman whose husband was off to war. Since her husband was such a loyal servant, it was only fitting that he, the king, should comfort the man's wife. Of course, Scripture tells us what was really going on in David's heart. Only when Nathan confronted him about his sin did it dawn on him how deceived he had really been.

In Harmony with God

I don't know if that is what David was thinking when he shared this verse, but it is clear that he knew he had to find *chasithi* (חסת), or *"refuge,"* in God, for he could not trust his own understanding.

In verse 2, David says, *"I have said unto the Lord* [Jehovah]: *'Thou art my Lord* [*'adoni* (אדני), meaning "master, guide, and instructor"]; *I have no good but in Thee.'"* That last phrase is difficult to translate because it literally says, "You, my goodness is not upon You." Translators have, I believe correctly, rendered this phrase as, *"I have no good but in Thee."* David knew that he could not depend upon any alleged goodness in himself, and that there is only One who is good, and that is the Lord God. Jesus said the same thing in Luke 18:19.

The Hebrew word for *"good," tov* (טוב), means "that which is in perfect harmony with God." Once you are *in tune with God*, or *in harmony with Him*, you will be able to enter His heart. Thus, I could paraphrase our study passage to read, "When I find my refuge in God, who examines me in complete detail so that I do not fall into sin, I am then indeed in tune with Him, and He can use me as a conduit."

Study 38

Treasures of Darkness: *Orsaroth Chosheke* (ארצרות חשך)

"And I will give thee the treasures of darkness, and hidden riches of secret places, that thou mayest know that I, the Lord, which call thee by name, am the God of Israel."
—Isaiah 45:3

Isaiah 45:2, the verse just prior to our study verse, indicates that God will blaze the trail for us as we journey in His plan and calling for our lives. Then, in verse 3, God explains how He is going to equip us—with the *"treasures of darkness"* and *"hidden riches of secret places."* That sounds so wonderful, but do we really know what the *"treasures of darkness"* and *"hidden riches of secret places"* are?

A Treasure of Knowledge

To understand these phrases, we need to examine the four Hebrew terms from which they are rendered. The first two are *orsaroth chosheke* (ארצרות חשך), or *"treasures of darkness."* My initial question is, why would God give us something from darkness? Is He not the Light? This verse almost suggests that we will reclaim the powers that were originally the property of the light, but which were stolen and perverted by the darkness. That sounds good; after all, is it not time to take our rod, throw it on the ground, and let it turn into a snake that eats up the snakes of the occult? (See Exodus 7:8–12.) I think we would all agree to that, but I am not sure this is what the passage is really saying.

The Hebrew word for "*treasures,*" *orsaroth* (ארצרות), comes from the root word *'asar* (אצר). This word has the idea of a *storehouse*, or *treasures that are laid up but are not hidden*. But "*treasures*" would really be the wrong word to use here, because the first thing that comes to mind in our culture when we hear the word *treasure* is something of monetary value, such as diamonds, jewelry, gold coins, and so forth. The treasure referred to here is a treasure of *knowledge*. The root word *'asar* (אצר) is spelled aleph (א), sade (צ), resh (ר). The combination of these letters tells us that this knowledge is specifically of God's love and power. The Hebrew word for "*darkness*" is *chosheke* (חשך) and expresses the idea of being obscure or hidden.

Isaiah is drawing a picture here. At the time when he gave this word, due to the sinfulness of the people, the Torah was hidden but not lost. Yet during the reign of Josiah, the Torah was discovered buried deep in the royal archives. I believe the "*treasures of darkness*" refer to the deep mysteries of God stored away in His Word. They are not hidden any more than a library book is hidden in your local library; it is there for you to take out anytime you want. You may have to check the library's computer for its location and even search around a little for it, but you will find it. For example, due to my ongoing research, I am very familiar with certain library catalogue numbers, and I can walk into any library and almost instantly find the section that contains works on the Torah and the Talmud. Similarly, with the Word of God, the more you study it, the easier it is to find its treasures of knowledge.

Deeper, Hidden Riches

The next two Hebrew words we will examine are *matemenu misetarim* (מטמני מסתרים), translated as "*hidden riches of secret places.*" *Misetarim* (מסתרים), or "*secret places,*" comes from the root word *satar* (סתר), which is the term for "hidden," "concealed," or "secret." *Matemenu* (מטמני) comes from the root word *taman* (טמן), which has the preposition *from* in front of it and is used to express *hidden, concealed, or protected treasures of knowledge.* We could thus express this phrase as "hidden riches of knowledge from concealed or protected places." In other words, *taman* (טמן), or knowledge, is not as easy to get to as is *'asar* (אצר), or treasure. All you have to do to get treasure is to search for it. But to get knowledge, you need the equivalent of a key card or an access code.

Maybe a better way to explain this is that there are some documents in our legal system that are referred to as being in the *public record.* This means that anyone may have access to them. Then there are records that are *classified,* which you need a certain amount of security clearance to access. To get that clearance, you must not only prove a need for the documents but also demonstrate that you have the integrity to be entrusted with the knowledge. You generally have to earn that trust.

Thus, certain knowledge about God is open to everyone, such as the knowledge of His love and of His plan of salvation. Then there is knowledge that is hidden—the *"hidden riches of secret places."* To gain this knowledge, you need to enter the very heart of God, as David did. Only when we understand God's heart can we access the hidden riches of His secret places. The important thing to remember is that there are two levels of knowledge. Many Christians are content with the laid-up treasure, but few are willing to earn the trust of God, to seek and to know His heart, so they can be entrusted with the hidden riches of His secret places.

I challenge you, dear reader: Are you content to seek just the treasure of God? Or do you hunger for His classified knowledge? To gain God's treasure, you just need to seek it. But to gain access to His hidden secrets, you need to discover His heart.

Study 39

Cherub: *Karav* (כרוב)

"And he rode upon a cherub, and did fly:
yea, he did fly upon the wings of the wind."
—Psalm 18:10

Somehow, the picture of God sitting on the back of an angel, rider's crop in hand, and zooming through the sky had just never sat well with me. I was sure He did not need an angel or a horse to carry Him. He had enough power to make it on His own. I knew this was just a metaphor, a poetic expression; nevertheless, I always felt it had to be an illustration of something that was very common or well-known to the people of David's day. Then, while researching for my doctoral dissertation, I ran across something very interesting in this regard.

Discovering Ancient Connections

Recent research into the vast Persepolis Fortification Archive at the Oriental Institute at the University of Chicago has unearthed Old Persian tablets. In the cuneiform script of the Akkadian Persian/Assyrian language, a forerunner of modern Arabic, a Semitic language related to Aramaic and Hebrew, we find a word that is identical to the Hebrew word for *"cherub."* This word has always fascinated me because the English word is merely a transliteration of the Hebrew word. Until recently, the origin of this word was unknown. Additionally, no attempt has ever been made to define the word, and hence it took on its own definition as some sort of angelic being.

Fresh discoveries, like those at the Oriental Institute at the University of Chicago, have given us some clue as to the origins of this word. This would follow the works of Ctesias, a Greek physician and historian who lived in the fifth century BC and wrote a history of Persia. In that history, we discover that the word *karv* (כרב) directly corresponds to the Hebrew word *karav* (כרוב), which is the root word for *"cherub."*

Karv (כרב) refers to a mythical creature that was considered a form of deity in the Persian and Assyrian Empires. It is also known as a *griffin*, a *simurgh*, a *homa*, or a *roc*. The karv is a gigantic, legendary bird creature found throughout Persian literature, art, and culture. It is believed that the ancient Assyrians found the bones of a dinosaur, possibly a protoceratops—a dinosaur that had a very large head with a frill at the back of the neck and a beak like a parrot. The protoceratops protected eggs in their nests, which have been found near gold-ore deposits. It is thought that from this ancient discovery the legend of the griffin evolved as a creature that represented the divine, guarding a treasure or a sacred space and serving as the protector of evil.

King David's archenemies were the Assyrians, and the Assyrians had an army of chariots that were far superior to that of Israel's chariots. The Assyrians spent twenty years breeding horses that could pull their chariots, and they were considered invincible. David and the people of Israel were very aware of the legend of the griffin as a creature that protected the Persian Empire. So, in Psalm 18, David is crying out to God for help from the threat of the Assyrian Empire. In verse 7, he declares that in the past, when God heard his cry, the earth *"shook and trembled"* from its foundations, and the mountains *"moved and were shaken"* by God's *"wroth."* The Hebrew word for *"wroth"* is *karah* (כרה). This is sort of a play on the word *karav* (כרוב), and hence would have more of the idea of God's zealousness to protect than an expression of His wrath. It is also the description in ancient Akkadian and Persian literature of the appearance of the griffin, the divine protector of Assyria.

God's Enemies Are Mere Tools in His Hands

In verse 10, we learn that God came to David's rescue riding on a *karav* (כרוב). Again, there is a play on words, because *karav* (כרוב) is a transposition of the word *rakav* (רכב), which means "chariot." God was riding this *karav* (כרוב), this "divine protector" of David's archenemy, as a chariot—as a mere implement of His personal design and creation. Note that the chariot was the chief weapon that gave the Assyrian army its military superiority, not unlike our nuclear arsenal is to us. Here, David is showing that the key weapon and protector of his enemies is nothing more than a tool to his own God Jehovah.

In light of what I know of ancient culture, this psalm is telling me that when I confront an enemy who is about to turn me into a grease spot due to his superior advantage, I can just call on my Protector, God Jehovah, who will appear in all His zeal, riding the so-called deity that my enemy is trusting in and using it as a simple tool to turn against my enemy and to protect me.

Study 40

Eagle: *Nesor* (נשׂר)

"But they that wait upon the Lord *shall renew their strength; they shall mount up with wings as eagles; they shall run, and not be weary; and they shall walk, and not faint."*
—Isaiah 40:31

Using the same approach as in the previous study, let us venture down the ancient pathway to see if this verse might have had some meaning to the people of Isaiah's day that has almost been lost to history. First, we must examine the Hebrew word translated *"wait,"* which is *qavah* (קוה). As I briefly explained in an earlier study, this word refers to *making rope.* In those days, as it is today, rope was made by tightly binding together strands of fabric or strands of animal hair, such as that of a camel. Thus, this waiting upon the Lord carries the idea of binding oneself to Him. In ancient times, the strands of fabric in the rope had a tendency to come loose, and on occasion had to be rebound. As they were rebound, the strength of the rope was renewed. Similarly, when we drift away from God and then return to Him and begin to bind ourselves to Him again, tightening that bond, we become stronger.

Mounting Up as...Vultures?

Next, we see that when we bind ourselves to God, we will not only *"renew* [our] *strength,"* but we will also *"mount up with wings as eagles.*" Let me point out that we may not be talking about an actual eagle here. The Hebrew word rendered *"eagles"* is *nesor* (נשׂר), which could be either an "eagle" or a "vulture." The word is really more descriptive of a *vulture*, because in its Semitic root, *nesor* (נשׂר) carries a sense of *sawing or ripping something apart*, the way a vulture uses its beak to rip apart its food. In a related way, I have heard old-time carpenters talk about "ripping apart" a board in reference to sawing it in half. In older times, saws were not as sharp as they are today, and you usually cut a board by a combination of sawing and ripping.

Normally, we would tend to shy away from the idea of "mounting up with wings as *vultures*," as our culture has a noble view of eagles and a negative view of vultures. I mean, I would much rather mount up with the wings of an eagle than with those of a vulture! However, in ancient times, we might have preferred the image of a vulture, and I believe that in the context of our study verse, this word should be rendered as "vulture." Let's look into this further.

Protected by God's "Feathers"

Isaiah might be referring to the pagan Egyptian goddess Nekhbet, just as we might refer to some pagan religion in order to show the superiority of our faith. For example, we might first point to a pagan religion whose followers wash themselves with physical water before worship, and then explain that we cleanse ourselves through the Water of Life, Jesus Christ. Thus, Isaiah could be saying that we will mount up with wings like the goddess Nekhbet, who served as the protector of Upper Egypt. This goddess wore the Shen ring, which in hieroglyphs is pictured as the loop of a rope, symbolizing eternal protection. The prophet might have been making a play on the word *qavah* (קוה), which is rendered as *"wait"* but refers to the looping and binding of rope.

One problem in interpretation lies in determining the root word for *"mount up."* The priestesses of Nekhbat wore the feathers of the white vulture, so that they appeared to have wings. They would spread their wings to show that their goddess Nekhbat was their eternal protection. Tradition tells us that the root word for *"mount up"* is *'alah* (עלה), which is really a commonsense decision. Anyone doing an initial reading of the original text would almost automatically say that the root word is *ya'al* (יעל). But *ya'al* (יעל) does not really fit the context, so translators move to the alternative, *'alah* (עלה), which means many things, including "to ascend" or "to mount up." It fits, but it does leave you wondering exactly what that means.

However, suppose we go with the first impression that the root word is *ya'al* (יעל), which denotes "to receive," "to profit," or "to benefit." With this interpretation, we could say that those who wait upon the Lord will benefit or profit from the wings of protection. In ancient Egypt, if a man were about to go to battle or leave on a long journey, he might be given a feather off the robe of a priestess of Nekhbet (a very rare and coveted gift), and thus he would be protected in battle or not grow weary on his journey.

Let's look at some additional background. Isaiah lived between 750–700 BC. The northern kingdom had fallen to the Assyrian Empire about twenty years before Isaiah began to prophesy to the southern kingdom of Judah. When the Assyrian Empire conquered the northern kingdom, its rulers pretty much left Ahaz, king of Judah, alone. They did this as long as Judah paid them well enough. But when Hezekiah, Ahaz's son, ascended to the throne, he was determined to end the tribute to Assyria, and he sought an alliance with Egypt to put the Assyrian Empire in its place. This prompted Isaiah to prophesy to King Hezekiah, telling him not to trust in or depend upon Egypt's "arm of flesh." History shows that Isaiah was right. Hezekiah ignored the prophet's warning and made an alliance with the Egyptians. When the Assyrians mounted an attack against Judah, Egypt fudged on the alliance and was a no-show in the conflict. Had Hezekiah not sought help from Egypt, Assyria probably would have remained at peace with Judah—albeit a peace at a monetary cost, but at least not at a cost in lives.

It was in this climate of warning against an alliance with Egypt that Isaiah would have made a reference to the goddess Nekhbet, declaring that Egypt might depend upon their false goddess for protection, but Judah had a God who would give them His powerful *'avar*

(אבר), or "feathers," for protection. The first two letters of *'avar* (אבר) are aleph beth (אב), or *ab*, which spell the word for "father." This is followed by a resh (ר), which represents renewal. The heavenly Father would *"renew their strength."*

Thus, if we allow the strands of fabric in our own binding to God to loosen, then we, too, will be tempted to look to the "arm of flesh" to deliver us. That arm of flesh could be someone's empty promises, a money market account, a job, or even a relationship. If we accept an *'avar* (אבר), or "feather," from the arm of flesh rather than from God, we put ourselves in danger, no less than the danger King Hezekiah brought upon his nation.

Study 41

The Difficult Path: *Linethiboth* (לנתבות)

"Thus said the Lord, Stand ye in the ways, and see,
and ask for the old paths, where is the good way,
and walk therein, and ye shall find rest for your souls.
But they said, We will not walk therein."
—Jeremiah 6:16

Most of our English translations render the Hebrew word *linethiboth* (לנתבות) simply as "paths." Yet in its Semitic root, it really has the idea of a *difficult* path, a path that is filled with *uncertainties.* The Hebrew word translated *"ways"* is *derekim* (דרכים); this is in a plural form preceded by the word *al* (אל), which is in a construct* form. The plural would indicate that the word is more appropriately rendered as a "crossroads." With *al* (אל) as a construct to *derekim* (דרכים), a picture would thus be created of one standing at a crossroads, trying to decide which road to take.

Contemplation at the Crossroads

In our study text, God instructs us first to *"stand."* There are a number of words in Hebrew that are translated as "stand": *yatsab*

(יצב) denotes "a standing to be seen"; *chamor* (חמר) refers to "standing in fear"; *quwam* (קום) signifies "rising up to stand"; *'aman* (אמן) means "standing firm, immoveable." But in this verse, the word translated *"stand"* is *'amad* (עמד), which means "standing or pausing to contemplate."

So, what do you *contemplate* when faced with a *crossroads*? The word *'amad* (עמד) is spelled ayin (ע), mem (מ), daleth (ד). Ayin (ע) speaks of God's omniscience, or all-knowing; mem (מ) signifies that God reveals some of this knowledge, which opens a daleth (ד), or a door, to His presence. Hence, what you contemplate is the revealed knowledge of God that will lead you through a doorway to His presence.

The next thing we are told to do is to *"see."* This word is *ra'ah* (ראה) and is often viewed as a *spiritual seeing*, as in discernment or as in seeing like a prophet or a seer. In this context, it would appear that one is to try to imagine what lies at the end of each road, or is looking at the consequences of taking each road.

Then we are to *"ask for the old paths."* Again, the Hebrew word for *"paths"* used in our study verse is *linethiboth* (לנתבות) and not *derek* (דרך). This word comes from the root word *nathav* (נתב), which is *a path of uncertainty. Nathav* (נתב) is spelled nun (נ), which shows a path that you follow in *faith*; taw (ת), which teaches us that this path is following *divine guidance*; and beth (ב), which whispers to us that this path will lead us to *God's heart.*

The Hebrew word that is rendered *"old,"* or "ancient," really caught my attention. It is *'olam* (עולם), which has a root meaning of "concealed," "hidden," or "secret." We get the idea of "old" from the fact that the past, like the future, is hidden from us. We can be certain only of the present. Hence, the word is also used for "eternity"—a concept that is hidden from our understanding. However, the way I read the word in this context is that we are told to ask for the path that is *uncertain* and *hidden*. The syntax would suggest that we are also to ask for the *good path*. The Hebrew word translated *"good," tov* (טוב), means a path that is in harmony with God.

Rest in the Midst of Turbulence

Ultimately, this is a path where we have to walk in complete faith. But this walk will lead to *"rest for our souls."* The Hebrew word for *"rest"* is *raga'* (רגע), which is a rest that comes suddenly upon you after you have gone through a turbulent time. It is a rest that comes after God has taken you through the fires. *Raga'* (רגע) is a play on the word *marak* (מרכ), which means "a threshing machine." In other words, it is the kind of rest that a prizefighter feels when the bell rings and he goes to his corner to regroup for the next round. He is still in the fight, but he has a moment—which is another way the word *raga'* (רגע) is used—to catch his breath, to receive instruction and encouragement, to take a sip of water, and to regain his strength. To use a different analogy, it is a picture of flying in an airplane through a hurricane and coming out into the eye of the storm. I read in *National Geographic* magazine about the scientists who fly into hurricanes. They said the worst turbulence comes just before they break through to the eye of the storm, and then everything becomes peaceful. That peacefulness is *raga'* (רגע). But while God will give us rest on our journey to His presence, we must also eventually get up and continue that journey—like the prizefighter who still has to get back into the ring to finish the fight, or the scientists who must fly back through the hurricane in order to get home again.

Choosing the Difficult, Hidden Path

But before taking a particular path, we must *'amad* (עמד), or pause, to prayerfully contemplate our journey and make sure we take the right path, the way that is in harmony with God. We must pause to consider our path, because left to ourselves, we will instinctively choose the path of least resistance and not the path that is *linethiboth* (לנתבות)—hidden or uncertain. God's perfect will might be the *linethiboth* (לנתבות), or the more difficult, hidden, or uncertain path. When we *'amad* (עמד), we face the same decision that Israel did: do we take the *linethiboth* (לנתבות), the difficult path, or do we take the easy path?

Let me tell you my personal application of this verse. When I worship God with others in the general ballroom of His heart, so to speak, we are all celebrating, cheering, dancing, and praising. But then I *'amad* (עמד)—I stand, or pause—to contemplate a small door hidden off in a corner of that ballroom. I *'amad* (עמד), or consider, whether to enter this room, for I know what is behind that door. It is a special room, a room apart from all that joy in the large ballroom; it is a place where Jesus separates Himself from the celebration of the outer room. It is His weeping room, the room where He goes to weep over those who are in pain and suffering and are not able to join in the joy in His ballroom.

Do I dare to leave this room of joy and praise to enter this hidden chamber and weep with my Savior for those who cannot attend the celebration? Do I dare to share in His suffering? (See Romans 8:17; Philippians 3:10.) Am I willing to leave this hall to take on the pain that my Savior feels and to intercede for those whom He loves and longs to bring into the joy of His salvation? Or am I going to be like Israel in Jeremiah 6:16 and say, "I will not walk there"?

If I do choose to walk into this special room and weep with Him, He will share with me *devar* (דבר), or *words from His heart*, that I can then share with those for whom He is weeping; and this knowledge will bring *raga'* (רגע), or *"rest,"* to me.

Study 42

I Have Sought Thee: *Derashetika* (דרשתיך)

"With {all my} *heart have I sought thee:*
O let me not wander from thy commandments."
—Psalm 119:10

What's interesting about the Hebrew word *bakal* (בכל), which I have translated as "with all," is that although it means "complete" or "whole" and expresses a totality, it can also mean "bride," "bridal state," and "espousal," which would describe the way in which God is being sought after with wholehearted, passionate love.

The Hebrew word for "sought" is *daresh* (דרש) and has the idea of consulting an oracle and inquiring of the Lord. The particular grammatical form in which this word is found would suggest that the author of the psalm is seeking God Himself rather than seeking something *from* God.

The word for *"wander"* is *shagah* (שגה) and means "to stray," "to be hindered," or "to sin or err out of ignorance." The word for *"not," 'alal* (אלל), comes from the same root from which we get the word for terebinth, or an oak tree. Here it expresses the desire to be firmly rooted and grounded in the Lord's commandments.

So, what does the word *"commandments"* suggest? The Hebrew word is *tsavah* (צוה) and has the idea of *appointing or making a decree or a commission.* All the different usages of this word have a military aspect, as in service in the military or in going forth to war. It is also used for "trial," "struggle," or "affliction."

"Your Desire Will Be Done"

I can see this verse expressing—or being epitomized by—Jesus in the garden of Gethsemane. I believe there is a direct correlation between Matthew 26:39, 42 and Psalm 119:10, which seems to prophetically speak of the moment Jesus was praying in that garden. Jesus spoke in the Aramaic language, and in the Aramaic Bible, Matthew 26:39 is rendered literally as, "Not as I want, but as You." The Hebrew word for "want" is often translated into English as "will." In the Aramaic, it is the word *tsava'* (צבא) and is the equivalent of the Hebrew word *tsavah* (צוה) from Psalm 119:10. This Aramaic word *tsava'* (צבא), which is often rendered as "want," gives us an even greater understanding of what Jesus was expressing, because it can also mean "to serve in the temple," "to go forth to war," "warriors," "soldiers," and "commander in chief." This word also carries the idea of "to will," "to find pleasure," or "to choose," denoting *divine design.*

The literal translation of what Jesus said in Matthew 26:42 is, "If it is not possible for this cup to pass over except I drink it, Your *desire* will be done." Once again, we have the Aramaic word *tsava'* (צבא), which in this case is rendered as "desire" and is the equivalent of the Hebrew word for *"commandments," tsavah* (צוה).

I can't count the number of times I've heard someone ask, "How do I know I'm being led by God?" I believe the best answer, as we find in this passage, is to let your heart be your compass—using Jesus as your example. When we yield our hearts to God and seek Him wholeheartedly, His desires become our desires. Our steps are in sync with His, and we are positioned to receive our "marching orders." However, if we give ourselves the role of commander in chief over our own lives and simply ask God to bless what we are doing, even if it may be good and godly, we cannot know for sure that it is His specific design for us. Rather, it is merely a matter of our will.

Love Sacrifices for Others

Looking more closely at Matthew 26:42, where Jesus says, "If it is not possible for this cup to pass over…," the word in Aramaic for "cup" is identical to the Hebrew word, which is *kavas* (כוס). There is a double meaning to this word for "cup," because it can denote either a cup or a pelican or stork.

To the ancient world, a pelican and a stork were considered the same bird, and both were noted for their tender care of their young. They would even care for young birds that were not their own. Hence came the legend of the stork delivering newborn babies. There was also the belief that when food was not available, the pelican would feed its young on its own blood. Additionally, there was the ancient idea that if one of its young died, a mother pelican would resurrect it with her own blood.

Returning to Jesus as our model, after He was arrested in the garden of Gethsemane, He said, *"Do you think I cannot call on my Father, and he will at once put at my disposal more than twelve legions of angels?"* (Matthew 26:53 NIV). In this verse, we see that Jesus had a choice whether or not to die on the cross, yet because He was a *prisoner of love*, His only option was to do the *tsava'* (צבא), or *"will"* of His Father. The cross was the only way, because love sacrifices for others. Will we love in the same way? Jesus said, *"Whoever finds their life will lose it, and whoever loses their life for my sake will find it"* (Matthew 10:39 NIV).

There is one additional meaning of the Hebrew word *tsavah* (צוה), which is translated as *"commandments."* That meaning is "a monument" or "a pillar," as well as the idea of a *signpost.* As I was working on this word study in a coffee shop, I noticed that it was raining outside. The moment I finished and left the coffee shop, the sun came out, and there was a big, beautiful rainbow in the sky. Sure, you can say it was just a coincidence, but for me it was a nod from God, a signpost, telling me that my study today was His *tsava'* (צבא), or desire.

Study 43

Rest: *Navch* (נוח)

"And he said, My presence shall go with thee,
and I will give thee rest."
—Exodus 33:14

It was late at night on a warm and beautiful December evening. I was in Southern Illinois on my way to a speaking engagement in Terre Haute, Indiana. I walked outside to spend some time alone with God, and as we sat under the stars and shared a few moments together, I was reminded of Exodus 33:14.

"My Presence Shall Go with Thee"

In studying the phrase *"My presence shall go with thee"* in that verse, a couple of things gave me pause. The first was that the Hebrew word translated as *"go"* is *yeleku* (ילכו), which is in a simple *qal* imperfect form. I would have expected God to have put this in a *piel* (intensive) form or to have added a nun (נ) at the end to make the word a paragogic. In other words, I would have expected Him to have intensified the word so that it would be rendered, "I will *most certainly* go...." The other question that came to my mind was why the Hebrew word rendered *"presence," pani* (פני), is in a plural form. Literally, it reads, "My presence, they shall go."

Probably one answer to this question we need to keep in mind is that the plural in Hebrew is a little different from the plural in English. In Hebrew, when something is in a plural form, it does not have to mean "more than one." It could also be used to express the uniqueness of something or to indicate that something is in its ultimate state or is supreme to all others. This would explain why the word *"go"* is not in an intensive form—the plural of *"presence"* more than makes up for it.

Perhaps what the Lord was saying to Moses is that he would be guided by God's unique presence. This would not merely be a feel-good presence or a counterfeit presence that Moses would drum up through fast music and wild dancing. He would not need to spend hours reciting "Praise God" over and over until he felt an emotional rush. This would be the genuine article. A picture is being drawn here of the presence of God coming softly and naturally, just as a husband steps quietly into the bedroom and embraces his sleeping wife, who quietly awakes in his arms and returns his affection. It is a concept that Christian fiction writer Janette Oke expressed in her first novel, *Love Comes Softly.* This book is about the growing affection and commitment between a husband and wife on the prairie who had married for convenience and survival but discovered an unexpected, deep love slowly developing between them.

God's Eyes Are Always upon Us

Exodus 33:11 says, *"And the Lord spake unto Moses face to face, as a man speaketh unto his friend."* The Hebrew word for *"friend"* is *ra'ah* (רעה), which means "to consume." In this verse, Moses and God are sharing a very intimate time on the mountain, totally absorbed with each other's presence. All of a sudden, God says, in effect, "Well, back to work getting these people to the Promised Land." Moses responds, "Okay, but under one condition: You continue to hold me, and we continue to be absorbed with each other." God says, "Of course, and not only that, but My eyes will never leave your eyes, and when the job is done, we will come together on this mountain again, and you can stay with Me forever. You will never have to leave." The image here is of two lovers gazing into each other's eyes, just consuming each other with their passion.

Let me give you another illustration. It is like a husband and wife who take a break from working on their house to lie on the grass in their backyard and look up at the stars together, dreaming of their future—a nicely furnished house with a white picket fence, several children, a family dog, and so forth. Then all of a sudden, the man says, "Well, we have to get back to work painting the living room." His wife responds by saying, "Okay, we will paint the living room under one condition: I hold a brush in one hand, and you hold a brush in the opposite hand, and we have our free arms around each other, and you just keep holding me as we complete this project. When it is done, then let's come back to this spot and lie here together again under the stars." The husband looks at his wife and says, "Of course, but I will not only continue to hold you—I will also never take my eyes off of you as we paint."

On that warm December evening, as God and I sat out under the stars talking of our journey together, He suddenly said to me, "Well, let's get to work encouraging My people to study My Word." I rebelled and said, "No, I like it here with You. If we have to go, I will go under one condition—that You just continue to hold me." God responded by saying, "Yes, I will not only continue to hold you on your journey, but I will never take My eyes off your eyes. And one day, the journey will end, and we can sit out under the stars together forever."

Oh, I almost forgot to talk about the word *"rest"*! You wonder where I get this "under the stars" stuff? The Hebrew word that is rendered as *"rest"* is *navch* (נוח). This word implies a rest that comes from just *lying down*, or *being in repose*. God says He will *"give"* us rest. The word for *"give"* is *nathan* (נתן). This term begins with a nun (נ) and ends with a (final) nun (ן), with a taw (ת) in the middle. It is circular, indicating that God will keep giving and giving. In other words, He is saying, "I will continue to hold you and look into your eyes, and no job that I give you will keep us from the times when we will just lie down on the ground and look up at the stars together. But one day, that work will be over, and then you can *navch* (נוח), or "*rest,*" with Me, and you will never have to leave to get back to work again."

Study 44

My Heart Is Fixed: *Nakon Livi* (נכון לבי)

"O God, my heart is fixed; I will sing and give praise, even with my glory."
—Psalm 108:1

Have you ever had a time when you carried such an overwhelming burden that you couldn't even pray? You tried to pray, but it was just such an effort because you felt so weighted down. This is apparently the way David felt when he started to write Psalm 108.

Praising God with Our Whole Being

At first, this psalm appears to express one of David's lighter moments. He seems so joyful, so happy. Yet the first verse actually gives his true emotions away. He calls out to God, saying that his heart is *"fixed."* The Hebrew word for *"fixed"* is *nakon* (נכון), which denotes the idea of *being established* or *directed*. Today, we would say that his heart was *focused*. Yet his heart was not focused on God but rather on his burden. It is for this reason that he will sing and give praise.

The word for *"praise"* here is *zamar* (זמר). This signifies *joyful praise*, but also a very *focused praise*. Additionally, the word *zamar*

(זמר) can be used for *cutting* or *pruning*. So, this is a very direct, specific praise, with no fluff and no disjointed or meaningless words. *Zamar* (זמר) is also in a *piel* (intensive) form with a paragogic hei (ה), making this direct praise very intense—David is putting his whole being into it. With everything he has, he is expressing his joy to the Lord.

Praising God with Our Burden

Then David says, *"Even with my glory."* The word for *"my glory"* is *kavodi* (כבודי), which can mean "heaviness," "burdensome," or "grievous." I suppose we could say that he praises God with his "glory," whatever that would mean. However, I would be more inclined to use *kavod* to express the idea of a *heavy burden* because it would fit the context better.

David is overwhelmed with some heavy burden. His heart is so fixed on this issue that he can hardly praise or worship God. So, he says he will sing a song of praise, and not just any praise. He could praise God for His power, for His majesty, and for similar attributes, which he has done many times. But right now, the praise he wants to offer is with his burden. The word for *"even"* in the phrase *"even with my glory"* is *'aph* (אפ), which is often translated as "indeed" or "furthermore." In other words, "I will praise You indeed, or furthermore, with my burden." Notwithstanding his heavy burden, he is praising God with joy.

David is not ignoring his burden or pretending it does not exist. He is simply bringing God into the picture. He is entering into intense praise with his burden right there, right out in front. He and God are going to share this burden while he digs down deep into his soul to find the joy of the Lord that he knows is resting there, covered by the weight of that burden. In the remainder of Psalm 108, David talks about the awesome power of God and His control over everything; with that perspective, the weight of his burden gets lighter and lighter, and the joy of the Lord begins to surface.

Sometimes, the burdens of this life can weigh you down so much, you just want to crawl under "yon rock from whence you came" and shut everything out. You can try that, but the burden will still be there. Or you could choose, like David, to worship and praise God in the midst of your burden. You could search your soul for the joy of the Lord that rests deep down inside you. You could let Him share the burden with you so that it will get lighter and lighter as His joy becomes brighter and brighter.

Study 45

Watchtower: *Mitspah* (מצפה)

"It was also called Mizpah {Mitspah}*, because he said, 'May the* Lord *keep watch between you and me when we are away from each other.'"*
—Genesis 31:49 (NIV)

A Tender, Emotional Bond

Valentine's Day is a special day when you say and do something special for your beloved. Might I suggest an endearment that you can express to your Valentine this year? It is the Hebrew word *mitspah* (מצפה), meaning "watchtower." I know it doesn't sound very romantic, telling your Valentine that he or she is a watchtower. I thought the same thing until I saw an old movie made during World War II called *Stage Door Canteen*. It's about celebrities who gather at an old theater set up as a nightclub to give soldiers about to go to war overseas an evening of relaxation and good food. At one point, a soldier comments that as he and his wife had parted, they had said "Mitspah" to each other. Another soldier, overhearing the conversation, asks what "Mitspah" means. Singer Francis Langford then gives a lengthy explanation that it means a tender, emotional bond between two people when they were separated either physically or by death. She goes on with her definition for a few more paragraphs. My first thought was, *All that from one word?*

If you look up the word *mizpah*, or *mitspah*, in your Bible notes or in a lexicon, the only definitions you will find will be "a place" or "a watchtower." Yet, like so many Hebrew words, it has a broad range of meaning. This is a prime example of how lexicographers rely mainly on the context of a word from a dead language to determine its meaning. The problem is that in examining this verse to determine the meaning of *mitspah* (מצפה), they went only as far as *"the Lord keep watch between you and me,"* and concluded that it meant "a watchtower." They overlooked the last phrase, *"when we are away from each other."* This, however, did not escape the attention of the Jewish sages, who included that last phrase in their definition, as well. In this way, we find the word *mitspah* (מצפה) used as a form of prayer. It is a word used by two people in love who are separated from each other. Accordingly, today, the word is sometimes engraved on jewelry, often on a necklace in the shape of half a heart, with a matching half-heart on a companion necklace, so that each can wear half a heart around their neck as a memorial to their bond while they are separated by distance, a long period of time, or even just several hours a day while they are at work.

Watching Over One's Beloved

In our Western Christian thought, we are often so scientific and cold that we see only the meaning that the Lord will keep watch over us, and we totally neglect the rest of the significance—that He will keep watch over those of us with whom He has bonded, as two lovers keep watch over their hearts while they are separated. When the soldier depicted in *Stage Door Canteen* went off to war, his wife would pray for him, think of him, keep a special place in their home ready for him, and send him letters, packages of cookies, and anything else she could in order to be a "watchtower" over his heart. In turn, he would remain faithful to his wife while they were separated—sending letters, words of encouragement, money, and anything else that would keep him as a "watchtower" over her heart.

When I leave a worship service where God and I have shared an intimate time together, we say "Mitspah" to each other. In that emotional word, God is committing to protecting me, to watching over me, to providing for me, and to keeping a special place ready for me for the next time we come together in worship. He is promising to be a "Watchtower" over my heart. In return, when I say "Mitspah" to Him, I am promising to be faithful to Him as my only God, to support His purposes, and to do what He desires. I am promising to be a "watchtower" over His heart.

Study 46

Hiss: *Sharak* (שׁרק)

"I will hiss for them, and gather them;
for I have redeemed them."
—Zechariah 10:8

Why the King James Version renders the Hebrew word *sharak* (שׁרק) as *"hiss"* is beyond my comprehension. Such a rendering creates a very curious passage and one that is difficult to understand, because we associate hissing with something sinister or degrading.

Yet *sharak* (שׁרק) can also be translated as "whistle" or "signal." This word is used seven times in the Old Testament. It is used negatively five times, and positively two times. As we have seen in previous studies, it is not unusual for a Hebrew word to have both a positive and a negative usage. In this passage in Zechariah, the context clearly indicates that it is used in a positive sense.

Gathering the Redeemed

When you trace *sharak* (שׁרק) back to its Semitic root, you find that it has its origin in describing the sound made through a reed. It came to be used for a musical instrument like a pipe or a flute. The context indicates that this sound will cause the redeemed to *"gather."*

This is interesting because we usually think of a gathering in the Bible being called for by a shofar.

We know that in ancient days, shepherds would make instruments from reeds and pass their time playing on these instruments. As a shepherd, David would have done the same. In Greek mythology, the god Pan was considered the god of shepherds, flocks, and rustic music. Pan is often pictured teaching shepherds to play the flute, and you also see pictures of Pan playing his flute and dancing with a flock of sheep gathered around him.

James Merryweather, the Scottish scholar and researcher, observed that when he went out to a field of sheep and played on his bagpipes a sound similar to that of a flute, all the sheep would stop what they were doing—usually grazing—and gather together. When he stopped playing, they would wander away from each other and go back to their grazing.

Sharing in Our Shepherd's Joy

The picture of Pan playing his flute and dancing among the sheep really has its origins in a more ancient depiction. We often view shepherds as old, bearded men barely able to walk, let alone dance. Yet the job of shepherding was often dumped on the youngest son of the family, as it was on David. I don't think it would stretch the imagination too much to picture David playing a flute and dancing among the sheep to gather them together. Perhaps the sheep instinctively desired to share in the shepherd's joy.

Zechariah 10:2 says, "*Therefore they went their way as a flock, they were troubled, because there was no shepherd.*" Our Shepherd, Jesus Christ, desires to gather us together to Himself. As Merryweather's sheep instinctively gathered at the sound of his pipes, we gather around our Lord to share the joy of our Shepherd. Thus, Zechariah 10:8 could be a messianic passage,** a picture of Jesus playing a flute for us and dancing for pure joy as we, His sheep who have been redeemed, gather close around Him to share in His joy.

Study 47

My Soul Melteth: *Dalephah Napheshi* (דלפה נפשי)

"My soul melteth for heaviness:
strengthen thou me according unto thy word."
—Psalm 119:28

The Hebrew word translated *"melteth"* is *dalaph* (דלף). This word actually has more of a connotation of *shedding tears* or *weeping*, or of *rain drops*. In this verse, *dalaph* (דלף) is in a *qal* verbal form, which means it is just a normal verb, with no intensification. It is a picture of tears shed gently out of feelings of deep sorrow. Since it is the soul weeping, the tears do not necessarily have to be literal. Think of the familiar saying, "I'm laughing on the outside but crying on the inside."

Renewing Our Minds in the Word

The Hebrew word translated *"heaviness,"* as in *oppressiveness*, is *yagah* (יגה). Looking at how this word is used in other verses, the idea is that of heaviness related to *feeling foolish*, *shameful*, or *disappointed*. It also signifies raindrops coming through the chinks of a roof. The constant dripping over time causes structural damage. This image reminds me of water torture, where simple drops of water fall in the same area of the forehead, causing pain and mental anguish.

In our study verse, David asks to be "strengthened." In this case, he uses the term *qum* (קום), which is in a *piel* verbal form, intensifying the word. *Qum* (קום) means "to arise" and can be explained as the type of strength needed when you're down for the count after a knockdown. This strengthening is *"according unto"*—or literally "like" or "as"—God's *"word."*

The Hebrew term translated *"word"* is *devar* (דבר), and one of the meanings from the root of this word is "oracle," "the place of speaking," or "inner sanctuary," which was an alternative name for the Holy of Holies in Solomon's temple. One way *devar* (דבר) can be summed up is *words spoken from the heart (inner place) of God.* What's interesting, as indicated above, is the use of the preposition *like* or *as* before *devar* (דבר). We would render this as "like God's words" or "as God's words." We are to renew our minds daily in the Word—both the whole of the Word of God and the specific promises spoken to us. Jesus, the Word, is the lifter of our heads. (See Psalm 3:3.) It's so important to view ourselves and our life situations from God's perspective.

God's Word Gives Us Life

A few verses earlier in Psalm 119, a similar sentiment is expressed: *"My soul cleaves to the dust; revive me according to Your word"* (verse 25 NASB). "Cleaving to the dust" denotes the idea of being close to death (see Genesis 3:19), and David is asking God to *"revive"* him according to His *devar* (דבר), or *"word."* The root word for *"revive"* is *chayah* (חיה), which also means "to give life." God's word is life, as we read in Deuteronomy:

> *He humbled you, causing you to hunger and then feeding you with manna, which neither you nor your ancestors had known, to teach you that man does not live on bread alone but on every word that comes from the mouth of the Lord.*
>
> (Deuteronomy 8:3 NIV)

Another meaning that we can draw from the same root word as *devar* (דבר) is "wilderness," which is *midbar* (מדבר) in Hebrew. God fed the Israelites manna in the wilderness; and Jesus said, *"But it is my Father who gives you the true bread out of heaven. For the bread of God is that which comes down out of heaven, and gives life to the world"* (John 6:32–33 NASB).

Lastly, we find from the root word *devar* (דבר) the word *dobar* (דבר), which is sometimes used in Scripture to mean "a pasture" or "a feeding ground for sheep." The Word, *devar* (דבר), feeds us, lifts us up, revives us, sustains us, and give us life. Jesus says, *"I am the door; if anyone enters through Me, he will be saved, and will go in and out and find pasture"* (John 10:9 NASB). Jesus also stands at the door of our hearts and invites us to *"sup"* with Him (see Revelation 3:20)—the very Word of God and true Bread of Life.

Study 48

Smitten: *Nakach* (נכח)

"Arise, O Lord*; save me, O my God:*
for thou hast smitten all mine enemies upon the cheek bone;
thou hast broken the teeth of the ungodly."
—Psalm 3:7

O, this is poison of deep grief: it springs
All from her father's death. And now behold—
O Gertrude, Gertrude,
When sorrows come, they come not single spies,
but in battalions.

—Hamlet, Act IV, Scene V[3]

If you read Psalm 3:7 closely, you will find something a little strange about the way it is worded. David is calling on the Lord to arise and save him, and then he says, "*For thou hast smitten all mine enemies.*" If the enemies are already destroyed, why is he calling on the Lord to save him? Practically every English translation puts the Hebrew word *nakach* (נכח) in the past tense, as "*smitten.*" And indeed, that is exactly the way it is in the Hebrew; it is in a perfect verbal form, considered as past tense.

3. Richard Jenkins, ed., *Hamlet*, The Arden Shakespeare (London: Thomson Learning, reprinted 2002; first published 1982 by Methuen & Co. LTD).

"O LORD, HELP!"

The apparent inconsistency becomes even more glaring when you look at the Hebrew words for *"arise"* and *"save me."* Both are in a *piel* (intensive) imperative (command) form. The word for *"arise"* even has a paragogic hei (ה), which increases its intensity. This shows David to be in a state of extreme desperation; he is in a state of total panic.

Have you ever been in a situation where it seemed like everything was coming at you at once—the kind described by Claudius in the play *Hamlet*, where he says, "When sorrows come, they come not single spies, but in battalions"? It is in the midst of such circumstances when you want to scream out, like the cartoon character Popeye, "That's all I can stands, 'cause I can't stands no more!" There are troublesome times when we pray, "O Lord, I need Your help—please help me now." And then there are desperate times when we shout, "O LORD, HELP!" That is the situation in Psalm 3.

What is odd is that in his extreme state of emergency and panic, David is so full of faith that he declares that God has already destroyed his enemies. As we noted, his enemies are not yet destroyed, but he puts the word *nakach* (נכח), or *"smitten,"* in a hiphil (causative) perfect (completed action or past) form. David is not speaking like a fool when he says his enemies are destroyed, even though they are not, but he is speaking in faith and making this affirmation to God: "The moment I called on You, You started the process of destroying my enemies, and their destruction is as certain as if it has already happened." You see, God does not live within the limitations of time; past, present, and future are all the same to Him. In God's realm, the deliverance has already been accomplished, and David is just recognizing that fact.

We Must Still Run the Race

I hear people say things like, "Well, that bill is paid," or "I am healed," when that is obviously not the case. That is not what is happening here with David. You may remember a situation from the book of Daniel where Daniel fasted and prayed, and the moment he prayed, an angel was dispatched with a response. However, the angel got "caught in traffic," so to speak—spiritual warfare traffic—which caused a delay in delivering it. (See Daniel 10.) Take note that the angel was not dispatched until Daniel prayed. It was the same way with David in Psalm 3; the process of his enemy's destruction did not begin until he prayed. We read in the book of James, "*Ye have not because ye ask not*" (James 4:2). And Jesus said, "*Ask, and it shall be given you; seek, and ye shall find; knock, and it shall be opened unto you*" (Matthew 7:7). We must ask, just as David asked, before the process can begin.

In David's case, remember that the destruction of his enemies is in a hiphil (causative) form; it is a process, and God sets into motion the events that bring it about. Likewise, the stage is set for the answer to your prayer, and when you pray, God begins the play. Here is the point: you never have to "wait" for God to answer your prayer; it is answered the moment you pray. It is, however, similar to a stage play in that sometimes it takes a little time for the actors to get into position. Sometimes angels get "stuck in traffic," but that doesn't mean your prayer was not answered. As he indicated in Psalm 3:7, David understood that his prayer had been answered the moment he called out to God; he knew that he was a sure victor. But he also had enough faith to know that even though his prayer had guaranteed that he would receive the "gold medal," there was still a race to be run before he received that medal.

Sometimes you will see immediate results from your prayers, and sometimes you won't. If you don't see immediate results, that does not mean your prayers are not answered; the outcome is sure, but you will have to run the race before you receive the prize. So, there's no problem in saying, "I've already won," but you will still have to jump over those hurdles, and that may take a little time. And even though you are already the winner, that doesn't mean you can just relax and run the race at an easy jog; it will take persistence and perseverance. After all, the "audience" does deserve a good show!

Study 49

God Is with Him: *YHWH Ethu* (יהוה אתו)

"And [Joseph's] *master saw that the* Lord *was with him, and that the* Lord *made all that he did to prosper in his hand."*
—Genesis 39:3

"Now I lay me down to rest, for tomorrow comes yet another test. If I die before I wake, that's at least one test I need not take."
—My bedtime prayer

Joseph and I have many things in common, but one thing we don't have in common is that the Lord doesn't make all that I do to prosper in my hand. Regardless, I decided that I would explore the meaning of this verse about Joseph, and there were a few things in it that caused me to stop and ponder.

Humbly, Prayerfully, and in Unity with God

First, Joseph's master, named Potiphar, *"saw that the* Lord *was with him."* The Hebrew word used for *"*Lord*"* is *Jehovah* or *YHWH* (יהוה). What did an Egyptian official know about the Hebrew God? How did he know it was God who was making everything Joseph did to prosper? And what is this prosperity business, anyway? Joseph was beaten by his brothers before they sold him into slavery, and he was later accused of a rape he did not commit and was thrown into prison for it. That does not sound very prosperous to me.

In Genesis 39:3, the Hebrew word for *"prosper"* is *tsalach* (צלח). This word does not mean to prosper as we would interpret the term in our culture—that is, to gain material possessions. Here the word *"prosper"* has the idea of *moving forward, making progress.* This is in a hiphal (causative) form, not a *piel* (intensive) form, so rather than having the connotation of gain, it would have more of the idea of *getting things accomplished*.

Tsalach (צלח) is spelled sade (צ), lamed (ל), chet (ח). These letters suggest that the word signifies *accomplishing things humbly, prayerfully, and in unity with God's will.* These qualities of Joseph may be what caught Potiphar's attention. Joseph's motivation in his work was not the same as that of the other slaves—whose motivation was perhaps to curry favor or to avoid punishment from their master. Joseph went about his work accomplishing his tasks for something—or Someone—much higher than Potiphar, and Potiphar recognized this. Prosperity in Joseph's case had to do with performing a task—even an earthly task for an earthly boss—as if he was serving God and not man. Thus, *tsalach* (צלח), or *"prosper,"* refers to doing any job as unto God humbly, prayerfully, and in unity with Him.

The Greatest Prosperity

Yet this does not really answer the question about how Potiphar knew it was God Jehovah who was prospering Joseph. I checked through Jewish literature and found something interesting in relation to this. In our study text, the words *"with him"* are translated from the Hebrew word *ethu* (אתו). The ancient rabbis saw the *'eth* (את) as a sign of a direct object and the *hu'* (הו) as a pronoun. In other words, the first part of the verse would be literally rendered, "Potiphar saw that the Lord is Joseph." That doesn't make much sense until you consider that the word *"saw"* is *ra'ah* (ראה), which could mean seeing in a spiritual sense, as well as in a natural sense. I am not sure of a proper rendering, but I do know what this verse is saying. When Potiphar saw Joseph, he saw God Jehovah. You may be familiar with the old slogan, "We are the only Jesus that people will ever see."

An eighteenth-century rabbi, Yisroel Ben Eliezer, rendered the verse in this way: "And his master saw that the name of God was always upon his lips." This is what drew Potiphar's attention. He saw a man who always performed his tasks humbly, prayerfully, and in unity with God, and always with the name of God, *YHWH* (יהוה), upon his lips. So, when Potiphar saw Joseph, he saw God.

The greatest prosperity we could have would be for someone to say to us, "I see Jesus in your face, and I hear Him upon your lips." For me, as for any believer, that would mean more than winning the mega-lottery.

Study 50

Turn: *Hafak* (הפך)

"How shall I give thee up, Ephraim? how shall I deliver thee, Israel? how shall I make thee as Admah? how shall I set thee as Zeboim? mine heart is turned within me, my repentings are kindled together."
—Hosea 11:8

Three Ways to Approach God

Jewish literature teaches three ways to approach God in prayer. We can approach Him as a child would to a parent, saying, "I want You to give to me and provide for me." This seems to be the most common form of prayer. A more mature approach to God in prayer is similar to what a wife feels toward her husband, so that we say, "God, I love You, and I want to attend to Your needs." Yet we often overlook a third approach in prayer, which is like a husband's concern for his wife. In that prayer, we ask God, "How can I protect Your heart?"

To reach this third approach to God, we must first understand His heart. If a husband really loves his wife, he will break down if he sees her dissolve into tears. For example, Esther 5:3 might be translated as, "The king looked into Esther's eyes and said, 'What to you?'"

While this response sounds coarse to us, "What to you?" is a very tender expression in Hebrew. In that moment, the king lost all his kingly protocol and expressed an emotion. Some translations insert the word "trouble" into the phrase, which is quite appropriate—"What is troubling you?" However, the compassion was much deeper than that. The king could not even say the word *trouble*; he could only get out something like, "What—is it?" Then he told Esther that he would give her up to half his kingdom to help her. (See Esther 5:1–3.) In the Persian Empire, that was the full extent of what a king could give up. In other words, he would grant her all he could possibly give.

Esther was greatly troubled over the impending tragedy that would fall on her people. The king saw this sadness in her eyes—maybe he even saw tears there—and was ready to give all he could to ease her trouble. He wanted to protect her heart.

As we have discussed in previous studies, God's heart is easily broken. If we truly love Him, would we not want to protect His heart? For example, we wish to reach our neighbor with the gospel message because we don't want him to go to hell. But do we want to reach that neighbor because we know it will break the heart of the God whom we love if that person were to die lost?

David was a man after God's heart because he knew and understood His heart. Too many of us spend so much time as a *child* to God that we never learn to understand God's heart. When we do, we can be not only like a *wife* to Him but also like a *husband*, seeking to protect His heart.

Sacrificial Giving

I have never heard a sermon based on our study verse, Hosea 11:8, yet its emotion truly reveals the heart of God. It begins, *"How shall I give thee up, Ephraim?"* The Hebrew word rendered *"give"* is *nathan* (נתן). The word itself simply means "to give," but when you consider it in its context, it would seem that this is sacrificial giving. *"Ephraim"* is a name for Israel that God uses to express a broken heart. The picture we have here is of a rejected spouse tearfully forced to sign divorce papers.

Next, God says, *"How shall I deliver thee, Israel?"* The word for *"Israel," Yisrael* (ישראל), means "prince of God." This is the name God uses when He wants to express His affection, just as a husband will call his wife "dear." The Hebrew word for *"deliver"* is *mogan* (מגן), which holds the idea of *setting up to examine and regard.* This is a picture of a woman who has placed her husband on a high pedestal and then learns that he has been unfaithful. How will she regard him now that her whole image of him has been shattered?

The Lord continues, *"How shall I make* [*"make"* is *nathan* (נתן) in the Hebrew, earlier rendered "to give," in a sacrificial sense] *thee as Admah? how shall I set thee as Zeboim?"* Contrary to popular belief, it was not just Sodom and Gomorrah that were destroyed in God's judgment during Abraham's time—about five other cities went down with them, including Admah and Zeboim. These two cities were like wealthy, privileged, upper-crust suburbs of Sodom and Gomorrah. God realizes that Israel has set itself up for destruction.

"Mine heart is turned within me." The Hebrew word translated *"turned"* is *hafak* (הפך). This term gives the impression of *ruin, being overthrown, destroyed.* Additionally, it is the word for *being imprisoned* or *put into stocks.* It is also used to express a *tumbling* or *churning.* I have heard some of the same words used by people who were suffering a broken heart. They declared that their lives were ruined or destroyed. They felt imprisoned by their love for the person who broke their heart. They said that their stomach was churning. So, when God expresses that His heart is "turned within Him," He is saying that Israel has broken His heart.

Then God says a curious thing: *"My repentings are kindled."* The word for *"repentings"* is *nacham* (נחם), a term expressing *sorrow* or *grief,* and the word for *"kindled"* is *kamar* (כמר), which means "kindling," as in *making a fire,* or *smoldering.* Many people who have a wounded heart talk of having a burning grief or sorrow, similar to what God is expressing as He speaks of His burning grief.

Again, when we choose to love someone and give our heart to them, we make ourselves vulnerable. We give that person the ability to deeply wound us, the ability to break our heart. When God chooses to love us, is He not making Himself just as vulnerable to us? When we give Him our heart, He gives us His heart in return. We and God make ourselves vulnerable to each other. Of course, we run no risk when we give our heart to God, for He will not abuse our feelings; He will accept our heart as a sacred gift and will protect it. We, on the other hand, often take His heart, toss it into a corner, and then go chasing after other gods to fulfill our needs, paying little attention to the heartbroken Lover who has been so faithful and loving toward us.

Read Hosea 11:8 again. Do you not see a Lover watching His beloved self-destruct without being able to do anything about it? Do you not hear Him weeping over the unfaithfulness of His loved ones who are about to destroy themselves? Do you not hear Him weeping for you?

Study 51

The Day That I Am Fearing: *Yom 'Ira* (יום אירא)

"What time I am afraid, I will trust in thee. In God I will praise his word, in God I have put my trust; I will not fear what flesh can do unto me."
—Psalm 56:3–4

Psalm 56:3 gives a rather strange combination of words. "*What time I am afraid*" sounds awkward, but the wording is very close to the original Hebrew. The expression is *yom 'ira* (יום אירא), which could be rendered literally as "The day that I am fearing." All of us have some day in the future that we dread. It may be the day of an important exam, a yearly job review, Tax Day, or even an approaching holiday season. Since it is a future event, we tend to put it out of our minds until some little occurrence jogs our memory, and instantly that sense of dread comes back. Some of us may even be in a state of constant stress over some future event, similar to the *Peanuts* character Charlie Brown, who walks around with a storm cloud over his head.

"I Will Trust in Thee"

In addition to the strange combination of words, the grammatical structure of Psalm 56:3 is a little odd for the context. David is reflecting on his capture by the Philistines at Gath, and he says, "The day that I am fearing...." But the event is over with, so what does he have to fear?

When Abraham Lincoln was president, there was a time when his wife got herself in a financial problem that could have been a real scandal for the presidency. Secretary of State William H. Seward managed to deflect the scandal and resolve the issue. He went to President Lincoln and reported that the scandal involving his wife was now resolved and closed. Lincoln showed no joy but only became very melancholy and went to his desk, sat down, and hung his head. Secretary Seward spoke up and said, "Mr. President, perhaps you misunderstood; the problem with your wife is resolved." Lincoln quietly replied, "I know it's resolved; I'm just getting ready to worry about the next problem she will cause." "What problem is that?" inquired Seward. "I don't know," Lincoln said, "but there will be one."

David was most likely feeling the same way. His problem with the Philistines had long been resolved, but he knew that his future held many similar problems. Reflecting on his experience with the Philistines probably reminded him that he would sooner or later have to face another stressful situation, but his response was, *"I will trust in thee."* I fully expected to find the Hebrew word for *"trust," batach* (בטח), to be in a participial form, but it is not. It is in a simple *qal* imperfect (future) form. David is confronting a future problem, and he is saying, "I will trust in the Lord."

At first, this didn't seem to me to be David's usual style of writing. To be typical of David's style, he would have made this a participle, which would be rendered in a present tense: "I *am trusting* in the Lord." But as I meditated on the verse, I realized that perhaps this was typical David, after all. In Matthew 6:34, Jesus instructed us not to worry about tomorrow, for tomorrow would take care of itself; each day had enough trouble of its own. David was simply living according to the same wisdom. There was no sense in worrying about something that hadn't yet appeared on the horizon. David could have said, "God, I am trusting You for the day when the Assyrians show up at my door. I am trusting You to take care of me; I am trusting

You for favor." Yet to do so would essentially be to worry and fret about the event rather than simply saying, "Hey, if that happens, I will trust God at that time in the same way I did when I was taken captive by the Philistines."

David refused to walk around with a storm cloud over his head. I don't know about you, but I tend to find myself in the Charlie Brown mode rather than in the David mode, saying, "Well, that problem is resolved; now what am I going to do when the next problem shows up?" The fact is, I am going to do with the next problem what I did with the last problem. I am going to trust God, and I am going to watch Him deliver me like He did with the previous problem.

Living from Glory to Glory

In Psalm 56, David was declaring that he was not going to live from problem to problem; rather, he was going to live from glory to glory. He was going to put all future problems in the hands of the God whom he loved. If a problem arose at some future day, he would simply say, "Lord, this is the problem I told You about a couple of months ago; at that time, I put it in Your hands—remember? Well, I am now going to just trust in You." In an earlier study, I mentioned the meaning of *betach* (בטח), or *"trust."* It means "to cling to," "to adhere to," or, in a modern sense, "to be welded to." So, David was also saying that he was melded, or welded, to God. His problems were God's problem.

Calvin Coolidge was once asked by a reporter why he appeared so calm when he was burdened with the office of the president. He replied, "When you see ten troubles rolling down the road, if you don't do anything, nine of them will roll into a ditch before they get to you."[4]

So, the next time you find yourself worrying over some future problem that hasn't even come down the road yet, just do what David did. Pray, "Well, Lord, if that problem ever reaches me, it is our problem. It is Your problem just as well as mine. I don't know what to do,

4. See http://www.calvincoolidge.us/quotations.html.

but if and when the difficulty arises, I am going to trust You to do something, just as You have done in the past when I have faced similar problems. In the meantime, I will deal solely with today."

Study 52

Angels' Food: *Lechem 'Abirim* (לחם אבירים)

"Man did eat angels' food: he sent them {food} *to the full."*
—Psalm 78:25

The psalmist is retelling the story of the exodus and of God's loving protection over His people. But rather than say that He gave them *manna* from heaven, he calls it *"angels' food."* Today, we have what is known as "angel food cake," so named because it is light and fluffy. The term was introduced just after the Civil War by a former slave who published a cookbook in which she had a recipe for what she called "angel food cake." She indicated that friends and relatives would often eat this type of cake after a funeral as a reminder that God had sent His angels to take their loved one home. Perhaps this former slave was closer to the mind of God than many of our translators, theologians, biblical historians, and lexicographers.

It is typical in Semitic storytelling for the narrator to replace a name with a descriptive word. For instance, in the story of Ruth, one of Elimelech and Naomi's sons was named *Mahlon* (מעלון), which means "sickness," and the other was named *Chilion* (כליון), which means "wasting away." It stands to reason that a Semitic father would never give his sons such names, particularly when there was a strong belief in that day that a name, when spoken, actually held the power to transform a person into what the name signified. For instance, if a man named his child *Ozaz* (אזז), or "powerful," he believed that just calling the child by that name throughout his youth would cause him to become *powerful*. Elimelech seemed to be a very loving, caring husband and father, and he never would have cursed his babies with such names. Yet the storyteller applied these names so the listener would have a better understanding that these two young men were suffering from serious health problems.

Considering the nature of Semitic storytelling, it would not be unreasonable or a threat to our understanding of the inspiration and infallibility of Scripture to read this term *"angels' food"* as a storytelling device, something that God is using to send us a very powerful message—especially since the usual term *"manna"* occurs in the previous verse, Psalm 78:24. The fact that God inspired the psalmist to call manna *"angels' food"* is what the sages would refer to as a *remez*,* or a hint of a deeper meaning.

The Perfect Food

To explore this deeper meaning, we need to examine the term *"angels' food"* in the original Hebrew. It is *lechem 'abirim* (לחם אבירים), which some translators render as "bread of the mighty ones" or "bread of princes." The Hebrew word that is commonly used for angels is *male'ak* (מלאך), which means "messengers." In our study verse, however, the word rendered as *"angels"* is *'abirim* (אבירים), which means "brave," "noble," or "strong." This is where commentators get the idea that the bread being referred to was eaten only by those in the nobility, kings, and princes. They may be right. Perhaps the psalmist was saying that God gave His people the best, most delicious food imaginable, and yet they grew tired of it and began to complain, demanding some variety. (See Numbers 11.)

But the Talmud teaches that this manna was something more than just the best food—it was the *perfect* food. It was food that could be completely absorbed by the body. Since the Israelites' bodies used this food entirely, there was no need for the people to eliminate waste. Had their bodies produced waste, it would have caused a very real sanitary problem, considering the fact that there were a million or so refugees camping out together. So God removed this problem by giving them food that was *'abirim* (אבירים)—"noble" or "strong."

You see, another meaning of *'abirim* (אבירים) is "feathers," or something that is *as light as feathers*. This manna drifted from heaven like a feather drifting off a bird onto the ground, and the idea is that this was something from God Himself that drifted to earth.

Actually, the sages take this idea further. Apart from the Masoretic text, we find that *'abirim* (אבירים) could also be a compound word meaning "the Father who overcomes." Like a feather off a bird, a feather that enables a bird to fly to the heavens, God shares His *feather* with His loved ones so that they can overcome the penalty of their sins and fly to heaven to be with Him. When Jesus said, "This is My body; do eat of it" (see, for example, Matthew 26:26), the disciples might very well have thought of the manna and how it was a part of God Himself that would allow them to overcome their sins and one day *fly to heaven*. Perhaps the old slave was right to name the cake that was eaten at funerals "angel food cake," because the departed souls were truly eating of the manna of heaven, taking on that "part" of God, His Son Jesus, who through His death on the cross provided their *transportation* to heaven.

I believe that the psalmist, under the inspiration of God, choose the words *lechem 'abirim* (לחם אבירים), or *"angels' food,"* to give a messianic picture of His Son who would one day come to earth. Just as the manna had given physical life to the people of Israel, the *lechem 'abirim* (לחם אבירים) would bring spiritual life to those who would trust and believe in Him.

The Best God Has to Offer

Sometimes, like the Israelites, I get tired of eating only *"angels' food."* I start demanding that God do something different with my life—that He would give me a new type of ministry or something more exciting to do. Yet every time I eat of the *"angels' food,"* I am reminded that what I have is the best that God has to offer me; He shares His *feathers*, or His *presence*, through the death and resurrection of His Son. Perhaps God whispers to me the question that I imagine He asked the Israelites: "You want more? I have given you My best, and that is not good enough for you?"

I try to take that reminder to heart. A little while ago, I traveled from my home in Illinois to the state of Kentucky, where angel food cake originated, to spend a week in a Benedictine monastery. For one week, I lived in silence; it was just God and me together, with no distractions. It was a special time of feasting on the manna from heaven, or the *lechem 'abirim* (לחם אבירים), *"angels' food."*

Study 53

The Fourth Generation: *Rova'* (רבע)

"Who can count the dust of Jacob, and the number of the fourth part of Israel?"
—Numbers 23:10

The context of the above verse is that Balak, king of Moab, had been trying to get the prophet Balaam to curse the Israelites, who had recently been freed from slavery in Egypt under Moses' leadership. Instead, Balaam ended up blessing Israel. It had not quite dawned on Balak that God is not at man's beck and call. He figured that if Balaam was a prophet, he would have some pull with God; and if he paid Balaam well enough, he could finagle God into putting a curse on the Israelites.

I know that sounds ridiculous. It is about as ridiculous as asking a pastor or a priest to pray for you because he should be able to persuade God to answer your prayer simply because he is a clergyman. But just because someone seems to be more holy than you or to have a special office does not mean that person has God at his beck and call. You have just as much clout with God as some popular television preacher does. Balaam knew he had no special pull with God, even though he was a prophet. That is why he said, *"Who can count the dust of Jacob, and the number of the fourth part of Israel?"*

The Hebrew word translated *"fourth part"* is simply *rova'* (רבע), which is the word for "four." Practically every English translation renders this term the same as the King James Version does. They assume that Balaam was making a reference to the number and might of Israel. One commentator even says that when Balaam referred to the *"fourth part,"* it was a reference to the four divisions of Israel, so that he was talking about Israel's military strength.

This interpretation does not make much sense to me, because it would seem that Balaam was telling Balak that he could not curse the Israelites because of their great numbers. But Balaam had previously asked, in effect, "How can I curse what God has not cursed?" (See Numbers 23:8.) The Israelites' numbers had nothing to do with whether or not Balaam could curse them.

The Promise of the Fourth Generation

When I researched this incident in Jewish literature, I found out some things that were quite amazing. First, the use of the words *"Jacob"* and *"Israel"* for the nation of God is a reference to the generations of Israel. Jacob represents the female aspect of the nation, and Israel represents the male aspect—the two who join together to conceive a child. The Hebrew word rendered *"dust"* is *'apar* (עפר), which is also used to denote "a young man." The numerical value of *'apar* (עפר) is 350, which is the same numerical value of *lan'ar* (לנער), meaning "a young woman." Hence, the sages consider Balaam's reference as an indication of the generations. But that is their deeper understanding of the word. In their literal understanding of it, they view the term for *"dust"* as a reference to humility and prayer to God.

The "sons of Jacob" were people who had humbled themselves and prayed before God. Balaam was looking to the up-and-coming generation, the generation that would have the faith to enter into the Promised Land. More than that, this new generation was the fourth generation of Israel—counting, as Balaam apparently did, from the birth of Moses. Note the four generations of Israel indicated here, with each generation representing forty years: The first generation consisted of the forty years during which Moses grew up in Pharaoh's court. The second generation was the forty years that Moses was in exile in Midian. The third generation was when Moses led the people out of slavery in Egypt, and they lived in the wilderness for forty years. And the fourth generation consisted of the children of the freed Israelites, who grew up to be the ones who would enter the Promised Land. There was a belief that the fourth generation would be the mightiest in the power and knowledge of God, because they would have the strongest faith. So Balaam was saying, in effect, "How can I curse a people who not only humble themselves in prayer to God but also represent the fourth and most powerful generation?"

While the Israelites wandered in the wilderness, there were times when they must have felt abandoned by God or pretty hopeless. Yet Balaam saw what even they did not see. He saw a praying people, and he was not about to curse a praying people—let alone one that had moved into that fourth generation.

Four "Generations" in Our Relationship with God

I remember watching a presentation on the television program *NOVA* about the monarch butterfly. Every year, the fourth generation of the monarch butterfly will take a three-month journey. These butterflies will travel fifty miles a day from all parts of Canada, converge in Texas, and then fly down to one spot on a mountain in Mexico, arriving at almost the same time. Millions of them all arrive on this one mountain. What caught my attention was that it is the fourth generation that makes this thirty-five-hundred-mile trip. The documentary explained how many of the butterflies suffer and die while making this journey. They perish from the elements or from predators. In fact, as I write this study, this year's monarch butterflies are currently on that journey to their "promised land," and they should be passing over my home in the Chicago area about now.

Is the monarch butterfly's yearly journey a sign, or reminder, from God? If so, what is the nature of this reminder? The sages teach that not only is there something special about each fourth generation, but there are also four "generations" in our relationship with God. The first is our spiritual birth—I consider this to be our rebirth in Jesus Christ. The second is our growth period. The third is our wilderness period. The fourth is our entrance into the Promised Land. If you feel like you've been wandering in the wilderness, as the Israelites were at the time of Balaam, and if you feel like you are getting nowhere and accomplishing nothing, as Israel must have felt, then you need to look up and see the monarch butterflies flying to Mexico, because they are a reminder that you are approaching that fourth generation, and the Promised Land is in sight. You may have to face a few more storms and a few more predators, but if you can continue your journey, you will arrive on the mountaintop where, like the monarchs, you can rest from your long journey.

Study 54

Soft Answer: *Ma'enkh Rak* (מענה רך)

"A soft answer turneth away wrath: but grievous words stir up anger."
—Proverbs 15:1

But soft, what light through yonder window breaks?
It is the east and Juliet is the sun!
—Romeo and Juliet, Act 2, Scene II[5]

Those who have been following my Hebrew word studies over the years are familiar with a little expression I use: "But soft...." In truth, in using this expression, I am just showing off my love of the language of Shakespeare; but I also use it because there is really no modern term that expresses what Shakespearean English can express in the word *soft*.

Shakespeare used *soft* in the context of Romeo seeking Juliet. One moment Romeo is feeling frustrated, and then suddenly he notices a light in his beloved's window. The way I read this scene, the

5. Brian Gibbons, ed., *Romeo and Juliet*, The Arden Shakespeare (London: Thomson Learning, reprinted 2002, 2003; first published 1980 by Methuen & Co. LTD).

very thought of her floods him with passion and love, and these feelings serve to *soften* his troubled heart.

"Nice Doggy..."

In Proverbs 15:1, most modern translations render the Hebrew word for *"soft," rak* (רך), as "gentle." Okay, "gentle" is a proper rendering of the word, but I do not believe it is the right word to use in this context. Then again, neither is the word *"soft."* In the days when the King James Version was written, *soft* was an appropriate word to use here; but over the last couple hundred years, it has lost the meaning it once had. Today, when we read this passage as "soft," we automatically think of a quiet, soothing answer that will appease someone's wrath. Sort of like the Will Rogers quotation that "Diplomacy is the art of saying 'Nice doggy' until you can find a rock." That might work on Sparky, my neighbor's pit bull, but it won't always work on human beings. I learned that much when I worked with troubled teens. Sometimes, a quiet answer enraged them all the more, because they thought they were being patronized. They felt they were being treated like some savage wild beast—and although they were acting like it, they still did not want to be seen that way.

The King James translators chose to render the Hebrew word *rak* (רך) as *"soft"* because they understood that *rak* (רך) comes from the root word *rakak* (רכך), which means "to be tender or delicate of heart." That idea is similar to how we often describe the way we feel when we see a wounded puppy, a child weeping, or the devastation and suffering a tornado has inflicted on people. We say things like, "My heart goes out to them." In other words, it is a response that is filled with the love and compassion that God feels.

Thus, this verse is not saying that if someone is expressing anger toward us, and we speak quietly, it will automatically cool them down. In some cases, it may; but in many cases, it will not. What the verse is saying is that when another driver cuts us off and gives us the one-finger salute, we do not return the gesture by shaking our fist, but rather respond with compassion and love; we consider why that person is behaving that way. It means that if we have wronged or offended someone, we apologize and make things right. And if a person's bad conduct is not the result of something we've done, we pray that God would heal that person of whatever is causing the dysfunctional behavior.

In other words, we do what Jesus taught us to do in Matthew 5:44: *"Love your enemies, bless them that curse you, do good to them that hate you, and pray for them which despitefully use you."* In the Northern dialect of Aramaic, the word Jesus used that is translated as *"good"* here is *tob* (טב). This term is identical to the Hebrew word *tov* (טוב), which means "to be in harmony with God." In other words, let your response to the one who hates you be in harmony with God's response—and God's response is always one of love.

Responding with God's Love

Let me give a personal illustration of this. The other day, I drove by an abortion clinic where Right to Life protesters stood outside with their signs and banners. One banner had a picture of the horribly mutilated body of a fetus at nearly full term. To be honest, I guess I had watched too many Hollywood B "horror" movies as a kid to be moved by such photos; I had become desensitized, so I noticed the photo and just drove on. But suddenly I felt my heart grieving, and I was weeping. I instantly knew that this was not my grief or my tears. I had never given much thought to the abortion issue; I had other concerns in my life. Yet I was now moved to tears. I knew and understood that these tears could only be God's.

In my journey to God's heart, I have discovered that I have to feel His heart to feel what He feels. When I do this, I experience *rakak* (רכך), or a tender heart. And at that moment in the car, I realized that God has given me a special gift as a result of my search for His heart. As I have expressed in earlier studies, He has allowed my heart to feel the pain in His heart. In this situation, He allowed my heart to see such pictures as His heart sees them, and He allowed my heart to hear the voices of the protesters as He hears them. Try as I might, I cannot help but weep as God weeps.

When we respond to other people's wrath with God's loving heart, that wrath will be turned away, for no one can resist God's love. First Corinthians 13:13 (ESV) says, *"So now faith, hope, and love abide, these three; but the greatest of these is* [God's] *love."* To know and experience God's love, to understand what that love is all about, has freed me from so many fears, for I know that I can rest in His love. When others experience God's love, it will do the same for them.

Rakak (רכך), or tenderness, expresses the very heart of God. Sharing His love is not something we work at or struggle to produce; rather, it is the natural result and gift of giving our hearts to God and letting Him share His heart with us. We Christians can be very good at giving our hearts to God, but do we really accept His heart in return? Do we dare to feel what His heart feels, to see what His heart sees, and to hear what His heart hears? Do we dare to experience the *rakak* (רכך) of God's heart for others?

Study 55

Naked: *'Aerom, 'Aram* (עירם)

"And the Lord *God called unto Adam, and said unto him, Where art thou? And he said, I heard thy voice in the garden, and I was afraid, because I was naked; and I hid myself."*
—Genesis 3:9–10

I have discovered that when I study Scripture with the purpose of learning about God's heart, I begin to find answers to questions that have troubled me in the past. For instance, somehow the idea of God wandering around the garden of Eden, apparently unable to find Adam and having to call out to him, hoping for some response so He could locate him, just never seemed to make much sense to me. I mean, if God had problems locating Adam because he was hiding in some bushes, that does not inspire much confidence that God can keep track of me 24/7.

"A Cry of Grief and Mourning"

Practically every modern English version translates the Hebrew word *'ayakah* (איכה) in our study passage as "Where are you?" But there is a rendering that would make more sense, at least to me in my search for God's heart. Translators will not use this rendering for two reasons: The first is that there are no English words to adequately communicate this alternative translation. The second is that even if we found some English words that could work to describe the emotion expressed, we certainly would not want to ascribe such an emotion to God, because it would come out something like this: "O, like woe is Me, like woe is Me!"

In your Bible, turn to the book of Lamentations. If your version includes the Hebrew rendering for "Lamentations," you will note that it is the same word translated "Where are you?" with just a difference in vowel pointing, so that it is spelled *'eyekah* (איכה) rather than *'ayakah* (איכה). The root word means "a lamentation," or "a cry of grief and mourning."

Can you picture God wandering through the garden, weeping and saying, "O woe is Me!"? But as I have previously emphasized, if we believe we are created in God's image, then we have a heart like His—a heart that can be broken. Haven't you ever lamented over a broken relationship? Most Christians seem to have a hard time picturing God as weeping over His lost children. Hence, we use the more appropriate rendering of "Where are you?" But while *'ayakah* (איכה) is an interrogative,* it is also an expression of grief. So, what is causing this grief? Adam and Eve were not hiding from God; they were hiding from the *presence* of God. They had willfully separated themselves from His presence. It was not their sin, in itself, that separated them from God, but rather their guilt. God didn't remove Himself from them; they removed themselves from Him.

Why did they hide from the presence of God? Adam told God it was because they were naked. That seems to be another little mystery—why did they not want God to see them naked? He is, after all, the Master Physician, and He knows human anatomy better than anyone. There should be nothing shameful about God seeing them naked. The Hebrew word translated *"naked"* comes from an uncertain root word. That root might be *'aram* (עירם), which means "naked" but could also mean "to act prudently, wisely, or cautiously." Or the root word could be *'ayar* (עיר), which means "to be in agony," as in the agony of death.

As I find myself drawn to the heart of God, I discover that I am more willing to step outside the box and assume possible alternative or secondary renderings that are not generally accepted by our translators. The standard translation of God's words is essentially, "Adam, where are you?" with the standard rendering of Adam's answer being, in effect, "I am hiding in the bushes because I am naked." But I find myself drawn to a secondary, or alternative, rendering. Since I cannot find any English words that would offer an adequate translation for this, I can only describe it with an illustration. These statements are like the cry of a lover who is separated from his beloved, while his beloved is hiding from her lover's presence because she is in agony over having betrayed him.

Arms Wide Open with Forgiveness

It's possible that many of the translations in English Bibles are renderings from those who see God as an angry God who is ready to whip you if you commit some sin. Yet as you draw closer to God's heart, keep in mind that there are secondary, or alternative, renderings that would show a God who is grief-stricken over your sins, not angry over them. He is grief-stricken because the sin has caused you to hide from His presence—the presence that He longs to share with you—and because He knows that sin is destructive to you. After searching for the heart of God and capturing a few glimpses of His heart, you may no longer see Him as a taskmaster ready to whip you into submission to His will, but as a Lover who has His arms open, ready to embrace you, to forgive you, and to win you over to submission to His perfect will through His passionate love for you.

Study 56

Sought: *Baqesh* (בקשׁ)

"But now thy kingdom shall not continue: the Lord hath sought him a man after his own heart."
—1 Samuel 13:14

When I look at the phrase *"a man after his own heart"* in the Hebrew, I find it is more correctly translated, "A man who has a heart like God's heart." Such a man is *sought after* by God. The Hebrew word translated *"sought"* in our study verse is *baqesh* (בקשׁ), which is found in a *piel* (intensive) form and would be a little more than just a seeking—it would be more like a *longing*. We should therefore render this sentence as, "The Lord has longed for a man who has a heart like His." I believe that most Christians long to have a heart like God's—not only because it would make us one with Him, but also because it would protect His heart. Believers who really love God desire to protect His heart.

If there has been one theme for my life in the last few years, it has been that of learning and understanding God's heart. So, I find myself on an ongoing journey to learn as much as I can about the heart of God and to pray that my heart will be like His. Now the question is, what happens when we have a heart like His? This is a completely new issue.

A Musician at One with His Instrument

Recently, via the Internet, I saw a piano recital by the brilliant late composer and pianist Glenn Gould, who was playing the Goldberg Variations on Bach. As I watched and listened, I found that I was not so much paying attention to Gould's style and performance as I was thinking about how someone could play for forty-five minutes without reading from any music sheets and not make one mistake. I play the piano a little, and I thought about how, after years of playing, your hands and fingers automatically seem to know where to go to make the sound that your mind is looking for. Thus, you are thinking more about what sound you want to make than about what notes you need to play. It is almost as if the musical instrument and you become one. Indeed, while watching Mr. Gould play, you cannot help but feel that he and the piano were one.

This started me thinking about God and about the Hebrew word *tov* (טוב), which is often rendered as "good" but really means "to be in harmony." Mr. Gould's ten fingers played ten different notes, yet they all seemed to be in harmony with each other. I then reflected on Jewish literature in which I remembered reading that *"a man after his own heart"* is a musical phrase. I began to understand what the rabbi was saying. And as I watched Glenn Gould play, I realized that he was not aware of his audience; he was off in his own world, somehow mystically joined with that piano, one with that instrument, through which his heart could express itself. The piano was the vehicle he used to communicate the depths of his heart—but to truly do this, that piano had to be in perfect tune.

When I was a child, we had a man in our church named Virgil who was a piano teacher at Moody Bible Institute. He also tuned the pianos at Orchestra Hall in Chicago where world-famous pianists would perform. Many artists would specifically ask for Virgil to tune the piano for their concerts, because they knew he would tune it to the standard of perfection they needed to perform. They required this perfect tuning so they could become one with the instrument.

Instruments Through Which God Shares His Heart

As I contemplated all this, I began to realize that I am God's "piano," His instrument, that He seeks, or *longs*, to use to express His heart. I also see that my sinfulness puts me out of tune with Him until I am restored again through Jesus Christ—like a piano that goes out of tune and needs to be re-tuned before each concert by someone who has the skill and talent to properly readjust it so the master musician can fully express his heart. The only way to become one with the Master so that He can express His heart through us is to be in tune with Him.

I may have spent years learning about the heart of God, but God cannot express His heart through me if I am out of tune with Him. I need His Son Jesus Christ to be called in to re-tune me. Through His shed blood, Jesus cleanses me of all the sins that keep me out of tune with God and brings all the keys of my life into perfect harmony with Him. In this way, the Master's heart can become one with my heart, and He can play the melody of His heart through me to others.

Study 57

God Left: *'Elohim 'Azavu* (אלוהים עזבו)

"Howbeit in the business of the ambassadors of the princes of Babylon, who sent unto him to enquire of the wonder that was done in the land, God left him, to try him, that he might know all that was in his heart."
—2 Chronicles 32:31

God had miraculously healed Hezekiah, the king of Judah, of an illness that had left him at death's door. Additionally, through God, Hezekiah had won a great victory over the Assyrian Empire. This was without the help of Egypt, which had allied itself with Judah and then chickened out at the last minute, leaving them to fend off the powerful Assyrians alone. The Babylonians were really impressed with Judah's victory, and as they faced their own threat from Assyria, they were curious about the God who had helped to pull that victory off. They were also likely interested in Hezekiah's health, because if he had died during his illness, having no heir to assume the throne, the nation of Judah might have been thrown into disarray, disrupting the stability of the region that Judah had produced. On top of that, the Babylonians were noted stargazers and were quite aware of the miracle of the sundial that God had performed when He moved the shadow of the dial back ten degrees as a sign of Hezekiah's recovery. I mean, God was letting the world know clearly that Judah was a nation of the most powerful God in the universe, and that it was He who established nations.

So, the Babylonians traveled to see Hezekiah, hat in hand, on the premise that they wished to congratulate him on his miraculous recovery. In truth, they wanted to learn of this powerful God who had delivered a nation that had only a second-rate military from the most powerful nation in the world. This was a great evangelistic opportunity for Hezekiah, but instead, what does he do? He shows off his armories and his wealth. He basically leaves God out of the formula for success as he seeks to win over the Babylonians, perhaps obtain an advantage, and position himself as a world ruler.

The Secrets of Hezekiah's Heart

This brings us to our study verse, 2 Chronicles 32:31. We learn that when these Babylonian ambassadors arrived, *"God left."* God wanted to *"try"* Hezekiah so He could know his heart. The Hebrew word for *"left"* is *'azavu* (עזבו), which can also mean "forsook." In this verse, *'azavu* (עזבו) is in a *qal* (simple verbal) form, but what is more telling is that it is in a perfect (past) tense and in a passive voice. In other words, God had already put Hezekiah's heart to the test. He knew what Hezekiah intended to do, and He could not be a part of this great act of disobedience in which Hezekiah was trying to impress the "arm of flesh," or those with human power. So, God had already *"left"* him.

There is significance in the fact that *'azavu* (עזבו) is in a simple *qal* form and not in a *piel* (intensive) form. To render it as "forsook" would be a little harsh for a *qal* form. In the simple verbal form, I would say it has more of the idea of *stepping back* than *forsaking*. The reason for this stepping back is found within the word itself. *'Azavu* (עזבו) is spelled ayin (ע), which, in its "shadow" form, or negative aspect, means "blindness"; zayin (ז), the shadow form of which indicates a dependence upon the arm of the flesh to defend you; beth (ב), which represents the heart; and vav (ו), which normally denotes a connection between earth and heaven, but whose shadow form reminds us of a codependency on the arm of flesh, rather than on heaven. Hezekiah was blinded to the fact that his heart was set upon the arm of flesh and not upon God. Babylon was the very nation that in a few years would take Judah captive, yet here was Hezekiah leaning on these pagan rulers to help him, instead of using the great miracles that God had performed to encourage them to put their trust in Jehovah.

When God Steps Back from Us

We need to understand that in the Hebrew language, syntax is built into the words; and in this verse, I believe that the inseparable pronouns point to Hezekiah, but the last pronoun points to God. In other words, God left Hezekiah to *"try him,"* which is rendered from the root word *nasah* (נסה) with a *piel* (intensive) infinitive. Although *nasah* (נסה) means "to tempt," or "to try," as well as "to probe," it is also used to denote "to write an essay." Thus, in the phrase *"that he might know all that was in his heart," "his heart"* refers to the heart of God, not to Hezekiah's heart. God was leaving Hezekiah so that the king could read or write an "essay" on His heart.

The picture here is of a lover who has faithfully given and cared for his beloved, only to see her take all his gifts and adorn herself to impress another lover. God is the forsaken Lover who steps back and lets His unfaithful beloved pursue another lover, hoping that in the process she will understand how she has broken His heart.

As Christians, we can too easily become complacent about our relationship with God. He answers our prayers and provides for us, but before long, we tend to take Him for granted. Consequently, we soon lose the sense of His presence, and suddenly it seems as if He has left us. Yet He does not abandon us in the sense of the *piel* (intensive) form but in the *qal* (simple) form. He is merely stepping back from us, hoping that we will see that He is our true Source. We may use the arm of flesh and try to impress others with our "godly experience" and testimony of God's provision, drawing attention to ourselves at God's expense. We may resort to natural means to obtain our positions of power and influence rather than be patient and allow God to control our lives and destinies. This is hard for us to do, because everything in us cries out to draw some comfort and encouragement from Babylon rather than declare to Babylon that our trust is in the Lord. But if we have to go to battle having "Babylon" as our ally, we must let it be known that our God is Jehovah and that we depend on Him to supply our needs—Babylon is only God's instrument to supply some of those needs.

Study 58

Vain Oblations: *Sheve' Minchcath* (שׁוא מנחת)

"Bring no more vain oblations; incense is an abomination unto me; the new moons and sabbaths, the calling of assemblies, I cannot away with; it is iniquity, even the solemn meeting."
—Isaiah 1:13

This verse pulls no punches—God is commanding His people not to bring any more *"vain oblations"* to Him. The Hebrew word for *"oblations"* is *minchcath* (מנחת), which means "an offering" and comes from the root word *manach* (מנח). The word is also used for a *tribute* or a *gift*. This particular word is late Hebrew and comes from a similar Phoenician* word. But if we go back to the time of Moses and see how the word was used at that time, we find that the root word would be *navch* (נוח) rather than *manach* (מנח). *Manach* (מנח) is an offering or a gift, while *navch* (נוח) is a *rest*, or a *repose*. I have read in Jewish literature that it has the idea of drawing near to God and resting in Him.

Navch (נוח) would be used to represent an offering or a gift in the sense of a sacrifice of something that you find comfort in, to demonstrate your surrender to the one receiving the sacrifice. In other words, a husband might give up his dream of owning a boat and use the money he'd planned to buy it with to purchase something for his wife instead. The *navch* (נוח) offering would be the husband's attempt to draw near to his wife by demonstrating that she, rather than the boat, is his source of comfort. That sacrifice would declare to her that he finds more joy in her than in any boat he wanted to buy.

Motivations for Coming to God

Thus, in our study verse, God is telling the Israelites not to bring worthless attempts to draw near to Him. The people are bringing him mere *manach*s rather than *navch*s. These gifts are for the purpose of winning God's favor rather than of drawing near to Him, so the motivation behind them is selfish.

Isaiah's play on the word for *"oblations," minchcath* (מנחת)—which had a modern root but, to the Hebrew people, also carried an ancient root—was a stroke of genius. (Okay, it was inspired.) It clearly showed why the people's offerings to God were an abomination to Him. Let's return to the analogy of the married couple. Suppose the husband gets a small bonus at work. He immediately thinks he could use that money to purchase a top-of-the-line fishing rod. Then he thinks of the opportunity to show his wife how much he loves her by using the bonus to purchase the expensive perfume she loves. He sacrifices his new graphite fishing rod and purchases the perfume. The wife naturally loves the gift and, in return, dips into her "mad money," which she was saving for a private shopping spree, and purchases the fishing rod for her husband. That is *navch* (נוח), and that is the type of sacrificial offering God wants.

Again, in the modern root meaning, *manach* (מנח) refers to a sacrifice or an offering, but the motive behind that sacrifice might be selfish, even mercenary. For example, if the husband gave a *manach* (מנח) gift rather than a *navch* (נוח) gift, he might use his bonus to purchase the expensive perfume for his wife rather than buy the fishing rod, but when he gave the gift to his wife, he would tell her, "See, I made this sacrifice of my bonus to get your perfume; and since I did this wonderful thing for you, you have to let me go on that fishing trip with my buddies."

What Gifts Are We Bringing?

Whenever we are tempted to throw rocks at Israel for presenting worthless offerings to God, I suggest that we remember a little saying that Jesus used: "He who is without sin, let him cast the first stone." (See John 8:7.) How many times have you forced yourself to go to church, pay your tithe, or do some worthy Christian service, hoping that God would be impressed with your sacrifice or offering so that He would grant you a favor? You thought that if you scratched His back, He would scratch yours. That is a *manach* (מנח), or an offering that is an abomination to God. To bring that kind of offering is to act like the jerk of a husband who made the "sacrifice" of buying the perfume for his wife just to butter her up so she would let him go on a fishing trip. He should have that expensive bottle of perfume "anointed" on his head with enough force to shatter the bottle!

However, if you take your offering to God and say, "Lord, I intended to use this offering for something else, but it is not nearly as important to me as You are, so I am giving it to You," then you have given a *navch* (נוח), the kind of gift that writer O. Henry expressed in *The Gift of the Magi.*

Study 59

Murmur: *Layan* (לין)

"How long shall I bear with this evil congregation, which murmur against me? I have heard the murmurings of the children of Israel, which they murmur against me."
—Numbers 14:27

Some modern translations of Numbers 14:27 say that the children of Israel "grumbled" against God, others say they "complained," and still others say they made an "outcry."

"*Bad* Israelites," we say. "How dare they grumble, murmur, complain, or even make an outcry against God after all the mighty miracles He had done for them! You surely can't blame God for not being able to bear such an evil congregation. I know that if I were God, my patience would certainly run pretty thin against a people who would keep demanding more and more and then bellyache because they felt they hadn't gotten enough!"

But was it the fact that Israel was acting like a spoiled child that made God declare they were *"evil"*? What did He mean by *"evil,"* anyway? Was God's patience really running thin?

Old Testament Relevance

While investigating our study verse, I thought of a Bible study I once attended where the group was going through a workbook.

Everyone seemed quite excited over the fact that they were actually studying the book of Numbers—one of those obscure books of the Bible that hardly anyone ever reads. One of the fill-in-the-blank questions in the workbook was, "God called the children of Israel evil because ________." Well, that was an easy one: "because they were murmuring against God."

Someone in the group then asked, "What does it mean to murmur?" Immediately, the response was, "Well, my translation says...." I thought, *Oh, good. Here is a group of people who really want to think and dig deep into the Scriptures to find out what the Word of God has to say.* I was really pleased until another member of the group asked, "Why is it that after all the miracles, someone would complain against God?" and someone answered, "Because they were evil." Everything started to go downhill from there. The discussion that followed can be summarized as follows: "We are Christians, and we have more revelation today than they did. Of course, we would never complain or murmur against God!" There was even the suggestion that since we are living in the time of the new covenant, there was really no need to study the Old Testament.

Bad Old Testament—it speaks nothing relevant to us today.

Okay, after forty years of studying, teaching, and earning a few academic degrees focused on the Old Testament, I will admit to some bias. But somebody has to speak out in defense of the poor Old Testament and show its relevance to our lives today. So, let us first look at the Hebrew word translated *"evil."* It is one of those *ra* (רע) words. *Ra* (רע) is a very common Semitic word for "evil." In the Hebraic form, a third letter following *ra* often tells what specific type of evil is being addressed. This particular *ra* (רע) word ends with a hei (ה) and describes *an evil of consumption.* It is an evil that comes from letting natural desires consume you—from being so preoccupied by the desires of the flesh that you fail to hear the voice of God. The *"evil congregation"* is one that focuses on their natural needs to the exclusion of addressing their spiritual needs. If you are like many people, you may be thinking—even subconsciously—that such things are not applicable to us today, because we are too spiritually enlightened to have such a thing happen to us or to the church. Well, I will let you ponder that idea as we move on.

Worrying and Fretting Denies God's Faithfulness

The people of Israel tended to do a lot of murmuring. The word in Hebrew that is used for "*murmur*" is *layan* (לין), which basically means "to remain," or "to stay." It is often used in Scripture to show a refusal to move forward due to a lack of faith after receiving divine instruction. Thus, we would have the idea of "murmuring" as *worrying* or *fretting*. Worry is nothing more than a lack of faith and a refusal to accept divine instruction. Does this bring us into the twenty-first century yet? I don't know about you, but that one causes me to start feeling the heat of relevance.

Finally, the word "*bear*" is not even in the Hebrew text. Actually, the literal rendering of the first part of Numbers 14:27 is, "Until when will this evil congregation murmur to Me?" In fact, let's look at this whole verse in a literal way: "Until when (or, "*How long*") will this congregation be so absorbed with or focused on their natural needs that they will continue to refuse to move forward to the Promised Land? I hear the children of Israel worrying and fretting, and they are fretting against Me."

As I wrote in the previous study, before we pick up rocks and get ready to stone Israel for their lack of faith, we need to heed this warning of Jesus: "He who is without sin, let him cast the first stone." (See John 8:7.) As Christians who belong to Jesus, when we worry or fret over our circumstances, we fret against our Lord. In all of my approximately threescore years of walking this earth, I have never known God to fail me. He is the one Person who has never let me down, who has never rejected me. Yet the moment my car breaks down, I begin to worry and fret, even after He has proven Himself trustworthy over so many years. When I worry and fret over my circumstances, I am taking all those years of faithfulness, throwing them back in His face, and saying, "I don't trust You." Yeah, the guy who is always talking about seeking the heart of God can actually break His heart in the cruelest way.

What? Am I the only unenlightened one here? Am I the only one who needs to examine the Old Testament to see my own reflection?

God Is Worthy of Our Trust

You see, Hebrew truly is a language of emotions. Thus, the words *'ad mati* (עד מתי), "Until when? or *"How long?"* are not an expression of anger but rather a cry of the heart, a heart that has been broken. God is not expressing anger at the children of Israel for their murmurings; He is expressing a broken heart over having given so much to prove Himself trustworthy, only to be told He cannot be trusted. Probably the most hurtful thing a spouse can say to his or her beloved is, "I don't trust you. I can't be intimate with you because you're not trustworthy enough."

If you are worrying and fretting over your circumstances, pause for just a moment, look beyond the natural, and consider God's heart. Is it worth all that time and effort to worry and fret—especially over something that will probably not exist fifty years from now—to break the heart of the God who has proven Himself worthy of your trust and of the intimacy that He longs to share with you?

Study 60

Tattoo on the Palm: *Kapayim Chaqothike* (כפים חקתיך)

"Can a woman forget her sucking child, that she should not have compassion on the son of her womb? yea, they may forget, yet will I not forget thee. Behold, I have engraven thee upon the palms of my hands; thy walls are continually before me."
—Isaiah 49:15–16

This is an awesome promise of the love of God. It is very unlikely that a mother would forget her child, but it could happen. Yet with God, it would never happen. The Hebrew word for "*forget*" is *shakach* (שכח), which has the idea of *leaving* or *neglecting*. If you peer into the heart of God, you will see a mother's heart—a heart that feels only compassion for her children.

My father regularly preached at a rescue mission, and he would often use the illustration of the man who was executed for murder and placed in an unmarked grave. No one ever paid a visit to that grave except for one elderly woman who faithfully came every week to lay flowers at the site. That woman, of course, was the man's mother.

Assyrian Tattoo Parlors

God says that even a mother could neglect her child, but He would never neglect His children. Then He says a curious thing: *"I have engraven thee upon the palms of my hands."* The Hebrew word for *"engraven"* is *chaqaq* (חקק). This is an unusual word because it means not only "to imprint" or "to engrave," but also "to imagine." This word has its roots in the Akkadian language, and the only way to understand it is to consider an unusual practice of the women in the ancient Assyrian Empire.

The Assyrians were a warlike people, and when a young man reached a certain age, he would usually be inducted into the Assyrian army. When a son left home to go off to war, his mother would long for some token to remind her of her absent child—so she would get a tattoo. Tattooing is an ancient art that was forbidden among the Hebrews but practiced among pagan cultures. The mother would go to the local "tattoo parlor," so to speak, and have her son's name tattooed on the right palm of her hand. As I mentioned earlier, the ancients believed that one's heart was found in one's right palm. Thus, this token, or symbol, that she would have permanently tattooed on her right palm would be a reminder of her son who was off fighting a war for her safety. According to Assyrian beliefs, that token was as close to her "heart" as possible. Since the palm of the hand is one of the parts of the body that we see most frequently, each time she looked at this little token, she would think of her son.

Of course, God does not have a physical hand, and He is speaking metaphorically when He says, *"I have engraven thee upon the palms of my hands."* By the way, I would not recommend using the above illustration with your local youth group, because they would probably take it as scriptural justification for getting a tattoo! And the Bible does strictly forbid the cutting of the skin or the printing of marks on it. (See Leviticus 19:28.)

What God is saying in this analogy is that we are closest to His heart, and He has a little token of us permanently "engraved" on His right hand as a continual reminder of us. He is imagining all the things He longs to do for us.

God Longs for Us

Let's conclude this study by looking at the second part of Isaiah 49:16: *"Thy walls are continually before me."* The Hebrew word rendered *"walls"* is *chamah* (חמה), which means "a barrier" or "a wall of defense." God has permanently engraved us near to His heart, yet too often we set up walls or barriers to His love. The picture is that of a mother longingly reaching out to her child, but the child refusing to acknowledge her love. Yet she continues to have compassion on that child. Her child may even spit on her or curse her, but she will still long to reach out to him or her.

Likewise, God longs for us and wants us to draw near to Him a million times more than we long for Him. So, keep the word *chaqaq* (חקק), "tattooed" or "engraved," in your mind the next time you feel as if God is not there or has abandoned you. You have His assurance, "I will not forget you."

Study 61

Ram in a Thicket: *'Aval Basavek* (איל בסבך)

"And Abraham lifted up his eyes, and looked, and behold behind him a ram caught in a thicket by his horns."
—Genesis 22:13

In reading about this incident from the life of Abraham, I had never really considered the significance of the ram being caught in a thicket. My initial thought was, *Well, God had to have the ram held in place by something.* But as I continued to think about it, I recalled something I had read while working on my doctoral dissertation. It concerned an archeological discovery made in the 1930s in Southern Iraq in the area that was known as Ur, which was Abraham's hometown.

British archeologist Charles Leonard Whoolley was excavating the Death Pit of Ur, which was the site of a graveyard for kings and nobility. He found an object guarding the tomb that he called "Ram in a Thicket," because he thought it resembled the story from Genesis 22. However, the image is not so much that of a ram, a goat, or a young bull being caught in a thicket, but rather a picture of a horned animal standing on its hind legs eating something at the top of a bush. This "Ram in a Thicket" object is dated circa 2050 BC. The picture of a horned animal reaching for a high branch would support this date, because it was within the period of a three-hundred-year drought in the land of Ur; goats and similar horned animals would have had to reach high on bushes to eat because vegetation to feed on in the wild would have been scarce.

Human Sacrifice Demanded for Help

Abraham was born about 1815 BC, so he, also, would have been born during the drought; and more significantly, he would have been alive when this figure of a horned animal reaching high on a branch in order to feed was a known symbol. No one really knows exactly what the symbol represented. One speculation is that it somehow signified the gods of that era taking a soul up to heaven. Another idea, which I think is more logical, is that the horned animal reaching up to the top of a thicket, trying to get a last morsel of food, is a picture of the struggle to survive during this centuries-long drought. The image could be a depiction of Amar-utu, a horned animal that represented one of the Mesopotamian/Akkadian gods. It was a common practice to offer the human sacrifice of a child to this god in return for food and water to sustain one's physical life, as well as to obtain eternal life. The horned animal reaching for that last bit of food could symbolize Amar-utu providing out of the scarcity of the land.

The Hebrew word translated *"thicket"* is *savek* (סבך), which means "to entwine" or "an entwining vine, tree, or bush." It is not really the type of bushy plant we might imagine a "thicket" to be. A fairly good picture of a *savek* (סבך) can be found on the Internet by searching "Ram in a Thicket." The Hebrew word for *"ram"* is derived from a sort of all-purpose root word, *'aval* (איל), which is used for any animal with horns. So, it could have been a goat, a deer, a ram, or a horned bull.

Putting to Death the Pagan God of His Youth

Considering the Hebrew words for *"ram"* and *"thicket,"* and looking at the picture of the Mesopotamian god guarding the Death Pit, I would not be surprised if, when Abraham was about to sacrifice his son, God told him to look behind him to see an image similar to one he might have seen as a child growing up in the land of Ur. He would have seen the image of Marduk, or Amar-utu, which means "the calf of Utu" (the sun god) or "the young bull of the sun." Amar-utu would fit the Hebrew word *'aval* (איל), which translators render as *"ram"* but could also be rendered as a young, horned bull. The god Utu is often pictured with horns. As I indicated earlier, many children were sacrificed to this god during the prolonged time of drought and famine; their parents hoped that the young bull of Utu would provide rain to keep them alive.

So, when Abraham took the ram or the young bull that was caught in the thicket and sacrificed it instead of his son, he was putting to death, so to speak, the pagan god Amar-utu, the god of his youth, and affirming his complete loyalty to the God Jehovah who had revealed Himself to him. The Lord was declaring that He was a God who did not demand child sacrifice from His followers for them to retain physical life and to receive eternal life. Utu demanded the sacrifice of one's son in order to grant life. God also demanded the sacrifice of a son—only He would give *His* Son as a sacrifice for the world, in order to grant not only temporal life but also eternal life for all who believe in Him.

Accepting the Free Gift of God's Son

When times get rough, as they now are for many believers, we tend to get desperate and turn to various earthly means in order to survive or to find security. Sometimes, we sacrifice things very dear to us in hopes that we will get God's attention. In making these sacrifices of, for example, our time or our finances, we may expect God to think, *Oy, what this person is willing to give up for Me! Surely I must provide what he wants.* Instead, He may be telling us to look behind us and see the *'aval* (איל) in the thicket. Whereas the gods of this world demand a sacrifice of what is most dear to us (money, health, time with family, and so forth) in exchange for the security we need, God makes no such demands of us. He only asks us to accept His Gift of what is most dear to Him—His Son. In accepting this Gift, we will find life, and life eternal.

Study 62

A Tender Heart: *Rakak Levav* (רכך לבב)

"Because thine heart was tender, and thou hast humbled thyself before the Lord, when thou heardest what I spake against this place...."
—2 Kings 22:19

King Josiah, who is being addressed in our study verse, not only sought to serve God, but he also loved God. He became king of Judah at the young age of eight. Ten years into his reign, he had the scribes begin some housecleaning and repairs to the temple of God. In the process, Hilkiah, the high priest, happened upon the book of the law, the Torah. He gave it to Shaphan, a scribe, probably because the scribe was the only one who could read. Shaphan took it with him and included its discovery in his report to the king. It seemed to be almost an afterthought: "Oh, by the way, the boys at the temple ran across this book. Looks like a good read." But when Shaphan read it to Josiah, the king immediately knew what it was and what it meant. He fell down before the Lord in repentance, knowing that the kingdom would come under the judgment of God for breaking the laws of God. (See 2 Kings 22:10–11.)

A Humble, Nurturing Heart

King Josiah then ordered the high priest, the scribe, and a couple of servants to go and seek a word from the Lord. They went to Huldah, a prophetess, who gave them a word from God, part of which is recorded in 2 Kings 22:19. King Josiah was assured that he would not live to see judgment fall on the nation, because his heart was *"tender"* and because he had *"humbled"* himself before the face, or presence, of the Lord. This sounds almost like the same "spiritual formula" as in 2 Chronicles 7:14—*"If my people...shall humble themselves, and pray, and seek my face, and turn from their wicked ways; then will I... forgive their sin, and will heal their land"*—except that it does not say anything about repentance.

I hate formulas. God is not a chemistry experiment that needs the right compounds to produce a reaction, or a computer that needs the right program to supply the information we need. Josiah averted the judgment of God for a time, but not because he followed a formula; it was because of something else—his heart was *"tender"* before God. The Hebrew word rendered *"tender"* is *rakak* (רכך), which means "to be delicate, dainty, gentle, and feminine." *Rakak* also carries the idea of *nurturing.* Josiah had a heart that was nurturing toward God. He was also humble before Him. The Hebrew word translated *"humbled"* is *kana'* (כנע), which contains the idea of *bundling* or *packaging.* Josiah put all the aspects of his heart into one "package" and presented it to God.

But soft: the word *kana'* (כנע) is in an imperfect (future) form. What God is saying is that Josiah had a heart that was *"tender"* before God, and as a result he *humbled or packaged his heart and presented it to God.* This was not a case of Josiah suddenly discovering that judgment was coming and quickly seeking to repent. Throughout his life, he had showed a heart tender before God, ready to package it up and give it to Him anytime He wanted it. (See 2 Kings 22:1–2.)

This Scripture passage does not say that because Josiah repented, he wouldn't suffer the judgment of God; rather, it says that because he *always had a tender heart before God*, a heart that was *nurturing toward God*, he would escape God's judgment. His deliverance by the Lord started long before the discovery of the forgotten law. From an early age, he had sought to understand the heart of God. I have often heard people say, "Well, I don't agree with that person, but his heart is in the right place." That was Josiah; he had not been doing things according to God's law, but his heart was in the right place; and once he knew the law, he was ready to *kana'* (כנע), or humble, himself before that law.

The Heart of the Author

The high priest and the scribe did not realize the importance of the book of the law they had found, but Josiah immediately recognized its significance. The reason he was able to discern the importance of the book better than the high priest and the scribe was that he was seeking to know the heart of God, and the book of the law was the book for which he had been unknowingly searching—a book that would tell him about the heart of the God whom he loved and about what he could do to bring pleasure to his God.

I once heard an interesting story from a science-fiction writer. When he first met the woman he would eventually marry, he gave her one of his books, but she placed it on the shelf of a bookcase and forgot about it because she hated science fiction. But then she fell in love with this writer, and the day they got engaged, she took the book off the shelf and read every word of it. In fact, she read through the book three times, staying up all night to do so. Isn't it odd that someone who hated science fiction would savor every word of a science-fiction novel? But you see, the difference is that she fell in love with its author.

In my approximately threescore years on earth, I have met people from many religious walks of life, from Jews to Mormons to Catholics, and I have known very few who subscribe to my brand of doctrine or theology; yet I could not question their sincerity toward God and their longing to love the Lord with all their hearts. One day, we will stand before God, and we will find out who had the right doctrine and/or theology. But you know what? (You can throw rocks at me if you wish.) Somehow, I suspect that God will be less interested in what our doctrine or theology was on this earth, and more interested in the same thing He was interested in with Josiah, and that is whether or not we had a *rakak* (רכך), or a *tender heart*, toward Him.

Study 63

The Wounded Lamb: *Tela'* (טלא)

"He shall feed his flock like a shepherd: he shall gather the lambs with his arm."
—Isaiah 40:11

The Hebrew words for *"feed"* and *"shepherd"* in our study text are the same, although one is used as a verb and the other as a noun. It is up to the translator to make the application so that it makes sense. The Hebrew word rendered *"shepherd"* is *ra'ah* (רעה). While this term can mean "shepherd," its Semitic root is the word *ra* (רע), which, as we saw in an earlier study, is the prime Hebrew word for *evil*. There are many words in Hebrew that begin with the letters resh, ayin (רע), as *ra'ah* (רעה) does, and each word reflects a different type of evil. *Ra'ah* (רעה) contains the idea of *a consuming passion*. As I wrote previously, a consuming passion can be evil if it is a passion for something that is not of God, such as an abuse of alcohol, drugs, or sex. We would use the word *ra'ah* (רעה) today to describe an addiction. A drug addict might sacrifice his job, his resources, and his family and friends in order to satisfy his passion for drugs.

Consumed with Love

Having a consuming passion can be evil, yet there are some senses in which a consuming passion can be good. For example, shepherds are consumed with caring for their sheep as they spend their lives leading them to green pastures and cool waters and protecting them. A good shepherd lays down his life for his sheep; hence the word *ra'ah* (רעה) is used for a *"shepherd."* In another example, a true friend is one who is "consumed" with love for his friends. Jesus said, *"Greater love hath no man than this, that a man lay down his life for his friends"* (John 15:13). Thus, the word *ra'ah* (רעה) is also often rendered as "friend." From a true friendship, one is fed pleasure, comfort, and delight. We are nourished emotionally from such a relationship. Accordingly, the word *ra'ah* (רעה) is also used to express *feeding*, just as a shepherd feeds his sheep.

Thus, we can see that this whole verse is a metaphor. God is not a literal shepherd, and we are not literal sheep. But it gives a picture of our relationship to Him. God is not a taskmaster, a dictator, or a tyrant; He is a Friend. He is One who has a consuming passion for us, as we should have for Him. Christianity and Judaism are the only religions in the world whose followers do not have to serve their God out of fear that He will withhold the necessities of life if they do not honor Him. Unfortunately, many Christians tend to behave according to that mindset, treating Christianity as if it were another pagan form of worship or a worldly religion. Only in Christianity and Judaism, whose followers worship the same God, can we serve our God because we *love* Him; only in Christianity and Judaism do we experience a personal relationship with our God. Only the God Jehovah is a God who calls Himself a *ra'ah* (רעה)*—one who has a consuming passion for His friends.*

Yet here is the most wonderful thing about this passage: the word for *"lambs"* is *tela'* (טלא). This is the only place this particular word is used in Scripture. There are about nine other words in the Hebrew that are used for "lamb." The most common of these is *kebes* (כבש), which simply refers to a "yearling sheep" or a lamb. Then, there are separate words for "ewe lamb," "sacrificial lamb," and "a lamb without spot or blemish."

Special Care for the Wounded Lamb

So, what is this particular type of lamb that the Good Shepherd (Friend) gathers in His arms? It is the *tela'* (טלא). Since the word is used only once in Scripture, I had to go to Hebrew writings outside of Scripture to see how it was used. *Tela'* (טלא) actually means "to be blemished, spotted, or wounded." The lamb that the Good Shepherd is carrying is one that is not perfect; it is flawed, or it has been wounded and cannot walk or feed on its own, nor keep up with the rest of the flock. Yet this is the one that has been honored to rest in the Shepherd's arms and be carried. The Shepherd takes care of His whole flock and feeds them by leading them to green pastures and cool waters, but it is the *tela'* (טלא), the *wounded lamb*, that He not only takes care of in a general way, but also carries, feeds with His own hand, and allows to drink water from the palm of His hand.

The Talmud teaches that the rich man needs to depend upon God only once for his wealth. Then, each day, he turns to his storehouse of wealth to be fed. But a poor man must depend upon God every day to be fed and sustained. Why did God send manna to the children of Israel on a daily basis? And why did the manna rot if they collected more than was necessary for the present day? It is because God wanted Israel to wake up every morning depending upon Him for their next meal—recognizing Him as their true Source.

Maybe you feel like you are a *tela'* (טלא), a *wounded lamb*, a little lamb that cannot keep up with the rest of the flock. If you are that wounded lamb, you are the one who gets to be carried by the Good Shepherd, the *ra'ah* (רעה), the One who has a consuming passion for you. You get to eat and drink from the palm of His hand. Although He loves His entire flock, you, the little *tela* (טלא), the *wounded lamb*, get special attention because you need His special care.

Study 64

Seek Him Early: *Meshachari* (משחרי)

"I love them that love me;
and those that seek me early shall find me."
—Proverbs 8:17

In our study verse, the phrase *"I love them"* is a little odd in the original Hebrew because it is in an imperfect (future) form. Thus, it would correctly be rendered as "I *will* love them." Of course, no one translates it that way because it is followed by the phrase *"that love me,"* which is in a participial form and means "those who are loving me." In other words, it literally says, "I will love those who are loving Me." This would suggest that until we start to love God, He will not love us. However, when put into the context of the subsequent phrase, *"those that seek me early…,"* it might make more sense.

A Heart Filled with God's Presence

The Hebrew word for *"love"* here is *'ahav* (אהב), which comes from a Semitic root that has the idea of a heart that is full and satisfied. Accordingly, in this case, you could say that it denotes *God filling your heart with His presence*. Because of the broad range of meanings that encompass the word *'ahav* (אהב), it is very difficult to come to a definitive rendering of the phrase *"I love them that love me."* But the idea that is being conveyed is, "I will fill with My presence the hearts of those who love Me."

We read that those who seek God early will find Him. The word *"find"* is *matsa* (מצא), which comes from a Semitic root meaning "to discover hidden or secret knowledge." It is in a hiphil (causative) form, which means that they will *be caused* to find God.

What this verse is saying is that God will fill with His presence the hearts of those who love Him; and if we seek Him early, we will discover His hidden secrets. Rabbinic writings teach that the hidden mysteries or secrets of God are like the taste of food. It is impossible to sufficiently describe how a particular food tastes to someone who has never tried it; you cannot explain in words exactly what it is like—thus, the taste is "hidden." In the same way, you can see a mystery or a secret of God in Scripture, you can read about it, and you can even hear teaching on it, but it remains hidden and a mystery for you until you actually *taste* or *experience* it, until God fills you with His presence, enabling you to experience it.

Entrusted with God's Secret Knowledge

So, what does it mean to seek God *"early"*? The Hebrew word used for *"early"* here is *shachar* (שׁחר), which literally means "black," as in *night*, *dawn*, or *early morning*. One interpretation of this phrase is that God speaks to us in our dreams. The Talmud teaches that the last dream you have, the one you have as you are awaking, is prophetic. The idea is that when you seek Him in your early-morning dream, you will discover His hidden mysteries or secrets.

Another interpretation, which I like better, is found in ancient rabbinic writings that teach that the Lord searches for His people and calls to them to draw close to Him. So, His people join together and enter a place of meeting. But whoever arrives earliest joins himself to the *Shekinah* (שׁכינה) in a single bond! This concept is explained in a parable. A king summons a minyan* to appear before him on a certain day and a certain place at a certain time. While everyone is preparing, one individual arrives early and alone. The king is present and waiting. He asks the man where the others are. The man explains that the others are coming, but he has arrived early. The king then sits down and shares with this man his thoughts and feelings in an unofficial way. After the others arrive, he takes on a more formal posture and conducts his business. After having a number of such meetings, for which this one individual makes it a continual practice to arrive early, the king recognizes the man's early arrival as a demonstration of his eagerness to serve and of his deep love for the king. This *causes* (hiphil) the king to open up to him and share things that he would not share with the others.

Hence, this statement about seeking God early is presented more as a picture than as something to be taken literally. Such a literal application would mean that the earlier you got up in the morning to have your devotions, the better chance you would have of learning the secrets of God. Rather, what is being expressed in seeking God early is an eagerness to serve Him and to meet with Him.

For example, if you were to arrive late for a job interview, you could pretty well write off your chances of getting that job. Why? Because your late arrival would be interpreted as a lack of desire for the position. But if you were to arrive early, you would be conveying the message that you are really interested in that job. You are so interested that you made it a priority over everything else to arrive not only on time, but ahead of time. The same applies in your relationship with God. If you really love Him and desire to serve Him, He will be first on your agenda, and He will be a priority over everything else you have to do; thus, you will arrive in His presence "early." To such individuals, God will entrust His secret knowledge.

Study 65

(God) Hides His Face: *Hasethar Pani* (הסתר פני)

"And I will surely hide my face in that day for all the evils which they shall have wrought, in that they are turned unto other gods."
—Deuteronomy 31:18

Jewish philosopher Abraham Heschel often referred to what he called "divine anthropopathy." We often speak of God as anthropomorphic, symbolically ascribing to Him a human body, but we rarely consider God anthropopathically, as having humanlike feelings. Heschel told a story of Rabbi Dov Baer, who was walking on a street accompanied by his disciples and saw a little girl hiding in an alcove, weeping. "Why are you crying, little girl?" asked the rabbi. She replied, "I was playing hide-and-seek with my friends, but they didn't come looking for me!" Rabbi Dov Baer sighed and said to his students, "In the answer and the tears of that little girl I heard the weeping of the Shekhinah, '"and I will surely *hide my face*." I, God, have hidden Myself too, as it were, but no one comes to look for Me.'"

In ancient times, a king would not weep in front of his subjects. He would turn away or hide himself so he could weep in private and not show his emotions. In a similar way, in Deuteronomy 31:18, I don't think God is hiding His face in order to punish His people for their evils—He is hiding His face because their evils have caused Him such grief that He must turn away to weep. Their evil is that they have turned to other gods. God was not "good enough" for them, so they committed spiritual adultery and gave themselves to other gods to meet their needs; and, like a rejected lover, God suffered such hurt that He wept.

"Twice Hiding"

In the original text, the word *"hide"* is actually repeated twice. The first time, it is written as an infinitive. In Hebrew, one way to communicate the intensity of a verb is to precede the verb with its own infinitive. Thus, our English translations render this as *"surely hide."* But a literal reading really speaks of "twice hiding." Certain sages suggest this means that the hiding itself is hidden. In the first hiding, God has hidden Himself like the little girl playing hide-and-seek, because only when we miss His presence will we come searching for Him. As David once wrote, "When You hid Yourself, I was terrified." (See Psalm 30:7.)

When I was in college, I was a reader for a student who had been blind since he was six years old. I once asked him, "What is it like to have been blind for all these years?" He said, "I have not seen the moon in twenty years." I remember walking outside that evening and looking up at the moon, thinking, *You know, you get used to the moon.* So, too, we get used to the light of God, His presence, but when we have to go without it, we realize just how important it is. Like David, we become terrified and desperately seek His presence.

The little girl playing hide-and-seek anticipated being found by her friends and experiencing the joy of their reunion. But when her friends did not seek her, she remained hidden in her hiding. She remained hidden for another reason—so that she could weep over the rejection by her friends. Likewise, if God removes His presence from us, and we do not search for Him, this rejection will cause Him such grief that He will hide in His hiding so that He may weep.

The Hebrew word translated *"hide"* is *satar* (סתר), which means "to conceal" or "to keep secret." The word is spelled samek (ס), taw (ת), resh (ר). The samek (ס) in this word would suggest that this concealment or keeping secret is meant for protection or for a shelter. God is hiding His presence to protect Himself from the next letter, which is taw (ת). The shadow meaning of the taw is to avoid the risk of intimacy. God's intimacy involves the resh (ר), which indicates the Holy Spirit, who reveals God's hidden secrets.

Seek His Presence Again

We are all well aware of the pain of being intimate with someone and then having that person draw away from us. But it is even more painful after you have shared your deep, hidden secrets with the person. If we are made in God's image, would not God feel the same pain of rejection if, after He has been intimate with us and shared His hidden secrets with us, we were to draw away from Him? In His grief, He would hide His face, or presence, from us. If we did not seek His presence again, He would *"surely hide,"* or *hide His hiddenness*, so that He might weep over His broken heart.

If you no longer feel God's presence, you must first determine if He is hidden merely in order to draw you to search for Him, or if He is hiding in His hiddenness so He may weep over His heart that has been broken by your complacency or rejection.

Study 66

Ninety and Nine: *Tish'im Shanah Vetesha' Shanih* (תשעים שנה ותשע שניה)

"And when Abram [Abraham] *was ninety years old and nine, the* Lord *appeared to Abram, and said unto him, I am the Almighty God; walk before me, and be thou perfect."*
—Genesis 17:1

The Hebrew words for *"ninety years old and nine"* are *tish'im shanah vetesha' shanih* (תשעים שנה ותשע שניה). Abraham's age may or may not have been ninety-nine years in the way we count people's ages today. People in the Semitic culture were not as concerned with being precise about ages, so when they gave a person's age, it was often just an approximate and/or symbolic. Still, there is no getting away from the fact that Abraham was an old man.

I drive an access bus for the disabled, and yesterday I drove a man to the food pantry. He had a caregiver with him and used a walker, and he told me that he was ninety-nine years old—and would be one hundred in a couple of weeks. I could not help but think how Abraham was that age when he fathered a child. I wondered what would happen if Abraham were alive today and was in that situation. The movie rights alone would set him up for life (such as he had left to live). But it is apparent in this story that Abraham did not have a caregiver and did not use a walker. At least, it doesn't appear that way. God told him, "*Walk before me,*" not "Walk before Me with your walker." There is no indication that he had any physical limitations or disability.

How Old Is Ninety-Nine?

Our study verse gives us a prime opportunity to discuss how we often apply Western thought to an ancient Semitic text. When the Bible says that Abraham was ninety-nine years old, we automatically think of someone like my friend whom I drove to the food pantry. But again, this does not mean Abraham was ninety-nine according to the Julian calendar or the Gregorian calendar, both of which did not come into existence until a couple of thousand years after this event was recorded. On top of this, the ancient Semites did not have birth certificates on record at the local courthouse.

In truth, we really don't know how people's ages were measured in ancient times or in ancient thinking. All we really know is that these cultures marked periods of time. For instance, the ancient Egyptians measured time by the consistent yearly overflow of the Nile River, as this was the best time for planting their crops. The pharaoh maintained his power by being able to accurately predict when the Nile would flood, and of course only a god could do that—at least one that employed a battery of mathematicians and maybe a couple of pyramids to record the movement of the sun. The ancient Assyrians measured time by the change in weather that presented the perfect time to go to war. These methods were quite unlike our measurement of time today, which is marked with extreme precision based upon the earth's path around the sun.

Days, however, were easy enough for the ancients to measure—sunup and sundown. Yet even considering this basic method of marking time, our understanding of ancient thinking is a bit murky, because the times of sunup and sundown gradually change with the seasons. So again, when the Bible speaks of days and hours, it is not speaking of days and hours as we know them in modern Western thought. It is merely speaking of periods of time, which could vary in length. A "day" mentioned in one part of Scripture might not be the same period of time represented by a "day" spoken of in another part of Scripture.

I have said all this to show why Abraham could have been older or younger than our modern-day measurement of ninety-nine years. So, we do not know how old Abraham was when he became a father. All we really know is that he and Sarah were of an age beyond the childbearing years, which would put them somewhere beyond forty or fifty years of age according to our system of measurement.

Unfulfilled—and Desiring Something More

This brings up the question as to why Scripture gives such an exact number for Abraham's age—one that isn't even a round number. Would not "beyond childbearing age" or simply "old" have been enough? Why ninety-nine and not one hundred? The problem with our exact Western mind-set is that we spend so much time contemplating the idea of a ninety-nine-year-old man becoming a father that we tend to overlook something very obvious: the number ninety-nine had some real significance to the ancient Semitic people.

For one thing, counting to one hundred was about as far as the average person could go. When you reached one hundred, that was it. Recall that Jesus gave a parable about the ninety-nine sheep and the one lost sheep. (See Luke 15:3–7.) There was something psychological about the number one hundred to the mind of the ancient Semitic people. One hundred sheep was the threshold to being rich. With ninety-nine sheep, you were not yet rich, but one hundred put you into a new tax bracket, so to speak. Thus, it was a psychological blow to a shepherd who had only one hundred sheep to lose one. If the number dropped to ninety-nine, the shepherd would feel incomplete. He would have fallen from the upper middle class to just the middle class, to put it into modern lingo. He would always carry around the nagging feeling that he was just one sheep under the social ladder.

Accordingly, ninety-nine was the number that left a person wanting, feeling unfulfilled, and desiring more. Within the ancient

Gematria, ninety is the number for *humility*, and nine represents *divine completeness*. Thus, we are to be divinely completed before we reach physical completion. Maybe God's delay in giving Abraham the promised child wasn't so much to test his faith (although it surely did that) as it was to wait for Abraham to reach a state of divine completeness in humility before bringing that special child into his life. The fact that he and Sarah were beyond the natural childbearing years was of little concern to God.

"Get Ready for the Next Event in Your Life!"

Let's return now to the Hebrew words for ninety-nine, *tish'im shanah vetesha' shanih* (תשעים שנה ותשע שניה), which come from a Semitic root word meaning "a moment in time" or "a pause before the next event." We've established that we do not know the true age of Abraham; but even if he was ninety-nine according to Western measurement, we would still need to look at the double meaning behind the use of this number. I believe God chose to use *tish'im shanah vetesha' shanih* (תשעים שנה ותשע שניה) in this passage not so much to assign a specific age for Abraham as to express the idea that even though Abraham was past his childbearing years—a period when many people just settle back, look forward to their retirement years, and wait for the man with the scythe—God appeared to him and said, "Hey, guy, this is just a moment in time—get ready for the next event in your life!"

Many of us may already feel like we are ninety-nine years old physically, just waiting for our one hundredth birthday to pop up. Yet God is saying to us, "Yep, you are indeed ninety-nine, but don't expect to take up your walker and get on Chaim Bentorah's bus to the food pantry yet; if you do, he will just drop you off at the next event in your life, which will blow your mind, as it did Abraham's."

Note that by Genesis 17:17, Abraham is one hundred years old. That must have been a long conversation with God if it lasted a full year! Okay, I suppose the traditional explanation is correct—that Abraham would have been one hundred when the child was born—but one hundred was also considered the number of completion. I think that what Abraham had been telling the Lord before He spoke to him in Genesis 17:1 was something like this: "Hey God, I'm finished; I've reached the end of the race. I'm an old man, I'm tired, and I'm ready to just join You and become that '*bosom*' that everyone will be talking about in generations to come." (See Luke 16:23.) But God said, "No, you are not finished. You are only ninety-nine, and you are going to stay ninety-nine until I say you reach one hundred [completion]. As long as I give you life, I am expecting some good things from you."

Study 67

Bride (and) Groom: *Kallah Chatan* (כלה חתן)

"For as a young man marrieth a virgin, so shall thy sons marry thee: and as the bridegroom rejoiceth over the bride, so shall thy God rejoice over thee."
—Isaiah 62:5

Joined in Complete Truth

The Hebrew word translated *"bridegroom"* in our study verse is *chatan* (חתן), which is also a word for "marriage." This word has the idea of joining together in *complete truth and honesty.* When God as the *Bridegroom* is married to us, He is joined to us in *complete truth.* As the Bible says, those who worship God *"must worship him in spirit and in truth"* (John 4:24).

Okay, that is God's side of the deal; He is the Bridegroom. But what are we as the *kallah* (כלה), or *"bride"*? In its Semitic root, *kallah* (כלה) has a double lamed (ל = לל), which represents prayer with uplifted hands. This word is a picture of reaching up to your Bridegroom with an open, expectant heart and asking Him to fill your heart with His presence. The Semitic root is a little strange because it can mean either a "filling," a "completion," or a "wasting away." Yet the sages chose this word to represent a *bride* because a bride is to fill her heart with the desires of her bridegroom, while her own desires *waste away*. I know this flies in the face of our modern feminist thinking, but hey, I'm just the messenger, and it really is a cultural illustration.

To Protect and Provide For

As I mentioned in a previous study, the sages teach that there are three types of prayer. There is the prayer that represents that of a child to a parent—which seems to fit the majority of us—such as the following: "O God, I know I don't go to church as much as I should, I know I don't read the Bible as much as I should, I know I only pray when I am in trouble, but if You answer this prayer, I promise...."

The second type of prayer represents that of a wife to her husband. Now, much has been written about how we relate to God as His bride. When I presented this idea to my Hebrew classes for their opinions, one response that seemed to be quite popular was that a husband would seek for his wife to accept the leadership role that God has established a man to take in the household. God does want us as His bride to accept His leadership, to understand that He does what He does because He loves us and that He acts in our best interests. Even if we do not like His decisions, we must support them 100 percent and be willing to abide by whatever decision He makes in answer to our prayers. Such a prayer might be, "Lord, not my will, but Yours, be done."

But the third type of prayer seems to have eluded Christians. This is for good reason, because we do not like to think of God as being vulnerable in any way. After all, He is perfect and complete in everything. Yet He has chosen to make Himself vulnerable to those whom He loves and who love Him in return. This third type of prayer reflects a gift that comes with salvation.

If we picture our salvation as a marriage ceremony, then we can follow this motif in our ongoing relationship with God. In a marriage relationship that is truly successful, the wife has given not only her hand to her husband in marriage, but also her heart. That is a second gift that we in Christianity do not often consider because, unfortunately, many Christian husbands do not think in those terms. The gift of one's heart is sacred, one that the wife can give to only one person, her husband. Unless a man really understands and appreciates the true nature of this gift, he cannot hope to possess it for very long. And if we consider God to be the "Bride" to us, as well as the "Bridegroom," as we discussed earlier, we understand how He has given us His heart, too. I have often discussed this idea in my Hebrew classes, and many of my students have come up with some interesting thoughts about what this gift of God's heart really means to us.

A husband wants to protect and provide for his wife. Now, how can we protect and provide for the Master of the universe? Well, for one thing, we can protect His feelings. A man can be just a dumb ox at times. He treads over his wife's feelings and then scratches his head, wondering, *What's wrong with her?* So, too, we Christians tread over the heart of God and then wonder, *Why don't I feel His presence?*

To pray to God as a husband to a wife is to seek to understand the heart of God. A loving husband will spend a lifetime seeking to understand the heart of his wife. He will take his wife's heart in the palm of his hand, examine it, protect it, care for it, and gently caress it. Likewise, as we pray, we are to take the heart of God as a precious gift, seeking to understand it, protect it, care for it, and gently caress it. I know that might sound a little weird in our cultural setting, but once you get used to the idea, you may grow comfortable with it. God gave us the marriage relationship to help us to understand our relationship with Him. But it cannot be merely one-sided; we cannot just look to God as a bride would to a bridegroom. There is another side of the coin to consider—our beloved God has a heart similar to the heart He breathed into us. As I have emphasized throughout this book, just as our hearts can be broken, we, too, have the ability to break God's heart. Let us always remember that He has given us His heart, and treat it as a priceless gift.

Study 68

Birds Singing and Dancing: *Tsiphar* (צפר)

"*And* [the Lord] *said unto* [Abraham], *Take me an heifer of three years old, and a she goat of three years old, and a ram of three years old, and a turtledove, and a young pigeon. And he took unto him all these, and divided them in the midst, and laid each piece one against another: but the birds* [this term is singular in the Hebrew] *divided he not.*"
—Genesis 15:9–10

God Himself Paid Sin's Penalty

In this passage from Genesis, God is forming the Abrahamic covenant, which is a blood covenant. In ancient times, when two individuals made a contract, they would kill an animal, cut it in half, and separate the two halves a few feet from each other. Then they would sprinkle the animal's blood within that separation. The two individuals entering into the contract would join hands and walk the path with the blood between the two separated parts of the animal, symbolizing their readiness to be cut in half like the animals if they transgressed the terms of the contract.

At the end of this path stood a priest who would listen to the conditions, vows, or promises each person would make in the contract.

The two entering into the contract would have ten witnesses standing on either side, and it was their job to listen to the terms or conditions. These ten witnesses were the "enforcers," so to speak. If either party broke a condition of the contract, it would be the job of the witnesses to pay a visit to the offender and make sure he held up his end of the contract.

When God made His covenant with Abraham, He caused him to fall into a deep sleep, and then He passed through the center of the sacrifices by Himself. God knew that His people would not keep their end of the bargain, so He did not make them a party to the penalty; instead, He bore the penalty Himself for their breaking of the covenant. That penalty was paid for two thousand years ago when God sent His Son to earth to die on the cross and to shed His blood as the sacrifice for our sins.

The Holy Spirit Explores Our Hearts

In our study verse, what is curious is that the heifer, the goat, and the ram were cut in half, but the birds were not. I was told in seminary that this was for practical reasons, because the birds were too small to cut in half. But, come on, you can cut even a grasshopper in half, so there had to be some other reason. Perhaps a little study of the Hebrew words for *"turtledove," "young pigeon,"* and *"birds"* might suggest a deeper meaning.

First, the word for *"turtledove"* is *tavar* (תור). This term, of course, means "turtledove," but it comes from a Semtic root word that is often used to signify "to go around," "to spy," "to investigate," or "to explore." Birds know no boundaries, and they can investigate, explore, and "spy" all around. They can fly from country to country without a passport. David envied the birds because they could fly right into the temple and the Holy of Holies and rest in the presence of God with no effort. (See Psalm 84:1–3.) Israel is located at the junction of three continents and is crossed by migrating birds on an unparalleled scale. Studies show that about five hundred million birds cross Israel's narrow airspace twice every year in the course of their migrations. Perhaps the birds sense the presence of God in that sacred land.

Furthermore, the word *tavar* (תור) is used to denote *searching out one's heart to discover the truth.* The lips can lie, but the heart cannot. If a person speaks his heart, he is not lying. In Judges 16, we read how Samson misled Delilah three times when she asked him about the source of his strength, but the fourth time he *"told her all his heart"* (verse 17)—he spoke what was true.

After the turtledove, a second bird, a *gozel* (גזל), or *"young pigeon,"* was laid down. Ornithologists say there is no scientific difference between a dove and a pigeon; they are really the same bird. That is why some translations will render *gozel* (גזל) as "a nesting bird." Genesis 15:10 says that Abraham did not separate the *tsiphar* (צפר)—a term that means "bird" and is in the *singular.* Two different Hebrew words were used for the two birds that were laid down, but when mentioning both, a singular form is used. So, the passage appears to be speaking of one species of bird. You can do that with the singular in Hebrew. Actually, plural and singular in Hebrew do not always mean the same thing that they do in English. Sometimes, a plural form can indicate something that is the ultimate or the most powerful, while two things in a singular form can mean two of one kind. Hence, we can assume that there was only one type of bird used here, rather than two.

So, why were two words used for the turtledove if only one bird was being referred to? Actually, the word *gozel* (גזל) can mean not only "pigeon" but also "to pass over." And the third time the dove is mentioned, the writer uses the word *tsiphar* (צפר), which means not just a bird, but a bird that is *happily chirping and dancing.* It can also signify a *humble or soft voice that brings the presence of the Holy Spirit.* So, the next time you are sitting outside Starbucks trying to share the love of God with a friend, and a little bird lands near you and starts to chirp and dance, take note—maybe it is telling you that the Holy Spirit is very present at that moment!

That last comment was for those of you who are into that sort of thing, but back to my more serious study. The writer is obviously making a play on words here and creating a hint of something much deeper. Buried in this little story lies the message that the bird was not divided into two halves because it represented the Holy Spirit, who *tavars* (תור), or *"spies out" our hearts, explores our hearts*, to identify the presence of sin there. Through the blood sacrifice of Jesus Christ, we are cleansed from our sin and redeemed, and God will *gozel* (גזל), or pass over, the penalty for that sin so that we may enter into the *tsiphar* (צפר), or the *joy and dancing* of Jehovah. This is just something to think about the next time you see a *tsiphar* (צפר), or bird, *tsiphar*-ing, or chirping and dancing. After all, God has given us every part of His creation to speak to us; we just need to listen to it with our hearts.

Study 69

(Holy) Laughter: *Tsachaq* (צחק)

"[God said,] *Is any thing too hard for the* L*ORD*?...*Then Sarah denied, saying, I laughed not; for she was afraid. And he said, Nay; but thou didst laugh.*"
—Genesis 18:14–15

When God told Abraham that Sarah was going to have a child at the age of ninety, Sarah was listening in on the conversation, and she "*laughed within herself*" (Genesis 18:12). In our study passage, the Hebrew word translated "*laugh*" in Genesis 18:15 is *tsachaq* (צחק). Lexicographers have debated the nature of this word to determine what type of laughter Sarah expressed. Was it mockery? Was it the incongruous idea of a ninety-year-old woman having a child that struck Sarah's funny bone? Or was it the laughter of unbelief?

Something Wonderful from God's Heart

God's response that nothing is too hard for Him suggests that it was the laughter of unbelief and possibly mockery. Yet the word for "*hard*" is *pala'* (פלא), which really refers to *something wonderful* or *marvelous.* It is in a niphal form, which would make it reflexive, so it could more correctly be rendered as, "A wonderful thing from the Lord." Note that the word rendered "*thing*" is *devar* (דבר), which, in its

Semitic root, has the idea of *a word or a saying that is an expression of the heart.* Thus, another rendering of this passage might be, "This is something wonderful coming from the heart of God."

What makes the syntax so difficult here is the fact that there is no verb in this sentence. In the Hebrew language, you can have a sentence without a verb; but in the English language, you can't do that, so you have to insert your own verb, which the translators did by using the word *is*. I am not certain that the sentence really needs to be interrogative, or in the form of a question, but let's suppose that it does and keep it that way. What I do find disturbing is that the preposition *from* that is in front of God's name in the original text has been completely ignored by translators.

I would suggest that an appropriate rendering would be, "Is anything that comes from the heart of God too wonderful or marvelous?" As the interrogative is uncertain, we might alternately render it as, "There is nothing more wonderful than an expression of the heart from God."

Laughing with God

Now let's look more closely at the word *tsachaq* (צחק), or "*laugh.*" It is spelled sade (צ), chet (ח), qof (ק). The sade (צ) shows *humility and submission to God*, the chet (ח) indicates *a joining with God*, and the qof (ק) represents *a new beginning with God*. The sade (צ) and chet (ח) would suggest that Sarah was laughing with God, not at God. The word would then imply that this laughter springs from the joy of the Lord. It would also suggest that God Himself was laughing. Perhaps Sarah was afraid to admit that she had laughed because she thought her laughter was out of context or inappropriate. This situation reminds me of that old Mary Tyler Moore TV episode where Chuckles the Clown was killed in a parade by being stepped on by an elephant. When it was explained that he had been dressed as a peanut, everyone at the TV station broke out laughing but then felt guilty because the laughter did not seem appropriate.

However, I think the reason Sarah was fearful was that she had broken protocol. You see, Sarah was not a part of the discussion between God and Abraham, and in Semitic culture, she should not have been listening to the conversation of two men. When God pointed out that she had laughed, she denied it. If she had not denied it, she would have admitted to having broken protocol, a violation of a cultural standard. Yet God was and is above all cultural standards, so that what might seem inappropriate in one's culture might be all right from God's standpoint.

One time, I was teaching a Hebrew class in the basement of an inner-city black church when suddenly, from the sanctuary, I heard joyful singing, hand-clapping, and feet shuffling, as if there was dancing. One of the church's pastors was in my class, and I asked him what was going on. He said that it was a funeral. Now, in my cultural background, you did not sing joyful songs, clap your hands, or dance at a funeral; that would have been considered inappropriate. Instead, you were supposed to be sad and quiet. But to the people of that congregation, someone had just entered into the presence of God, and it was appropriate to have a time of joyful expression.

The Joy of God's Promise

I think God was reminding Sarah that He had given her a word and a promise. Perhaps He was encouraging her to laugh, and to continue to laugh, with *the joy of His wonderful promise.* Is anything more wonderful than a promise or a word from God? The Lord's comment, *"Nay; but thou didst laugh,"* could also be rendered as, "No, just keep *laughing.*" Maybe this passage is suggesting such a thing as *holy laughter*—laughter that comes from God but, according to our minds or cultural norms, seems inappropriate for that moment. God has a sense of humor, and we are, after all, made in His image, so laughter is a part of that image. Yet God does not live in either a Western culture or an Eastern culture; He is not subject to any culture. So, He might just laugh at what to us seems an inappropriate moment. If we happen to enter His heart at that point, we will discover ourselves laughing along at such an "inappropriate" time.

It is curious that God had previously told Abraham to name the promised child *"Isaac"* (see Genesis 17:19), because *Isaac* is the same word as *tsachaq* (צחק) and literally means "he will laugh." The only difference in the word for Isaac is that it has a yod (י) in front of it. The yod (י) represents a message from heaven. In other words, this message from heaven brings laughter. Perhaps God told Abraham and Sarah to name the child "laughter" with a yod (י) as a description of this heavenly, holy laughter.

I believe the name *Isaac* was more than just a memorial to that moment of revelation; it was a reminder that God wanted to share His joy with Abraham and Sarah. The use of the word *devar* (דבר), or *"thing"*—a word or a saying that is an expression of the heart—suggests that Sarah entered God's heart at the moment He told Abraham that she would have a son, and she began to laugh. Not realizing that God was laughing and that she was really laughing with Him, she recognized her cultural indiscretion, stopped laughing, and felt embarrassed. But God said, in effect, "Hey, forget your petty cultural norms; come on, laugh it up with Me!"

As we have seen, in this journey to discover God's heart, when you enter His heart, you begin to mimic what He is feeling. If He is weeping, you weep; if He is dancing, you dance; and if He is laughing, you laugh. Even if it seems inappropriate or culturally wrong in your mind, God is saying, "It's okay, I want you to share with Me what I am feeling." When you love someone, you want to share your most emotional times with that person, whether those times are joyful or sorrowful.

Actually, what was inappropriate wasn't Sarah laughing but the fact that she *stopped* laughing.

Study 70

Producing Something: *Lama'anehu* (למענהו)

"The Lord *hath made all things for himself."*
—Proverbs 16:4

On the surface, this verse would appear to indicate that God is a very selfish God. However, you could say there is a good type of "selfishness." Do we not purchase a gift for someone for "selfish" reasons, because we long to express our love for that person, and because doing so makes us feel good? As I wrote in an earlier study, there is *self-interest* in pleasing the one we love, but it is not the same as *selfishness.*

Working for a Reward

The Hebrew word for *"made"* in Proverbs 16:4 is curious. It is not the usual term that you find translated as "make," as in "to produce something" or "to create something," which would be *'anah* (ענה). Rather, it is the word *pa'al* (פעל), which means "working for a reward or a commission." For this sense of the word, we would use the term *employed.* I remember when I was working in building construction, and my foreman handed me an envelope with my paycheck in it and said, "Well, this is what it is all about." I thought, *Isn't it about building these houses, the feeling of accomplishment, and the chance to use the muscles God gave me and to exercise my brain?* But when it came down to it, I would not have been on that job site for one moment if I had not expected a paycheck at the end of the week. The bottom line was that if I was going to eat and keep a roof over my head, I had to work, and this particular job was available to meet that need.

The word *"things"* is not in the original Hebrew; the text simply says that "God made all," followed by the word *lama'anehu* (למענהו), translated "for himself." *Lama'anehu* (למענהו) literally means "for His answering," but it is used to denote *producing something.* The root of this word is the common term mentioned earlier for making something, which is *'anah* (ענה); yet when you trace the word to its Semitic root, you find that it has the idea of an *impartation.* It reminds me of the story of when Jimmy Durante asked a friend, "Who are you working for?" and his friend replied, "The same people: the wife and the kids." Thus, I don't think the English translation of "*the* LORD *hath made all things for himself*" goes far enough. The statement is true, but the word *'anah* (ענה) suggests even more. God is working, laboring for His own pleasure, but His pleasure is in being able to impart the blessings of His labor to us. Similarly, a man goes to work every day to provide for his family members because he finds joy and pleasure in them; all the fruits of his labor are passed along to them so that he can enjoy their love and draw pleasure from their pleasure.

God's Works Convey His Love for Us

When I was a pastor, I was asked by the children of an elderly woman to speak with their mother to try to convince her that it would be the best thing for her to sell her house and move into a retirement community. Her husband had passed away, she was alone in the house, and it was just too much for her to maintain. I felt this was a good idea, because she would really be more comfortable in a retirement community. Yet as I spoke with this woman, I began to change my thinking on the matter. She told me how her husband had built that house when they were first married. And throughout their marriage, he had continued to add on to the house and to make improvements to it, all of which were for the express purpose of pleasing her. The house, its additions, and its improvements had been made to meet her desires for a house, not his. This woman got up and walked to a wall, touched it, and said, "Don't you see—every wall, every door, every window was built for me; every wall, every door, and every window is my husband saying to me, 'I love you.' Every morning when we would get up, my husband would say to me, 'I love you.' He is gone now, but he has left me this house that he built for me; and now every morning when I wake up in this house, he is still saying to me, 'I love you.'"

What I find Proverbs 16:4 telling me is that, yes, God made everything for Himself. But He made it for Himself so that He could feel the joy and the pleasure of saying to us, "I love you." That is His greatest joy and His greatest pleasure. He created us and breathed into us His very breath of life so that He could have someone to whom He would be able to say, "I love you." Every tree; every blade of grass; every little squirrel that runs up to you, looks at you, and then runs away; every bird on your porch that sings and dances; is God saying to you, "I love you."

God built this world, His whole creation, to be our home for a short time, the time of our "engagement" or "betrothal" to Him. During this engagement period, we live in a world filled with all his *pa'al* (פעל), or "works," which He made to impart His love. As we spend our years in this home that He built for us, surrounded by the many examples of His love—as He sends His birds to sing to us, His trees to wave to us in the winds, His rains to refresh us, and His sun to strengthen us—we grow more and more in love with Him. In the ancient Hebrew tradition, a young woman would grow more and more in love with her betrothed during her year of betrothal, to the point that she just could not stand being alone without him; and one night, her beloved would come for her and take her to his father's house and consummate their marriage.

So, too, as we live in this world during our betrothal period to Jesus, our Bridegroom, we grow more and more in love with Him;

and every day, through His *pa'al* (פעל), or works of creation, He tells us that He loves us. As He keeps telling us how much He loves us, we reach the point where we just can't stand not being in His very presence. And one night, Jesus will come and take us to live in His Father's house. We will then be allowed to consummate our marriage with Him and spend eternity living in His heart.

Study 71

An Evil Heart: *Livo Hara'* (לבו הרע)

"And they said, There is no hope:
but we will walk after our own devices,
and we will every one do the imagination of his evil heart."
—Jeremiah 18:12

"If I do it, I get a vippin'—I do it."
—Comedian Red Skelton in *Mean Little Kid*

That is quite a thing for the people of Israel to say. Some translations render Jeremiah 18:12 in such a way as to suggest that the people are telling Jeremiah, "Forget it; you have no hope of reaching us, and we don't want to hear about God. We want to live in our sins, so we are just going to go ahead and sin anyway." Had the people fallen so far as to admit to having an *"evil heart"* and following those evil inclinations?

When reading this verse, most of us feel it has nothing to do with us. We say, "Well, at least I have never reached the point of saying I am *evil* and that I don't care." We would never just boldly reject God in that way!

Feeling Hopeless

Grammatically, this verse might be rendered to suggest the people are telling Jeremiah that his attempts to turn them to God are hopeless; however, it would also be grammatically correct to render it as the people saying that *they are the ones who feel hopeless.* The word used for *"no hope"* is *y'ash* (יאש), which means "to be despondent" or "to be in despair." Was the people's desire to follow their own devices and imaginations the result of hopelessness? Just what was it that brought them to this state of feeling that there was no hope, that it was pointless to follow God?

The use of the English word *"evil"* might be misleading in this verse. The Hebrew word is *ra'a'* (רעע), which comes from a Semitic root word meaning "to be broken." The people could be saying that they will follow the imaginations of their *broken heart.* They had apparently reached the point of feeling broken because God had not done for them what they had expected Him to do, and so they said, "There is no hope."

Do you ever feel like you have a *broken heart* because God seemingly did not come through for you? He did not provide for that financial need or for that healing; therefore, similar to Red Skelton's "mean little kid," you sniff, wipe away your tears, and say, "Okay for You, God, I'll show You. I'm gonna really go out and sin, and then You will be sorry." If you stop to consider those moments when you have felt in despair because God did not come through for you, you might have to admit, at least to yourself, that you sometimes have had the urge to go out and seek your own devices, following the imaginations of your *ra'a'* (רעע), or your *evil, broken heart.*

Perhaps you have been unemployed, and it seemed as if God was not coming through with a job, so you were tempted to fudge a little on your experience or skills in a resume or on an employment application. I once had a student who had spent three years in prison before God changed his life. He was desperately looking for a job because he had a wife and child to support, and he was also trying to pay off a school bill. But every employment application included the question, "Have you ever been arrested?" He became so discouraged that he came to me and said, "I am beginning to believe that I should lie on an application, because if I mention my arrest record, even getting through the door is hopeless."

Many people feel free to stretch the truth on documents like tax forms, employment applications, and insurance claims—all the time saying, "Well, God certainly hasn't provided the resources, so what is wrong with a little white lie? Everyone does it. If I am caught, I will just shrug my shoulders. They won't arrest me for a little error; I will just pay a fine." That doesn't sound as brazen as what the people said in Jeremiah 18:12, but it does amount to the same thing.

Clinging to Our Own Devices

Lets get some additional insight into the Hebrew word *y'ash* (יאשׁ), meaning *"no hope,"* "hopeless," or "despair," by looking at the built-in commentary of this term, which is spelled yod (י), aleph (א), shin (שׁ). Hopelessness comes when we allow the shadow connotation of the yod (י)—*being ungrounded in the Word of God*—to influence us. We then permit the shadow aspect of the aleph (א)—*ambivalence*—to consume us, letting our *feelings of uncertainty* join us to the last letter, the shin (שׁ), which represents a consuming fire. Thus, this built-in commentary tells us that the danger of *hopelessness* is that when we are not grounded in the Word of God and then face a seemingly hopeless situation, we are prone to allow fear and uncertainty to consume us to the point where we will cling to our own devices and the imaginations of our hearts to deliver us, rather than clinging to God and relying on Him for deliverance.

In a sense, the people of Israel were not much different from us. They said to Jeremiah, in effect, "Listen, we tried to trust God, and it didn't work; we have these problems, and God didn't lift a finger to help, so why should we bother with Him? We will follow our own *chatsav* (חצב), or *'devices,'*—the thoughts, ideas, and imaginations of our broken hearts." In other words, they were saying, "God, You didn't come through for us, and our hearts are broken over Your abandonment, so we are going to do it our own way. We'll show You."

Two Broken Hearts

Okay, maybe you have never said anything like that, but I know I have. In moments of anger, I have declared, "Well, You broke my heart, so I will just break Yours." And then I have gone about feeling justified seeking my own way. But in such a situation, the only thing we end up with is two broken hearts—that of a loving God because His child doesn't trust Him and has turned away from Him, and that of a "mean little kid" getting a "vippin'" because he wanted things to go his own way and make his life comfortable on his own terms.

Study 72

Wonderful [,] Counselor: *Pele' Ya'ats* (פלא יועץ)

"His name shall be called Wonderful, Counsellor."
—Isaiah 9:6

"Never ask your barber if you need a haircut."
—Daniel Greenberg, educator and columnist

Well now, here is a real twist. Fifty percent of our modern English translations disagree with the Masoretic Text and the King James Version on the rendering of Isaiah 9:6. Yet I, who often seem to disagree with the Masoretic Text and the King James Version, happen to side with them in this case. Then again, I also side with the other 50 percent of the modern English translations!

Half of the translations render the descriptive term for the Messiah as "Wonderful Counselor," with no comma separating the terms, indicating that Jesus is a Wonderful Counselor, with *Wonderful* used as an adjective. The other half, including the King James Version, insert a comma in between, indicating that Jesus is both Wonderful and a Counselor.

But can they both be right?

In our culture, we seem to believe we must choose between the two—that one interpretation has to be wrong and the other has to be right: Jesus either has to be a Wonderful Counselor or He has to be Wonderful and a Counselor. With our Western, precise, scientific, mathematical mind-set, we cannot accept two different interpretations as being valid.

This is one reason why many people cling to the King James as the Authorized Version. They claim that we need one standard as the truly inspired and accurate Word of God, and this translation should be the King James Version, which has endured and proven itself over the centuries. Modern translations are okay, but if they do not line up with the King James, then they are either mistranslations, wrong—or even of the devil. They believe contemporary versions change the true teaching of the Bible. (Forget the fact that even the King James Version has been through half a dozen revisions, the last being just a few years ago, with the final product not always squaring up with the original version.) Even though I understand this line of thinking and these concerns, I think they do tend to apply Western Platonic logic to a Semitic mind-set.

I have a brother who spent fifteen years in the jungles of Papua New Guinea (or is it "Papua, New Guinea"?) translating the Bible into the Amanad language, and if the 1611 English version of the Bible is the only accurate rendering, then he should really have spent his time teaching the people English. To be really correct, he should have taught them the seventeenth-century dialect of King James English. Okay, I know the King James Only group has an answer to that, but I am not here to debate their argument. I am just glad they love and respect the Word of God; that is all that matters to me. I welcome any disagreement they may have with me on certain issues of translation and will hear them out.

Language in Flux

Let's now discuss the modern, "progressive" translations that leave the comma off, making the word *Wonderful* an adjective. Linguistically, this would be correct if we want to stay in tune with our English lexicographers. But who is to say these lexicographers are always right? They are also the ones who would probably tell me that I was wrong to start my last sentence with the word *but*. *But*, after all, our language is in a constant state of flux, and many of the grammatical rules advocated by your old, gray-haired English teacher, such as using *whom* instead of *who*, are destined to evolve, particularly with the explosion of Internet blogging, where anyone can be a "writer"—with or without an English or journalism degree or an innate writing ability.

In fact, it wasn't until the seventeenth century that people began to think about the need to codify the English language, and even then no one was sure how to go about it or even who should regulate it. Thus, the edible by-products of chickens were known as *egges* in Northern England, while in the Southern region they retained the old Anglo Saxon form of *eyres*. It was not until the English colonies codified the word that *eggs* became the standard spelling. So, navigating the dense jungle of translating an ancient language into modern English would be enough to give even your old, gray-haired (or should it be grey-haired?) English teacher a heart attack.

Almost all of our modern Bible translators agree that the truly inspired Word of God was the original documents, which no longer exist. Those documents were written in Hebrew, Greek, and Aramaic, and these are all dead languages. As with any dead language—even Latin—translations and renderings of words are subject to much debate and speculation regarding their preciseness. So, we cannot really know with precision how to render many passages of Scripture and what would be the best English word to apply to many of the ancient Hebrew words.

I personally subscribe to the school of thought that God designed Scripture to carry a degree of ambiguity, and I hold up our study verse in Isaiah as an example. The Hebrew word translated "*Wonderful*" is *pele'* (פלא). The Masoretic Text places a *segol** (ֶ), or three dots arranged as a triangle, under the lamed (ל), making it a noun. However, 50 percent of our modern translations ignore the Masoretic Text and put a *chiriq** (ִ), or one dot, under the lamed (ל), making it *peli* (פלאי),

which turns it into an adjective. The problem is that the original text did not have commas—but neither did it have *segol*s or *chiriq*s. Those markings were not added until seven hundred years after the birth of Christ. So, no one can know for certain if the original, inspired passage from Isaiah in the Word of God intended to convey the idea that Jesus was both Wonderful and a Counselor, or that He was a Wonderful Counselor.

With 50 percent of our modern translations using *Wonderful* as an adjective and 50 percent using it as a noun—and with the Masoretic Text standing in the center of the storm being about as impotent as the United Nations trying to resolve the Middle East conflict—we can only reach one conclusion: *no one knows.*

Now, I could walk up to the two opposing sides in this issue and give my own suggestion, saying, "Guys, put down your rocks. You are both right." But then they would throw the rocks at me! Yet as I raised my shield of faith to deflect the rocks, I would cry out, "Listen, according to any English translation that I read, all of which record the life of Christ, I find that when Jesus walked this earth—and as He lives in my heart today—He is Wonderful, or *pele'* (פלא) in the Hebrew, signifying *a miraculous one*, or *one who performs miracles*; and He is also a Counselor—*ya'ats* (יועצ) in the Hebrew, denoting *one who gives advice on righteousness.* But any translation will also clearly show that He is a *peli ya'ats* (פלא יועצ), a *Wonderful Counselor*, or *one who gives perfect or supernatural, straight-from-the-lips-of-God advice on righteousness.* The Semites to whom this verse was originally written had no problem with a double meaning; they were a romantic and poetic people. Again, it is we in the Western world who seem to have a problem with double meanings.

In our precise way of thinking, 1+1+1 must equal 3. Yet in Hebrew terms, 1+1+1 can equal 1 (1 Father + 1 Son + 1 Holy Spirit = 1 Perfect Love). So, what is so wrong with stepping out of our cultural box and saying that God's Word is infinite, that there could be more than one correct rendering for a passage, and that Jesus is Wonderful (the miraculous or marvelous One), Counselor (One who will guide into righteousness) and also One who is the Wonderful Counselor (the miraculous, marvelous, perfect Guide into righteousness).

"You're Right!"

There is a story in Jewish tradition about a man who asked a rabbi a certain question. The rabbi gave his answer, and the man excitedly said, "You're right!" Then another rabbi, overhearing the answer, joined the conversation and explained why the first rabbi was wrong and gave his own answer, which was the total opposite of the first. The man who'd asked the original question got excited again and declared to the second rabbi, "You're right!" A third rabbi entered the conversation and said, "He's right, *and* he's right? They both can't be right." The man pointed to the third rabbi and announced, "You're right."

So, I say to the King James Version, "You're right!" and to the revisionist translator, "You're right!" If you say to me, "They can't *both* be right," my only reply to you is, "You're right, because it means all that—and much more."

Study 73

Return unto the Lord: *Shaveta 'ad YHWH* (שבת עד יהוה)

"[When thou] *shalt return unto the LORD thy God,*
and shalt obey his voice according to all that I command thee
this day, thou and thy children, with all thine heart,
and with all thy soul; that then the LORD thy God will turn thy
captivity, and have compassion upon thee,
and will return and gather thee from all the nations,
whither the LORD thy God hath scattered thee."
—Deuteronomy 30:2–3

"*Draw nigh to God, and he will draw nigh to you.*"
—James 4:8

There is one striking similarity among Bible verses that talk about returning to God or drawing near to Him: it is we who must make the first step toward God. The syntax of Deuteronomy 30:2 suggests that returning to the Lord is a separate step from obeying His voice. In other words, the first step is to return to the Lord, after which we must obey with all our heart and soul.

Return and Rest

There is an interesting play on words in the Hebrew word for *"return,"* which is *shabbata* (שׁבת). This term comes from the same root as the word for *Sabbath*, which means "to rest," except that the Masoretes pointed the word with a *pathah* (ַ) under the shin (שׁ) rather than a *qammits* (ָ), which made the root word *shuv* (שׁוב), meaning "to return" or "to restore." In the unpointed text, this word could come from either the root word *shabbat* (שׁבת) or the root word *shuv* (שׁוב), and I believe the intent was both. We are to return to resting upon God and not upon the arm of flesh.

Return with Heart and Soul

Note that we must return and obey with all our heart and soul. When the Hebrew word for *"heart," lavav* (לבב), is used with the word for *"soul," nepesh* (נפש), it refers to both the intellect, or understanding, and the passions. It's possible to return to God with one's intellect but not with one's passions, or to return to God with one's passions but not with one's intellect. God is expressing that we must return to Him with both. There is an old saying that "loving" someone is not the same as "being in love" with that person. Similarly, it is not enough for us just to love God. We can do that intellectually, or with our souls. We must also *be in love with God*, which we can do only with our hearts.

Our study passage also says that we are to return to "the Lord our God." In Hebrew, the word for "LORD" is *YHWH* (יהוה) and the word for God is *'Elohim* (אלוהים). There seems to be a new fad among Christians to use the name *YHWH* (יהוה) when speaking about God or addressing Him, as if there were some mystical benefit to saying it. I have no problem if you wish to use God's Hebrew name, but I draw the line at the suggestion that you are receiving some special or supernatural benefit from Him by using that particular form of His name. Furthermore, no one knows the correct pronunciation for this name of God. As I have previously noted, vowel pointings were not added until seven hundred years after the birth of Jesus, and then the

Masoretes just added the vowels from the word *'adoni* (אדני), meaning "lord," to the word *YHWH* (יהוה), creating the word *Yehoah*, or as we say in the Western world, *Jehovah*.

What is interesting about the word *YHWH* (יהוה), however, is that it is in a feminine form. The word *'Elohim* (אלוהים) is in a masculine form. The sages teach that when the word *YHWH* (יהוה) is used, it represents the feminine nature of God, which reflects His mercy, His loving-kindness, and His nurture of us. The word *'Elohim* (אלוהים) represents the masculine nature of God, which reflects His protection, His provision, and His discipline. So, the syntax suggests that we are to return to *YHWH* (יהוה) with our hearts—we are to be *in love with YHWH* (יהוה), God's feminine nature, the part of Him that is nurturing, caring, and loving. Then, with our soul, or mind, we are to *love 'Elohim* (אלוהים), God's masculine nature, the part of Him that guards us, provides for us, and corrects us. We are not to be "gold diggers," marrying God for His money and His free ticket out of hell. We must allow ourselves to fall in love with Him.

A common scene played out in the movies and in novels is a young man calling on his sweetheart, who refuses to see him because, as she tells him, "You don't love me." The young man pleads, "But I do love ya, baby." She still responds, "You love me not." Here is an example of how God created woman to be an *'ezer* (עזר), or a "*help meet*" (Genesis 2:18) for man. An *'ezer* (עזר) is one who helps someone to understand something. In the case of Eve, the woman was to help Adam to understand God—more specifically to understand the love of God and how to love Him in return.

A woman is able to sense, more than a man can, if he loves her merely superficially. In other words, she knows if he loves her simply because she is beautiful, because he is attracted to her sexually, or because he is attracted to her wealth. She knows that if he loves her only in that way, he does not love her with his *heart*. She will wonder if he will continue to love her even if her beauty fades, if she becomes physically incapable of providing sexual companionship, or if she loses all her money. She will never be confident of his love if he loves her only with his soul and his mind, and not with his heart.

When we can love God not only because He is a good Provider and will keep us out of hell, but also because we love Him with our heart—that is to say, even if there were no hell to escape, or if God were not to "reward" our love with a new car, a big house, and great prosperity—then He will return to us.

Return as Best You Can

There is just one issue in relation to our study passage from Deuteronomy that bothers me. This business of "returning" seems very ambiguous. How do we really know that we do return to God and love Him with all our heart and soul?

I have a friend who is a widow and who lost everything of material value. She lost her home in foreclosure, and her late husband's hundred-thousand-dollar life insurance policy went to his former wife, so she ended up homeless. Yet she still clings to God; she still loves Him. She has not cursed God because He did not enable her to keep her home and be financially solvent. In her case, it is easy to see that she truly loves God not only with her soul but also with her heart. The same is true for many Christians who accept Jesus as their Savior and subsequently have their whole world fall apart. But how about those who seem to gain great financial and material benefits after accepting Jesus as their Savior? In a sense, it makes it hard for them to judge whether they love God not only with their soul but also with their heart.

I think there is a clue for us in the Hebrew word for "*return*," which is in a *qal* (simple) verbal form and not in a *piel* (intensive). This is a return with all our heart and soul that is the best we can give, even if it may not be perfect and even if it may fall short. But if we come to God in the best possible way that we can, telling Him that we want to offer our heart and soul to Him as best we can, that is enough. Accordingly, that young man who has just been rebuffed by his sweetheart because she believes he loves her only with his soul, or mind, and not with his heart, can be honest and say, "Honey, I am not sure how I love you, but I am sure of one thing—I want to love you with all my soul and heart, and I will do my best to love you with all my heart. Come on, give this poor slob a chance to really learn how to love you with all my heart!" That may just be enough to draw the young woman to him, particularly if she loves him with all her heart and soul. In the case of God, He loves us with both His heart and soul; therefore, all we must do is desire to love Him with all our heart and soul, and He will draw near to us; and we will soon learn to love Him with all our heart and soul, too.

In James 4:8, the apostle James tells us that we just need to draw near to God, and He will then move into action to draw near to us. We just need to start the process and do our best. The Lord will take care of the rest.

Study 74

The Lame Horse: *Yagun* (יגון)

"For my life is spent with grief, and my years with sighing:
my strength faileth because of mine iniquity,
and my bones are consumed."
—Psalm 31:10

David is saying here that his life is filled with *"grief."* Some translations use the word "pain," others use "sorrow," while one uses "misery." In our English language, there is a difference between *grief, pain, sorrow,* and *misery.* You can be in pain if you hit your thumb with a hammer, but you may not be in grief. You can be in misery without having sorrow or grief. By why split hairs? David is essentially saying that he is feeling absolutely *lousy.*

"Spent with Grief"

I woke up this morning after having had a horrible dream where it was as if all the iniquities of my life were packed into one event. When I awoke, I really felt miserable—I didn't feel pain or grief, just misery—until I realized it was all a dream, and I was not really in that situation. Afterward, I was drawn to our study verse, and I suspect that *accumulated grief* is what David is addressing in Psalm 31. David is saying that his life is *"spent with grief."* This is not just a onetime event; it is a lifelong event. We learn further that it is due to some *"iniquity."* Some commentators say that he is referring specifically to his sinful nature, but I don't think so. We don't usually get that depressed over our sin nature. This has to be some sin from his past that still haunts him.

The Hebrew word for *"grief"* is *yagun* (יגון). As indicated above, this word can also mean "pain," "sorrow," or "misery," with each term tending to signify something a little different. When you trace this word to its Semitic root, you find that it comes from an ancient Persian word used to describe a horse that has such pain in its hoof that it has become lame. A lame horse is useless for performing any work or function. This lameness could be caused by something as simple as a thorn or a small blister or sore. David is saying that from taking counsel in his own soul, he has become useless; he is so crippled by his feelings that he cannot function or perform any work. Somewhere there is a sin in David's life that just keeps coming back to haunt him. Even though it is forgiven, the enemy continues bringing it back to his mind such that it has a paralyzing effect.

"Thorn in the Flesh"

Perhaps the *"thorn in the flesh"* that the apostle Paul talks about in 2 Corinthians 12:7–10 is something like David's *"grief."* The Greek word for *"thorn"* is *skolops*, which means "a pointed stake" or "a thorn." In extrabiblical literature, such as the works of Plato, *skolops* can be a reference to anything with a sharp point. Paul may have written the book of 2 Corinthians in Greek, but his native language was Aramaic, and he might have had the Aramaic word *shaphaya* (שפיא) in mind, which really denotes a sharp splinter. A splinter is something that is very small but can be such a continual irritant that it interferes with your well-being and can even affect your work.

Paul does not say what this thorn in the flesh is, and there has been much speculation as to what it was, such as an eye problem or some physical deformity. However, he does tell us that it is something that kept him from becoming conceited. For this reason, I don't think he is referring to something physical. I base this opinion purely on my own experience. I have a physical affliction that does affect my appearance, and as such, it keeps me from being conceited over my appearance; but when someone praises my writings, that particular physical thorn in the flesh doesn't seem to prevent my becoming conceited over my insights into Scripture.

Thus, I suspect Paul's thorn in the flesh had to do with past iniquities. My own pet theory is that it was some sin in his background, and although God had forgiven him, it kept haunting him when he *sought counsel in his soul*. He calls it a messenger of Satan. God has forgiven Paul, cleansing him from the most horrendous sins, and yet Satan still brings back this memory, sending Paul the message, "Hey, *Saul*, look at you—you are a mass murderer. Those Christians you want to fellowship with, you probably killed one of their loved ones simply because of their belief in Jesus; maybe it was their father, son, or dear friend. Yes, Paul, they will not really accept you; they will never forgive you for such a crime and will hate you." In the midst of this, perhaps poor Paul sat there, scratched his head, and said, "You know, you're right; maybe I should just sidestep this town because there are too many bad memories here."

Freedom Through Worship

Can you relate to such thoughts? Like David and Paul, even though God has forgiven you for all your sins, the enemy might still bring up the past to try to haunt you to the point where you cannot even serve God. That dream I had last night crippled me at first. I usually spend three to four hours every morning studying the Word of God in Hebrew, Greek, and Aramaic, but this morning I could not get up and begin my study because the dream of my past sins and iniquities reminded me of my thorn in the flesh, my *yagun* (יגון). Yes, it does keep me from conceit, as Paul's did for him. Actually, it is for this reason that I will not put my picture on my books or use my real name. I use the pseudonym Chaim Bentorah to declare that all my writings come from my life in Jesus Christ and not from my past. When the enemy sneaks in and continually brings my past failures to mind, I find myself crippled and unable to serve God until I finally take my forgiveness by faith and rest in His presence, knowing I could not experience His presence if He had not forgiven me.

We all have our personal *yaguns*; one cannot make it through life without acquiring some. We all make mistakes, and we all sin. We may not be a mass murderer, like Paul, or be unable to build a temple in God's honor because we have so much blood on our hands, like David. Yet we have enough iniquities that the enemy can subtly creep in, perhaps through an accusing thought or a troubling dream, to make us emotionally and spiritually crippled, and thereby ineffective for God. Remember that even a powerful, well-trained horse can be brought down by a simple thorn or sore in its hoof.

In such circumstances, the answer for us is to worship God. We shouldn't go to a worship service seeking the presence of God only to "feel good" for an hour, like a junkie shooting drugs into his system to get a pleasurable rush. Rather, when we worship God and feel His presence, we can defeat our *thorn in our flesh*, our *yagun* (יגון). For when we feel His sweet presence, we are reminded that our failures, our sins, and our iniquities were nailed to the cross two thousand years ago. We recall the truth about our forgiveness and righteousness in Jesus Christ. Thus, when the enemy comes to us and says, "Who do you think you are, with all *your* sins and iniquities, to tell this person about God's love, or to preach a sermon or teach a Sunday School class?" we can turn right around and say, "Satan, you're a liar; those iniquities were nailed to the cross of Jesus Christ two thousand years ago, and I stand pure before the God I love. The fact that I feel His presence right now is proof and a reminder that I have been forgiven."

Study 75

Collapsing: *Mot* (מוט)

"Cast your burden on the Lord*, and he will sustain you; he will never permit the righteous to be moved* {to collapse}."
—Psalm 55:22 (ESV)

There is a story in the Talmud of a poor man who had no wagon or donkey to carry his heavy bundles, so he had to walk the many miles back to his village with his bundles on his back. While the poor man was walking, a wealthy man with a large wagon rode by. Seeing the poor man struggle with his load, he stopped and offered him a ride. The man was more than grateful to have his burdens eased.

After they had traveled for some time, the wealthy man noticed that his companion was sitting with his bundles still upon his shoulders. "Why don't you put your belongings down?" asked the wealthy man. "There is plenty of room in my wagon to lay your burdens down. Are they not heavy?"

"Indeed they are," sighed the poor man. "But you have been more than gracious to offer me a ride, and I do not wish to take advantage of you by weighing down your wagon."

When you accepted Jesus as your personal Savior, He not only received your life, but He also took on your burdens. To not take your burdens off your own shoulders and lay them upon Jesus makes you about as foolish as that poor man riding in the wealthy man's wagon with his heavy bundles still on his shoulders.

Once, when I translated Psalm 55:22 in one of my Hebrew classes, one rather insightful student pointed out, "There are conditions to casting your burden upon the Lord." If you examine our study verse, I think you will indeed discover the conditions that will allow you to release your burdens and place them upon Jesus.

Continually Cast Your Burdens on Jesus

The first condition is that we must *"cast"* our burdens on Him. The Hebrew word for *"cast"* is *hasheleke* (השלך). This term is in an imperative (command) form. It is not that we just have the opportunity to cast our burdens upon Him; rather, we are *commanded* to do it. God is literally ordering us to do so. Let's face it—we are not going to accomplish much service for Him if we walk around with a heavy burden.

You may be thinking, *Yeah, yeah, "cast your burden upon the Lord." I tried that. I threw my burden on the Lord, but for some reason it still weighs on my shoulders.* Well, the Bible does not say to *throw* your burden on the Lord but to *"cast"* your burden on Him. It is not the same thing.

Hasheleke (השלך), or *"cast,"* is in an infinitive form, giving us the idea that we are to *continually* be casting our burdens upon Him. This is more than just going to the front of the church every Sunday and having the preacher pray over you. This is a day-by-day, moment-by-moment discipline. Our burdens are sort of like a magnet—they keep jumping back on our shoulders, so we need to repeatedly remove them and give them back to God. There is a fringe benefit to constantly casting your burden upon the Lord: if you follow this practice, it will keep you continually before God's presence.

Let the Spirit Blow Your Burdens Away

Hasheleke (השלך) comes from the root word *shalak* (שלך). In its Semitic root, it gives a picture of a flower being blown away from its plant by the wind. In other words, you do not do the casting yourself; rather, you expose yourself to the wind and let the wind blow your burdens away from you. I wonder if Jesus had this in mind when He said, *"The wind blows where it wishes, and you hear its sound, but you do not know where it comes from or where it goes. So it is with everyone who is born of the Spirit"* (John 3:8 ESV). The Holy Spirit is depicted as the *"wind."* We cannot control the Spirit or order Him around; we just have to expose ourselves to Him and let Him blow away our burdens.

Interestingly, the Hebrew word for *"burden"* is *yehabeka* (יהבך), which literally means "He has given you." It is from the root word *yahab* (יהב), meaning "to give." The most common word in Hebrew for "to give" is *nathan* (נתן). However, in this context, *yahab* (יהב) has the idea of *a giving of responsibility.* Think about it: most of the burdens you carry are really the result of responsibilities you have. You are weighed down by your job because of the responsibility it entails. You feel stressed in regard to your family because of the challenge of meeting your responsibilities to them. Then, when you begin to feel you are failing in your responsibilities, you become burdened. But when God gives you a responsibility, He also gives you a large "wagon" to carry the burden of that responsibility. We are only called to fulfill our responsibility—not to carry the burdens that come with it; that's the Lord's job. We are to just sit back and enjoy the responsibilities God has given to us.

Seek to Do the Right Thing

Here is the last condition: *"He will never permit the righteous to be moved."* I know it sounds more like a statement of fact than a condition, but note that it refers to "the *righteous.*" The final condition is that you must be righteous; in other words, you must be seeking to *do the right thing.* Whenever you seek to do the right thing, even if you are wrong in what you are doing, and you expose yourself to the *wind* of the Holy Spirit, He will blow that burden upon the Father, who will make all things work together for good (see Romans 8:28), and you will not be *"moved."* The Hebrew word translated as *"moved"* in our study verse is *mot* (מוט), which means "to fall down" or "to collapse." This is sort of a play on another word, *moth* (מות), that is also pronounced "mot" but means "death." He will never let the righteous *collapse* under their burden. He won't let it kill them off.

Study 76

Love Eternal Love: *'Ahaveth 'Olam 'Ahavethik* (אהבת עולם אהבתיך)

"The Lord *hath appeared of old unto me, saying, Yea, I have loved thee with an everlasting love: therefore with lovingkindness have I drawn thee."*
—Jeremiah 31:3

Neither love me for
Thine own dear pity's wiping my cheeks dry:
A creature forget to weep, who bore
Thy comfort long, and lose thy love thereby!
But love me for love's sake, that evermore
Thou mayest love on, through love's eternity.
—Elizabeth Barrett Browning[6]

Seeing, Hearing, and Experiencing God's Love

Once you have translated a passage from the Hebrew, you are sometimes left scratching your head, more confused than ever as to what the passage really means. That is when you need to apply the

6. *Sonnets from the Portuguese*, IV, "If thou must love me, let it be for naught," http://www.bartleby.com/336/119.html.

principles of biblical exegesis. This involves looking at the context, at usages throughout Scripture, and at extrabiblical passages. You consider grammar, tradition, the opinions of others, and so forth. In short—you make an educated guess. As I have indicated throughout this *Hebrew Word Study*, that is why we have so many different Bible translations, each with its own exegetical twist.

A phrase from our study verse, *"The Lord hath appeared of old unto me, saying..."* is one such expression that is open to debate. The literal rendering would be "The Lord has appeared from afar to me." The Hebrew words translated *"appeared"* and *"of old"*—or literally "from afar"—each have a broad range of meanings. The term for *"appeared"* is *ra'ah* (ראה), which is often used to express the idea of spiritual insights. Sometimes it is translated as "visions." The Hebrew word for *"from afar"* is *rachaq* (רחק), which means "to be far off" or "to be far away." The word *"saying"* is not in the original text; it was included to allow the sentence to flow and make sense. However, the implication is that the prophet is seeing *a vision of the everlasting love of God*. The question is, how can you see "everlasting love" in a vision?

I remember reading in Jewish literature where certain rabbis attempted to resolve this issue. They presented the idea that in the spirit, our five senses are all combined into one sense. Thus, the prophet Jeremiah is not only hearing these words, but he is also seeing them and experiencing them. "From afar" would create a picture of taking a journey through God's everlasting love. Love can be very hard to understand, especially everlasting love. The context of this verse is that the people of Judah are going through some very difficult times. Just telling them "God loves you" isn't going to cut it. So the Lord gives Jeremiah a vision and takes him on a spiritual journey where he sees, hears, and experiences the love of God.

Loved for Love's Sake

This is not your everyday, off-the-shelf love. This is *everlasting* love. It is *'ahaveth 'olam 'ahavethik* (אהבת עולם אהבתיך), which literally means "love eternal love." How do we translate that phrase into

English? *"Everlasting love"* is a good way to render it, but it still falls short. I think Elizabeth Barrett Browning touched on the idea when she wrote, "Love me for love's sake." God loves us just for the sake of love. He does not love us out of pity, so that we "lose [His] love thereby," nor does He love us because we serve Him, pay our tithes, go to church, pray, fast, read the Bible, or perform any other duty. He will not love us one ounce more for doing any of those things. His *"everlasting love,"* or "love eternal love," is not built upon what we do. He loves us "because." Everlasting love has only one *because*, and that is *because He is Love*, and therefore *"we love him, because he first loved us"* (1 John 4:19).

You cannot help but love that which is perfect in love. I believe this is one reason why the enemy encourages abortion. A baby is as perfect in love as a human can get, and the enemy certainly doesn't want such a being influencing someone. Likewise, marriage is the closest picture to our love relationship with God that we can experience in the natural, so the enemy makes an all-out assault against marriages, using pornography and other devices to destroy them. Pornography perverts love, yet in our culture, perverted sexual acts are called "making love." It is often hard for people who have been exposed to such distorted love to respond when we tell them, "God loves you." They say, "That's nice, but what's the big deal? What's in it for me?"

That is why we must truly meditate on the meaning of God's *"everlasting love."* Maybe He won't give us a vision or take us on a spiritual journey, as He did for Jeremiah, but He has given all of us some type of creative capacity with which we can explore the reality of His eternal love. Some people, like Elizabeth Browning, can write poetically about love, others can paint a picture of love, and others can sing about love—but in some way we need to explore what this *everlasting love* really means. Then, the next time we hear the phrase "God loves you," we will begin to see just how special that love really is, and we can learn to love Him in return, purely for love's sake.

Study 77

The Queen in God's Palm: *Melekah Bekap Elohayike* (מלכה בכף אלהיך)

"You will also be a crown of beauty in the hand of the Lord, *and a royal diadem in the hand of your God."*
—Isaiah 62:3 (NASB)

In ancient Hebrew culture, there were two types of crowns. There was an enduring crown and a temporary crown. The enduring, or permanent, crowns were worn by royalty and priests, while the temporary crowns were worn by brides and grooms—temporary because they were made of flowers or leafy branches, which quickly wilted. The Hebrew word translated *"crown"* in our study verse is *'aterat* (עטרת), referring to a crown that entirely circles the head. It is a crown of *"beauty,"* or *pa'ar* (פאר), a word that denotes "beauty, glory, and/or honor." It can also mean "green bough" or "branch." Thus, it refers to the temporary crown worn by a bride or groom.

Protected by God

This crown is in the *yad* (יד), or *"hand,"* of Jehovah. The *yad* (יד) is a symbol of power and/or protection, and in relationship to a bride, it would specifically signify *protection*. The prophet Isaiah is saying that God will protect us as a husband would protect his bride. It is interesting to note that a groom also wears such a crown. In light of previous studies, we might infer that we are not only a "bride" to God but also a "husband" to Him. Whereas God will protect us as a husband would protect his bride, the role is also reversed in which we as a husband need to protect God as our bride; that is, as a husband would protect his bride's heart, we should protect the heart of God.

The verse continues by saying we will be a *"royal diadem"* in the hand of our God. The word for *"diadem"* is *tsenif* (צניפ), which is usually rendered as "turban" because it means "to wrap around." But this is a *"royal"* turban. The word translated *"royal"* is *melekah* (מלכה), which is often rendered as "a queen." A queen did not wear a turban, and that is why the word is generally translated as "royal."

Disciplined by God

Yet why does the Hebrew use a word that literally means "a queen"? Note how the verse concludes: *"...in the hand of your God."* We are a *crown* to Jehovah and a *diadem* to *'Elohim*. As I indicated in an earlier study, for the Hebrews, the name *Jehovah* represents mercy and the name *'Elohim* represents discipline or judgment. The term in Hebrew translated as *"hand"* is *kap* (כפ), which actually signifies the palm of the hand. Here again, we have a picture of a God who both protects and judges.

Protection we understand, but judgment has such a harsh sound to it. Yet this judgment is administered *in the palm of God's hand*. This reminds me of the incident when the wife of the president of the United States created quite a snafu by placing her arm around the queen of England in response to the queen lightly putting her hand on the back of the president's wife as they talked. The shock waves were heard around the world: the president's wife touched the queen! Somebody in the president's protocol department probably lost a job over that one. A very basic principle, known to everyone except Americans, who have no concept of royalty, is that one is never to touch a queen, except on rare occasions when one may touch her hand, if it is offered. The only one who can touch a queen is someone who shares a deep intimacy with the monarch. In Isaiah 62:3, we find a picture of a queen *in the palm of God's hand*. Whatever the judgment, it is offered in deep intimacy with God.

I look at it in this way: we are protected by God as a husband would protect his bride. If we do face some form of judgment, it will be done safely in His palm. So, if God brings His judgment on our nation, for instance, we will experience that judgment simply because of our geographical location. Yet we need never fear, for we will be *His queen*, resting safely in the palm of His hand.

Study 78

Trusting (God): *Yachal* (יחל)

"Though he slay me, yet will I trust in him."
—Job 13:15

Job's affirmation in our study verse is much stronger in the original Hebrew than it appears to be in English, even though it might seem as if there couldn't be a much stronger statement than this one. Translating the Hebrew word *hen* (הן) as *"though"* makes the phrase come across as "Even if God slays me...." but the word *hen* (הן) is often translated as "behold." The word for *"slay me"* is *yeketeleni* (יקטלני), which is in a simple *qal* imperfect (future) form. In other words, we would be correct to translate the phrase as "Behold, He will slay me," or "Surely, He will slay me."

The root word for *"slay"* is *qatal* (קטל), which is used only three times in the Old Testament. This is not the usual word used for "kill," which would be *ratsach* (רצח) for "murder" or *harag* (הרג) for "manslaughter." All three words refer to a physical killing, but *qatal* (קטל) can mean not only a physical killing but also a killing of the spirit or a killing of all hope. It can also denote "to make small" or "to be of little value."

Waiting and Hoping Expectantly

It is very interesting that Job used the word *qatal* (קטל) here. Like him, we can boldly say, in effect, "Though God does the worst to me,

I will still trust Him." But Job actually takes it one step further in his use of this word. He is essentially saying, "Though He breaks every promise, fails me in every way, treats me like I am simply worthless, I am still going to trust in Him." The Hebrew word translated as *"trust"* is also an unusual word. It is *yachal* (יחל), which means "to have an expectant hope." You see, Job fully expects to die; the use of the *qal* imperfect (future) implies that God is going to take his life—to Job, it is not a question of *if* but *when*. And he is expressing that when God takes his life, he will be hoping and expectantly waiting to be with Him.

I was raised as a Baptist, and I was well trained in the art of evangelism. In fact, I remember sitting in classes on evangelism taught by a successful salesman from the secular world on how to "market" God. First, you establish the person's need for the product. Second, you demonstrate how the product works, often through testimonials. Third, you show how your product meets your client's need. Of course, finally, you get the client to sign on the dotted line (i.e., say "the sinner's prayer"), and *bingo*—you have wrapped up another sale. Of course, if the product doesn't work, there is no refund. We sold God as a means to an end, not as Someone whom you can love and hope to live with one day.

If Job had similarly signed on the dotted line with God to receive all the benefits of the "product," he certainly would have been seeking a refund. As I've expressed previously, how many of us cling to the promises of God, only to find that He just doesn't seem to be fulfilling them? What happens if He doesn't apparently bring them to fruition? It is easy to love Him when He gives wonderful promises and fulfills them quickly. But would we still love Him if He appeared to break those promises? We cannot help but love Him when preachers tell us how much He loves us and how we are the center of His world. But suppose He *qatal*s (קטל) us, or doesn't seem to answer us, so that we feel worthless? This is what Job is referring to. Yet he says he will still *yachal* (יחל), or trust, God. He will still continue to hope and to place his life and future in God's hands, even if He seems to treat him like he is worthless and appears never to fulfill His promises.

Job's relationship with God obviously did not depend upon all the "benefits" he would receive. Without fail, when I speak on the book of Job, some Christian will always say, "Yeah, but remember, once Job came through it all, God restored everything to him, and more." To say something like this means you have missed the whole point of the story. That restoration part is an epilogue; it is just information that is added at the end, separate from the story and not intended to take away from its theme. The theme of the story of Job is that when everything was taken away from him, and it seemed like his life was going to end in poverty and shame, he still trusted God; he was waiting and hoping expectantly to be with the God whom he loved.

What Is Most Precious to You?

There is a story in Jewish literature about a married man who longed to be single again and not be burdened with a wife. One day, he learned that under Jewish law, he could divorce his wife if she did not give him a child after ten years of marriage. Finding his escape, the man decided he would seize this loophole, because he and his wife were childless—not that he had really cared or tried. He went to the rabbi and demanded that he be granted a divorce based upon this Jewish law.

The rabbi knew the couple, and he said that he would grant the divorce only after speaking to the man's wife. After meeting with her, the rabbi called the man to his office and told him he would grant the divorce under one condition. The man was crestfallen—he knew there was a catch. The rabbi explained the condition: the husband was to allow his wife to go into the house and pick out the one thing that was most precious to her, and he was to let her have it. The man's apprehensions turned to joy. "That's it? That's all? Just let her have the one thing that is most precious to her? I'm free!" the man exclaimed excitedly. He ran out into the streets and grabbed his drinking buddies and had a big party at his house that night to celebrate his new freedom.

Unfortunately, the old boy made a little too merry and passed out in a drunken stupor. When he awoke, he found himself in bed at his father-in-law's home, with his wife sitting next to him. He looked around, saw his wife, and asked what he was doing there. His wife replied, "The rabbi said I could go to your house and take what was most precious to me." The man brightened up and asked, "Did you find it?" She said, "Yes, it was you." The story goes that the man did not get the divorce but thereafter remained contentedly married to his wife.

Sometimes, as with Job, God has to allow everything to be taken away from us so we can discover what is most precious to us. It is then that we learn that nothing—neither the enemy nor any human being, "*neither death, nor life, nor angels, nor principalities, nor powers, nor things present, nor things to come, nor height, nor depth, nor any other creature, shall be able to separate us from* [what is most precious to us] ***the love of God****, which is in Christ Jesus our Lord*" (Romans 8:38–39).

Study 79

Beauty of God upon Us: *No'am 'Elohanu 'Alinu* (נעם אלוהני עלינו)

"Let thy work appear unto thy servants, and thy glory unto their children. And let the beauty of the LORD our God be upon us: and establish thou the work of our hands upon us; yea, the work of our hands establish thou it."
—Psalm 90:16–17

Many Bible scholars attribute the authorship of Psalm 90 to Moses. Moses knew a few things about the glory of God. He had asked God to reveal His glory to him, and God did—well, kind of. The Bible says God revealed to Moses His *chasad* (חסד), which signifies His *loving-kindness*, not His *kavod* (כבד), or His *glory*. (See Exodus 33:18–23.) In our study passage, Moses is saying that God will reveal His *hadar* (הדר) to his children. Some translations render this word as "glory," yet *hadar* (הדר) really means "beauty," "majesty," or "splendor."

Servants and Children

Psalm 90:16 begins, *"Let thy work appear unto thy servants."* The Hebrew word for *"work"* is *pa'al* (פאל), which refers to one's activity or deeds, what one has done. To His servants, He shows what He has done and will do for them, but to their children He shows His *beauty.*

In verse 17, Moses talks about the beauty of the Lord being upon us. The Hebrew word translated "*beauty*" is *noam* (נעם), which is a word for "pleasure." This, like the other words, is in a cohortative* form and thus should be rendered in the form of a blessing: "*May* God do good works for His servants, and *may* His splendor and majesty be upon their children, and *may* the pleasure of God be upon us all."

The rest of the verse is a little difficult to translate. The King James Version renders it, "*And establish thou the work of our hands upon us; yea, the work of our hands establish thou it.*" The word "*establish*" is *kun* (כון), which comes from a Semitic root that has a variety of applications. I feel the best application for this context is "success" or "prosperous." Thus, Moses is saying, "And make the work of our hands *successful* or *prosperous.*"

Taking a very close look at the syntax of verse 17, it would appear that this success or prosperity is related to the *beauty* or *pleasure* of God being upon us. In other words: *May all our works be successful in bringing pleasure to God.* Both the servants and the children bring *pleasure* to God, but there is a difference between the two. God will do good deeds for His servants, and His beauty will be revealed to their children, so that all they do will bring pleasure to God. Based upon that understanding, we might choose to be a servant of God rather than a child of God. A servant gets to experience the *works* of God in his or her life. But all you get by being a child of God is His *beauty*—you know, like, big deal.

Besides that, many of us are so caught up in life's many problems and cares that we certainly are not bringing much pleasure to God with our negative attitudes about our situations. We tend to just sit around feeling sorry for ourselves and worrying about the future. So we start crying out to God that we are His *servants*, and it is about time that He starts doing some of this good *work* in us, like healing us, giving us a good job, and blessing us financially. Once that is done, then we can get down to the business of bringing Him some pleasure.

Yet I wonder if God is not bringing us into the state of a child. The word for *"servant"* is *'abad* (עבד), which literally means "slave" or "bondage." Do we really allow ourselves to be in total bondage to God, or to be a slave to Him? Moses understood this word *'abad* (עבד); he knew about slavery. He understood the slavery of God's people in Egypt. As a slave, you were totally dependent upon your master for everything. Your life, your existence, your next meal were all in the hands of the slave master. When the children of Israel left Egypt, they were free to experience the beauty and splendor of God. They had a new Slave Master, one who fed them and took loving care of them. This new Slave Master was beautiful and majestic. But they were so wrapped up in getting their basic needs met from their new Master, just like from their old Egyptian masters, that they did not bother to see His majesty. In fact, they told Moses, "You go in the cloud and find out what our new Master wants from us and report back to us." (See Exodus 20:18–21.) I imagine that when Moses returned from the cloud, he told the people, "Our Master is so beautiful, splendid, and wonderful. You have to see it; you just have to see it." But the people were not interested in their new Master's beauty; they were only concerned about their next meal.

Take Time to See God's Beauty

The application for us is that we have been redeemed from our old slave master of sin. We have a new Master who is beautiful and splendid and wants to show us His *hadar* (הדר), or His *beauty*, but we are so focused on our personal needs, desires, and wants that we never take time to see His beauty. And we would rather that someone else go into that cloud and tell us what God is saying. Once we get our needs met, then maybe we will appreciate the cloud better.

Most of us pick up our Bible and read it when we need something—perhaps comfort or some key to getting our prayers answered—or when we have the idea that by reading God's Word, we can sort of brownnose Him into doing us a favor or a *pa'al* (פאל)—a work or a miracle. Do we ever really read the Word of God to seek His *hadar* (הדר), His *beauty*, rather than His *pa'al* (פאל), His *works*?

All of the Hebrew word studies in this book originated as entries in my daily journal. Sometimes, I look back on them and notice that, at times, they center on God's works rather than on His beauty and splendor. There are plenty of websites, blogs, books, and other materials that center on God's *works* and how to get Him *working* in our lives. I really don't need to add another voice to those. I would like to move beyond being His *'avad* (עבד), His servant or slave, and offer a voice that is not commonly heard because it does not address the idea of meeting one's personal needs, desires, or wants. I would like my writings to be the voice of one who looks to God as a Father, as one who simply wants to have a relationship with Him as His child and to see His *hadar* (הדר), His *beauty* and *majesty.*

Rather than focus on how to get things from God, we need to focus on bringing pleasure to His heart by admiring His beauty and majesty and not just the good works He performs in our lives. I know that if I were to post on my Facebook page, "God gave me a brand-new red Porsche so I can drive little children to Sunday school," I would get a thousand "likes" and hundreds of "praise God, hallelujahs." But if I were to say, "I looked up in the sky tonight and saw the beauty and majesty of God," I could count on one hand the number of likes I would receive. But you know what? I believe that if we were to look deep into our hearts and then be given the choice between receiving a new red Porsche or seeing and experiencing the beauty and majesty of God, we would probably choose the latter in a heartbeat.

Study 80

He Carried Our Sorrows: *Hu Nasa' Make'ovanu* (הוא נשׂא מכאבינו)

"Surely he hath borne our griefs, and carried our sorrows."
—Isaiah 53:4

Have you ever heard a Scripture verse all your life—read it, memorized it, sung it as a chorus, and heard it preached on numerous times—but then one day looked at it and said, "Is that really in the Bible?"

Our study text was one of those verses for me. Clearly, the literal interpretation is that Jesus our Messiah has borne our griefs and carried our sorrows. That sounds really good, but when you stop to think about it, what does it actually mean? Does it mean He feels sorry for us or pities us? Does it mean that He removes those griefs and sorrows from us?

Our Sufferings Exalted

Let's explore the meanings of the words *"griefs"* and *"sorrows"* and then answer the question, do "bearing" and "carrying" mean the same thing? The Hebrew word for *"griefs"* is *chalah* (חלה), which means physical sickness and pain, as well as mental anguish. Jesus *bears* these. The word for *"borne"* is *nasa'* (נשׂא), which contains the idea of *being made high or exalted.* It can also be used to express the idea of *to bear* or *to carry away*—but what about this idea of being lifted up or exalted?

There are many Christians today who have lost jobs or are in the process of losing jobs that they know God gave them. Other Christians are losing the ministry given to them by God. Still others are losing spouses, through death or divorce, that God gave them. It is one thing to suffer sickness or grief as a result of selfish decisions you have made, but what about when you have made good decisions and done your very best to do the right thing, and you end up getting blasted through no fault of your own? Perhaps our study verse is also addressing that situation by saying that God will exalt your suffering—will lift it up, or honor it—just as He honored Job for enduring the suffering he went through, which was no fault of his own. The apostle Paul talks about sharing in the sufferings of Jesus. (See Romans 8:17; Philippians 3:10.)

Shifting Our Burdens to Jesus

Next, we read that Jesus *"carried our sorrows."* The Hebrew word for *"carried"* is *saval* (סבל), which means "to carry" and is the same word used for *a porter* or *one who carries a heavy load for another person.* The baggage does not belong to the porter—another person still owns it—but the porter bears its weight. The word for *"sorrows"* is *k'ab* (כאב), which refers to *a deep inner pain, sorrow, or burden.*

Do you have a deep sorrow or a burden? Jesus is our celestial "Porter" who will carry our baggage for us. That knowledge is all well and good, but I personally have a terrible time giving my burdens over to Him. Sometimes I think I do, but then I find myself fretting over the issue all over again. So, how do we let Jesus pick up our burdens? Perhaps there is a clue in the word for *"carried," saval* (סבל), which is spelled samek (ס), beth (ב), lamed (ל). This combination of letters suggests that through prayer, we enter into the shelter of God's heart. It is knowing and understanding God's heart, His real love for us, His concern and longing for us, that allows us to shift our burden to Him. Like the protagonist Christian in the classic work *The Pilgrim's Progress*, we take that heavy burden off our back and lay it at the cross. Then we enter the narrow gate, which brings us into the heart of God, and we find rest.

Resting in the Shelter of God's Heart

Once we enter God's heart, whatever happens really does not matter, because it is all part of His plan. In God's heart, we can see His loving-kindness, and although we may not understand His reasoning behind our afflictions, we are resting in the shelter of His heart. To dwell in the heart of God is to be in constant prayer, even if we are not speaking actual words to Him and do not have our hands folded and our eyes closed. We can be busy doing our daily tasks, but if we are in the heart of God, we are in prayer. Perhaps this is one more application of what Paul meant when he said, *"Pray without ceasing"* (1 Thessalonians 5:17).

Study 81

Return with All Your Heart: *Shavah Bekal Livah* (שבה בכל לבה)

"And yet for all this her treacherous sister Judah hath not turned unto me with her whole heart, but feignedly, saith the Lord*."*
—Jeremiah 3:10

We have to realize that at the time of this prophecy, Judah was a very religious and prosperous nation. The people had the temple of God in Jerusalem where they faithfully worshipped. From all outward appearances, they were a godly people, yet God said *they had not turned to Him with their whole heart.*

Take a look at the phrase *"sister Judah hath not turned."* There is an amazing play on words here. Every English translation renders the Hebrew word *shavah* (שבה) as "return" or "turn back." What the translators are doing is looking at the qamtes (ָ), or the vowel *a*, at the end of the word *shavah* (שבה) and assuming that it is a feminine ending based upon the fact that Judah is referred to as *"sister."* That, after all, follows good grammar and is proper. Yet this dusty old Christian professor cannot help but ask, "Why is God referring to Judah as a '*sister*' to Israel?" I believe this is a hint that a much deeper insight into our relationship with God is tucked away in this verse.

Remember that the original Hebrew texts had no vowel pointings. These were added several hundred years after Jesus lived on earth, when the Masorites feared that oral tradition would get lost due to the Jews being scattered throughout the world. Feeling the need to preserve the spoken Hebrew language in some written form, they added vowel pointings to the original Hebrew texts, which had only consonants, in order to maintain a correct pronunciation. Thus, oral tradition provided the vowel pointings, and there was some dispute over what the proper vowel pointings should be. At the same time, these pointings narrowed down the playing field when it came to translation.

In the original text of our study verse, the Hebrew word we translate as "*turned*," or "returned," is *shavah* (שׁבה), spelled shin (שׁ), beth (ב), hei (ה). Interestingly, this word is usually rendered as "to take captive," while the word translated "to return" would normally be *shavav* (שׁוב), spelled shin (שׁ), vav (ו) beth (ב). But again, because we assume the *qamtes* (vowel pointing for *a*) in the Masoritic text for this word to be a feminine suffix,* we then assume that the triliteral root* of *shavav* (שׁוב) should take on the form of *shavah* (שׁבה), so that it is spelled shin (שׁ), beth (ב), hei (ה). This gives it the same spelling as the word for "to take captive," *shavah* (שׁבה), even though it has a different meaning. As I have said, this usage is all very proper and correct. But again, when we hold up the Masoritic text to be *the* inspired word of God (which it is not), we start to limit ourselves.

So, let's just say that the word really is *shavah* (שׁבה)—shin (שׁ), beth (ב), hei (ה), as found in the original text. This particular word comes from a root that means "captive" or "imprisoned" rather than "return." One root that comes from this word is *yashab* (ישׁב), which means "to dwell." Another is *shavuh* (שׁוה), which means "to make oneself like another."

Outward and Inward Appearances

Lately, I have been struggling with the idea of what it means to give God my *whole heart* when I pray, "God take my whole heart. That is the best I can give You—my whole heart." Even as I say those words, I still feel like I am falling short. I guess I feel that way because

I do not really understand what I am saying. Looking at Jeremiah 3:10, I have to admit that I am like Judah—I am acting *treacherously* toward God. The Hebrew word rendered *"treacherous"* is *bagad* (בגד), which, in its Semitic root, carries the idea of *a covering or a wrapper.* Thus, I am only letting God have my wrapper, my outward appearance, and not what is inside of me—my fears, my pride, my fleshly concerns, and so on. As the passage says, I feel like I only *"feignedly"* give Him my heart. The Hebrew word translated *"feignedly"* is *shaqar* (שקר), which means "to be deceptive."

Judah looked godly on the outside. The people gave their tithes, their sacrifices, and their praises to God. They kept the law, they attended worship services, and they appeared very holy, but they had given God only their top layer. They were faking the rest.

Our Hearts Taken Captive by God

Like most Christians, I sincerely want to give God my whole heart; I don't want to fake it. But what does it really mean to give Him my *whole heart*? Does it mean to live some kind of monastic lifestyle, never enjoying life itself because you are too busy praying and studying the Word, afraid that watching even a half hour of TV will turn your heart away from God?

To help me discover the answer, I looked at the various plays on the word *shavah* (שבה). To give God our whole heart means *to be taken captive by Him, to be His prisoner.* A prisoner's life is ordered. In fact, many people who spend years in prison have a real problem adjusting to life on the outside because they suddenly have much more freedom and many more options; they sometimes cannot make a decision on their own because decisions were always made for them by the warden and the prison guards. Another play on the word *shavah* (שבה) is *to dwell.* If God has our whole heart, He dwells in our heart; *He holds it captive.* The third play on words is that *we seek to make ourselves like Him.*

I find Western Christians spending too much time trying to win God's favor through all their good works, their tithes, their prayers, and even their Bible reading and study, rather than letting God take their hearts captive. In my search for God's heart, I am discovering that the only way I can know His heart is to allow my heart to be held captive by His.

You see, if you worry that watching a half hour of TV will turn your heart away from God, then you are like a person in prison worrying that he will accidentally walk out of the prison. It won't happen—the only way out before being paroled is to escape. If I have no desire to escape from the prison of God's heart, then I don't have to worry that by watching a half hour of television I will accidently walk out of my confinement, any more than a prisoner has to worry about inadvertently walking out of prison. God holds me captive. The only way out is to make a conscious decision to escape, to *want* that separation.

Therein lay the sin of Judah—the people did not want to be held a prisoner of God's heart. But if you truly want to give God your whole heart, He will make you His *shavah* (שׁבה), or captive, and put you in the prison of His heart. He won't let you escape if you don't want to. Since I want God to have my whole heart, He has it; my problem is that, like Judah, I sometimes find myself trying to escape so I can watch some particular half hour of television that would be offensive to His heart. But again, when we sincerely give Him our heart, He will not let us stray from His. As Paul wrote, *"If we are faithless, he remains faithful, for he cannot disown himself"* (2 Timothy 2:13 NIV).

Study 82

A Thing of Nought: *K'ayim Uke'epes* (כאים וכאפס)

"Thou shalt seek them, and shalt not find them,
even them that contended with thee: they that war against
thee shall be as nothing, and as a thing of nought.
For I the Lord *thy God will hold thy right hand,*
saying unto thee, Fear not; I will help thee."
—Isaiah 41:12–13

I occasionally drive a rather delightful little lady named "Janice" to her doctor's appointment in my disability bus. She loves to tell stories about her life, and one day she told me how she used to walk to her doctor's office before her legs got so weak that she had to start using our bus service. She related an incident that occurred one day when she was crossing Cicero Avenue and Cermak Road to get to the doctor's office. Cicero Avenue is a main artery through the center of Chicago and a direct link to the interstate highway that leads out of town. Hence, many large semitrailers travel down Cicero, usually at a rapid pace. Just as Janice was preparing to cross the street, three large tractor trailers came roaring by. Poor Janice had a panic attack. Those trucks were so big and so loud, they scared her half to death. She screamed and ran into the doctor's office in tears, crying, "Help,

help; you've got to help me!!" The nurse ran up to her and asked, "Janice, what's wrong?" In between tears of panic, she said, "They're after me." By this time, the doctor had come out, and he said, "Now, now, Janice, who's after you?" With absolute terror in her eyes, she said, "Trucks, big trucks; they're trying to run over me." The doctor motioned to the nurse, who picked up a phone, and within a few minutes our hapless Janice found herself strapped to a gurney, on her way to the hospital in an ambulance, where she was put in restraints and given an injection. She commented, "They thought I was crazy."

Living in Constant Fear

Many Christians live in constant, often unreasonable fear. They fear for their jobs, for the safety of a family member, or for their health; they fear being the victim of a natural disaster, a crime, or even a terrorist attack. In our study passage from Isaiah, God is saying, in essence, "I am in charge, I love you, and I will not let anything happen to you." But even with such assurances, we are still afraid. We carry around the thought that maybe God wants us to go through poverty, pain, or suffering. I know some Christians who live in constant fear that they will go to hell. Recently, I was transporting an elderly lady to and from Sunday Mass in my disability bus. She had had a stroke and now had difficulty keeping her balance. As she walked out of the sanctuary, she accidently knocked over the holy water. In tears, her first comment was, "Oh no, I'm going to hell." The enemy wants to fill us with unreasonable fear and dread so that he can destroy our faith. Yet God is telling us that all these enemies that try to create fear in us are *"a thing of nought"*—they are totally unreasonable.

Trampling the Enemy Underfoot

The Hebrew phrase translated *"a thing of nought," k'ayim uke'epes* (כאים וכאפס), is a very interesting expression. Practically every English translation renders this phrase as "nothing." It's true that these words could be rendered as "nothing," but when you trace them to their Semitic root, you find they have the idea of *the bottom of the foot*, or *the sole of the foot*. As the words evolved through the various Semitic languages, they eventually carried the idea of the extreme portion of your body that is the ankle or the sole of the foot. The word *k'ayim* is prefixed with a kap (כ), indicating the preposition *like* or *as*. So, all your enemies are like the sole of your foot; in other words, the sole of your foot will crush them, like walking on an ant. God isn't saying that your enemies are not really out there—they are out there, and they are real; but they are at such an extreme length from you that they hardly matter. I wrote in a previous study that Calvin Coolidge was asked how he could remain so calm as the president of the United States when every hour a new crisis seemed to arise. He replied, "When you see ten troubles rolling down the road, if you don't do anything, nine of them will roll into a ditch before they get to you."[7] If the enemy does reach you, then all you have to do is to simply step on him.

The words translated as *"a thing of nought"* are also used to signify something that is *limited*. That problem that you see walking down the road toward you may appear very fearsome and frightening, but God is going to make it *k'ayim uke'epes* (כאים וכאפס). He is going to *limit* its power over you so that you can crush it under the soles of your feet.

Nothing Can Separate Us from God's Love

The apostle Paul understood this concept very well. When he became a believer, man took everything away from him. He lost his status, his reputation, his wealth, and his family; he became an itinerant preacher who was subsequently stoned, beaten, and shipwrecked. Yet through it all, as we read in a previous study, he was *"persuaded, that neither death, nor life, nor angels, nor principalities, nor powers, nor things present, nor things to come, nor height, nor depth, nor any other creature, shall be able to separate us from the love of God, which is in Christ Jesus our Lord"* (Romans 8:38–39).

Paul had nothing to fear, for fear is often based on our concern over losing something that is of value to us. It might be our job, our

7. See http://www.calvincoolidge.us/quotations.html.

health, our money market account—you fill in the blank. Yet the only thing of real value to Paul was the love of God in Christ Jesus. Man could take away his wealth, his influence, and his health, but the one thing they could not touch was the love of God in Christ Jesus. The Greek word for "*love*" in Romans 8:39 is *agape*. Paul's native language was Aramaic, and in my Aramaic Bible, the word used for "*love*" there is *chav* (חב). With *chav* (חב), the emphasis is on giving out of love more than on receiving love. God is constantly giving out His love, and nothing can prevent Him from doing so. No matter what forces might try to block His love, His *chav* (חב) will still flow through.

If God's love is the most important thing in your life, then what do you really have to fear? His love is something you can never lose. Nothing will ever separate you from what is most important to you if it is the love of God in Christ Jesus.

Study 83

I Will Allure Her: *'Anoki Mephateha* (אנכי מפתיה)

"Therefore, behold, I will allure her, bring her into the wilderness and speak kindly to her."
—Hosea 2:14[8]

In context, our study verse refers to Hosea's adulterous wife, Gomer, who represents God's unfaithful bride, Israel. God has instructed Hosea to take a harlot for a wife so that he can embody the very message he is to convey to the people, which is to feel what God feels and to understand what He thinks. Knowing God's heart is what gives Hosea his prophetic voice. I've heard people say things like, "Poor Hosea, to have such an unfortunate marriage and such personal tragedy." I guess it's just a matter of perspective. You can look at his story from a temporal viewpoint or from an eternal one. For myself, I say that it would be an honor to have God share the sufferings of His heart in this way. The apostle Paul considered it an honor to share in the sufferings of Jesus. I don't believe this means physical suffering as much as experiencing the sorrow and heartbreak that God feels for this world. That is what God allowed Hosea to share in as he suffered the heartbreak of having an unfaithful wife.

8. All the Scripture verses in this word study, including the main Scripture text, are taken from the *New American Standard Bible*.

Speaking Kind Words of Truth

In Hosea 2:14, God is speaking through Hosea, saying, *"I will allure her."* The Hebrew word translated *"allure"* is *pathah* (פתה); it is in a *piel* form, which intensifies its meaning, so it should read something like, "I will seduce her into the wilderness and speak...." How will He "seduce" her? Let's look at the built-in commentary of the word *pathah* (פתה). The first letter is pe (פ), which refers to speaking words in relation to the next letter, which is taw (ת), representing truth; He will speak these words of truth while she is in a place of weakness and brokenness, which is expressed by the last letter, hei (ה).

The Hebrew word for *"wilderness"* is *midbar* (מדבר), and the word for *"speak"* is *devar* (דבר). These two words are very similar and serve as a play on words. The root word *devar* (דבר) can mean "a dry, uninhabited land," "a pasture where sheep go to feed," or "words spoken from the heart of God." So, this is a picture of God bringing His beloved to a desolate place so that she will feed on His words, which are described as *"kindly."* Actually, the Hebrew word translated as *"kindly"* is *levav* (לבב), which is the same word for "heart." The double beths (בב) indicate that He wants to speak to her *heart to heart*, just as a husband who loves his wife and desperately desires her faithfulness would want to speak to her. Additionally, another meaning for *pathah* (פתה), or *"allure,"* is "to open wide"; in this verse, it is as if God (and/or Hosea) is trying to open her mind and persuade her to see the reality of her choices.

Earlier, Israel had said, *"I will go after my lovers, who give me my bread and my water, my wool and my flax, my oil and my drink"* (Hosea 2:5). In a heart-wrenching reply, God said, *"For she does not know that it was I who gave her the grain, the new wine and the oil,... which they used for Baal"* (verse 8). As a result, God said He would *"destroy her vines and fig trees, of which she said, 'These are my wages...'"* (verse 12) and would *"punish her"* (verse 13).

The Hebrew word translated *"punish"* is *paqad* (פקד), which is in a simple *qal* verbal form. Thus, it would not mean "punish" as much as "examine"—to see if there is any hope for a restored relationship. The first time this word is used in Scripture is in Genesis 21:1, where the Lord intervened on behalf of Sarah in a miraculous way so that she could conceive a child at an advanced age. The underlying meaning of this word is an action on the part of God that produces a beneficial result to His people.

Returning to the Time of First Love

After God draws His bride into the wilderness, He says, "*Then I will give her her vineyards from there, and the valley of Achor as a door of hope. And she will sing there as in the days of her youth, as in the day when she came up from the land of Egypt*" (Hosea 2:15). Jeremiah 2:2 later echoed the same sentiment: "*Go and proclaim in the ears of Jerusalem, saying, 'Thus says the LORD, "I remember concerning you the devotion of your youth, the love of your betrothals, your following after Me in the wilderness, through a land not sown.*" God reflects on the time of Israel's wandering in the wilderness as if it were a honeymoon with His bride. He considers it a time when they were alone together, and she was fully dependent upon Him. He is expressing not just a desire but a longing to return to that time of first love.

In an earlier study, I mentioned how I spent a week in a Benedictine monastery living in silence in God's presence. During this silent retreat, I took a walk every morning and early evening. There was a long road with an open pasture on both sides and a vast, open sky above. I could see the sun prominently on one side of the road and the moon prominently on the other, with the long path in front of me and behind me. The scene was as simplistic as a child's painting, yet as beautiful as a masterpiece.

That is a picture of where I now find myself in life. I'm in a time of great transition; I am somewhere in between the *old day* and the *new day*. (You may find yourself in the same situation.) The Lord has reminded me of the words "*I will...speak kindly* [or "tenderly," as many translations put it] *to her.*" In the Hebrew, this phrase is literally saying, "I will speak *over* her heart." The Hebrew term for "over," *'al* (על), might come from a Semitic root word that makes it function as a preposition; or it could come from a different root word that means "to blossom" or "to arise like the dawn"; or from a root word that means "the setting of the sun." Thus, this is a perfect time to be reminded of the romance of walking by faith and how God cherishes our love and faithfulness, just as when we first began our walk with Him.

Study 84

Enlarge My Heart: *Tarechib Livi* (תרחיב לבי)

"I will run the way of thy commandments, when thou shalt enlarge my heart."
—Psalm 119:32

When I first studied this verse, it appeared to say that David would follow God's commandments only if God *enlarged his heart*. Was this just a poetic expression, or was David really striking a bargain with God in order to obtain a larger heart? And why would he want a larger heart?

An Enlargement of Understanding

The Hebrew word for *"enlarge"* is *rachab* (רחיב), which signifies *an enlargement of understanding*. The word for *"when"* is *ki* (כי), which really means "because" rather than "when." It would seem that the translators rendered *ki* (כי) as *"when"* because the word *rachab* (רחיב) is in a hiphal imperfect (causative future) form, and to express *ki* (כי) as "because," you would really need to put the verb in a perfect (past tense) form. In other words, it would be more proper to say, "...when you shall enlarge the understanding of my heart" rather than "...when you have already enlarged the understanding of my heart." To say, "...*because* you will enlarge the understanding of my heart" would suggest more confidence in an act being done than if you said "*when* you will enlarge...." Yet David seems to live a life in which his heart is very close to the heart of God, and he is very confident about what God is doing in His life. I would suggest that we stay with the original intent of the word *ki* (כי) and render this phrase as: "...*because* you will enlarge the understanding of my heart."

If the word "*enlarge*" means to enlarge in understanding, then this would suggest that David is going to keep the way of God's commandments whether he understands it or not, because he knows that at some later date it will all make sense. God's commandments to wash one's hands before eating, and to wash one's dishes with hot water after eating, constitute a good example. In David's day, people did those things ceremonially because God commanded it. I imagine that an Israelite living at that time might have said to a friend, "Why is God making us do these crazy things?" And I picture the friend answering, "Don't ask—just do it. God said to do it, and that should be good enough for us."

Today, we understand what the people in those days did not realize—that washing with hot water kills germs that can cause illnesses and diseases. The very idea of a world of microscopic life that you cannot see with the naked eye but has the ability to harm you would be the equivalent of science fiction to the ancient mind, which had no concept of microbes. Yet it is common knowledge to modern man who, through technology, can see this invisible world.

Even today, there are things that God commands us not to do that we perhaps don't understand; yet because the Bible forbids then, we will not do them. One day, God will *rachab* (רחיב) my heart (enlarge its understanding), and these things will make sense. For example, I don't fully understand how and when life begins, but I do know that if there is human life inside the womb, and the Bible teaches that to destroy human life is murder, whether that life is in the womb or not, then I will stand against abortion. Call me a fanatic if you wish, but I am in good company with David, who was willing to trust and believe God whether or not he fully understood what God had in mind. He knew that one day he would understand.

In another example, the Bible instructs that a man should not have relations with another man like he does with a woman. I don't really understand why such a thing is an abomination to God. If two people love each other, and no one is getting hurt, why not? Just because it doesn't seem natural or doesn't fit into our cultural context, does that make it wrong? Yet the Bible clearly teaches that it is wrong, so although I do not understand the mind of God, if the Bible says it, then, like David, I will believe it and abide by it.

"Lean Not on Your Own Understanding"

David's own son, Solomon, who was the wisest man on earth, said, *"Trust in the Lord with all your heart and lean not on your own understanding"* (Proverbs 3:5 NIV). Even the wisest man who ever lived faced things beyond his own understanding, and he realized he had to trust the Lord with these things, believing that one day God would *rachab* (רחיב), or *"enlarge,"* the understanding of his heart.

I don't understand why I face certain physical afflictions, why my financial situation is not as blessed as others', why my relationships do not run as smoothly as others'—and on and on. There is so much in my life that I do not comprehend. Some people say I am a smart guy, that I can figure things out. But you know what? There are just some things one can never figure out, so I know there are certain things I will never find the answers to in this life. But, like David, I have no doubt in my mind that one day I will understand them. With that firm confidence, I will follow God's Word as He reveals it to me through the Holy Spirit and not question why. For me, it is not a matter of obeying *when* I understand, but rather *because* God is one day going to *rachab* (רחיב), or *"enlarge,"* the understanding of my heart. Jesus and I have an appointment a hundred years from now to sit on a park bench in heaven where He will explain it all to me. But until that time, I plan to live as if I already have all the answers and fully understand the big "Why?" *because*, *ki* (כי), one day I will.

Study 85

Deal Bountifully: *Gamal* (גמל)

"Deal bountifully with thy servant, that I may live,
and keep thy word."
—Psalm 119:17

Tending the Garden of Our Heart

The Hebrew word translated as *"Deal bountifully"* is *gamal* (גמל), which means "to mature," "a ripened fruit," or "a child weaned from its mother." *Gamal* (גמל) has the idea of *being nourished until completely ripe.* As we have seen throughout this book, Hebrew is a very colorful and picturesque language, and this verse expresses the motif of *maturing in God* through the image of a vineyard with grapes ripening to maturity.

The word for *"with"* is *'al* (על) and is a play on the word *gamal* (גמל). *'Al* (על) is a preposition, yet it comes from the root word *'alah* (עלה). As we have previously seen, *'alah* (עלה) has a number of meanings, one of which is "to grow up." Unless a vine grows and bears fruit to maturity, it is of no use or value.

The word rendered *"servant"* comes from the root word *'abad* (עבד), which, when speaking of the ground, refers to *tilling, cultivating, or dressing a vineyard.* The purpose of tilling is to prepare the soil for planting. Tilling agitates and breaks up the soil, serves to mix in organic matter to produce a base for seeds, and helps to remove weeds. *'Abad* (עבד) can also mean "servant of the Lord," one doing the will of God, as a true worshipper or as one executing the purpose of God. Tending the garden of our heart, walking in step with the purposes and plans of God, is an act of worship.

The word translated *"may live"* is *chayah* (חיה) and means "to live," "to become strong," "food," and "restored from sickness." When considering the motif of the maturing vineyard, this is a picture of a healthy, vibrant, nourishing fruit ready for the picking, as opposed to grapes rotting on the vine, which are worthless and will never be used for what they were intended.

Then we have the word *"keep,"* translated from the Hebrew term *shamar* (שׁמר), which means "watchman," "to keep," "to preserve," and "to guard." Interestingly, it can also mean "lees of wine," which refers to the residue that separates from the wine and settles at the bottom of the vat after fermentation and aging.

Last, the Hebrew term translated as *"word"* is *devar* (דבר), which can be explained as *words spoken from the heart of God.* In the parable of the sower, which would perhaps be better titled "the parable of the soil," we know that the seed represents the Word of God:

> *The seed which fell among the thorns, these are the ones who have heard, and as they go on their way they are choked with worries and riches and pleasures of this life, and bring no fruit to maturity. But the seed in the good soil, these are the ones who have heard the word in an honest and good heart, and hold it fast, and bear fruit with perseverance.*
>
> (Luke 8:14–15 NASB)

Eternal Fruit That Remains

In order for grapes to fully mature, their plants need to be carefully watched over and pruned. If they are not regularly pruned, they will become wild and overgrown; consequently, they will never reach maturity. Not only will the crop be useless, but it could also spread disease to the rest of the vineyard, making it difficult to produce again the following season. Isaiah speaks of God giving everything that was needed to yield good fruit, but instead only worthless grapes were produced:

> *He dug it all around, removed its stones, and planted it with the choicest vine. And He built a tower in the middle of it and also hewed out a wine vat in it; then He expected it to produce good grapes, but it produced only worthless ones.*
>
> (Isaiah 5:2 NASB)

God's plans are for us to bear fruit—eternal fruit that remains. (See John 15:16.) We must abide in God, yielded to His timing and pruning process, which will bring us into full maturity, reaching our potential and fulfilling our purpose in Him.

Study 86

Weep: *Dama'* (דמא), *Baki* (בכי)

"When Jesus therefore saw her weeping,
and the Jews also weeping which came with her,
he groaned in the spirit, and was troubled."
—John 11:33

"Jesus wept."
—John 11:35

I was recently listening to a segment of talk radio where a guest was discussing his new organization, which was trying to raise a million dollars to get off the ground. This organization is being started by a former government undercover agent and a team of former Navy Seals. Their mission is to rescue young children, many between the ages of six and ten, who are being kidnapped right here in America and sold into sexual slavery. After the former undercover agent had finished his appeal, a listener called in and said that nothing ever affects him enough to cause him to weep, but when he heard about the plight of these children, he wept. He added that he has listened to many appeals, but this is the first time he has ever cried over an appeal. When I heard his comments, I instantly thought of the Hebrew and Aramaic word *dama'* (דמא).

Entering Into Someone Else's Heart

In Hebrew, the word for "I weep" is *baki* (בכי), which has a numerical value of 32. The word for heart, *lev* (לב), also has a numerical value of 32. The ancient Jewish sages used to teach that weeping and the heart are related, for weeping comes from the heart. The root word for *baki* (בכי) is *bakah* (בכה), which is *a weeping in the presence of someone*. In both Hebrew and Aramaic, there are two other words for weeping. One is *baka'* (בכא) and refers to *a weeping over one's own grief*. The other is *dama'* (דמא), which is *a weeping over the grieving heart of someone else*. The latter is the kind of weeping that the caller experienced when he heard of the tragedy of those children. He himself was not a child who was being sold into slavery to be sexually abused, yet he grieved over the suffering of children who were in that dire situation, to the point that he was ready to take some action to relieve their suffering.

In John 11:33, we see that Jesus found Mary and others weeping over the loss of Lazarus, Mary's brother and a friend to many in their hometown. When Jesus saw their tears, He also wept. In this passage, two different Greek words are used to express weeping. The word used for the weeping of Mary and the others is *klaiousan*, which is a loud, lamenting, audible type of weeping. The word used for when Jesus wept is *edakrysen*, which comes from the root word *dakryo*, signifying to weep quietly, to shed tears in silence.

The Aramaic Bible uses the word *baka'* (בכא) for the weeping of Mary and the others. This word likewise denotes loud weeping and lamenting, but it also signifies weeping that is in relation to one's own grief. When Jesus wept, the Aramaic word that is used is *dama'* (דמא), which is a weeping over the grief of another. Jesus did not mourn the loss of His friend, because He knew where Lazarus was and that death was only a doorway to the presence of God. But He was still deeply moved by the grief of those who did not fully understand this and of those who were going to miss the immediate presence of this brother and friend. His *dama'* (דמא) for others moved Him to action.

However, while the Aramaic word *dama'* (דמא) is very similar to the Greek word *dakryo*, it goes much further in its Semitic roots, because *dama'* (דמא) has the idea of *entering into someone's heart* and feeling their grief and pain. The man on talk radio who wept over those children claimed he had never wept over any other appeals. He also said that he wanted to present the organization's mission to his church and get them to commit to offering financial support for the work. I began to think that if this man was not normally driven to tears by ministry appeals and was a member of a church where he must have heard numerous such appeals, then perhaps it was not just the grief and pain of the children that he was feeling; it was possible that he had allowed himself to enter God's heart and feel His grief over this tragedy.

Shedding God's Tears

During my week of silence at the Benedictine monastery, I made a deal with God: we would cry on each other's shoulders. If He would weep for me when my heart was broken, I would weep for Him when His heart was broken. Listening to the story of the man attempting to fund his organization to rescue children being sold into sexual slavery was such a moment when God called me to keep my end of the bargain, for I, too, wept as I heard the story of these children. However, I knew and recognized that I had once again entered God's heart and found Him weeping over the suffering of children and their families.

I have heard many Christians relate how, either during worship or at other times, they suddenly found themselves crying for no reason at all. Some say they wake up in the middle of the night sobbing but not knowing why. Or maybe some event that they would normally take little notice of or not be affected by will suddenly drive them into deep sorrow, where they weep heavy, grieving tears. Have you ever experienced anything like that? If you are a follower of Jesus, I am sure that you have at one time or another. We call this empathy; humans have the ability to mourn for others; they have the ability to *dama'* (דמא). But sometimes you need to recognize that these are not your tears. They are the tears of the ones you are weeping over. Then too, you must recognize that they could be the tears of God, who is suffering over the same tragedy. There are times when God will invite you into His heart to share His grief and His sorrow, and to weep with Him.

For many of us, our time of worshipping God is "*Happy Hour,* happy, happy, happy, oh so joyful!" Indeed, to use an analogy from a previous study, when you worship God, He invites you into His heart to share His joy, to experience this joy with others, and to dance in His grand ballroom of celebration. Yet remember that there is another room to His heart, His quiet room, His weeping room; sometimes He will trust you enough to invite you into that room. Let me ask you once more: Are you willing to weep with Him? Are you willing to share in His sorrow, to share in His suffering, as Paul expressed in Philippians 3:10?

Study 87

(God) Will Not Fail: *Lo Yarefeka* (לא ירפך)

"And the Lord, *he it is that doth go before thee; he will be with thee, he will not fail thee, neither forsake thee: fear not, neither be dismayed."*
—Deuteronomy 31:8

"Abused children will always protect the abuser, because it is all they know. They fear the person, hate the circumstances, but anything is better in their eyes than abandonment."
—"Lil K," a woman who spent her childhood in foster care

In our study verse, Moses is encouraging Joshua in front of all the people of Israel as they are about to begin their invasion of the Promised Land. He offers Joshua two assurances, giving him courage and removing any fear. He promises that God will not "*fail*" him or "*forsake*" him. Those two assurances sound like the same thing, and thus seem a bit redundant. I mean, if God will not fail us, that means He has not forsaken us or abandoned us, right?

But in Hebrew, there is a real distinction between failing someone and abandoning someone. The Hebrew word for "*fail*" is *raphah* (רפה). This word is used when someone is pulling on a rope and his strength is beginning to fail. It is used for someone who is growing tired and weary of doing a task.

Failing—or Forsaking?

As a pastor, I would make frequent visits to a member of my church who was bedridden with rheumatoid arthritis. Her name was Daisy, and her husband's name was Harold. I always found Harold at her bedside, caring for his Daisy, cooking meals for her, emptying her bedpan, bathing her, and holding her hand every opportunity he had. Harold never *raphah* (רפה), or *failed*, her. He never grew weary or tired of caring for his Daisy.

But one day, Harold had a heart attack and was admitted to the hospital. When I went to visit him there, the first question he asked was about the well-being of his Daisy and whether she being cared for. I sat and listened to him as he talked about being in the hospital and failing his wife. He wept as his heart broke over the fact that he was unable to care for her. Harold had not failed his Daisy emotionally; neither had he grown mentally tired of caring for her. Rather, his body had failed because it had become weary from its caretaking tasks. That is an example of *raphah* (רפה), growing weary and tired in relation to a task, either mentally or physically. Sometimes, we are just not physically up to a task; that is *raphah* (רפה).

Harold's whole life was caring for his Daisy; she was his reason for living. He did not come out of that hospital but went to be with the Lord shortly after my visit. And although Daisy did not have a life-threatening illness and was given good care in a nursing home, she joined her Harold only a month later.

We know that God never grows emotionally weary or physically tired, although we sometimes think He will grow tired of putting up with us. Yet He will never give up on us, either emotionally or physically. We have the assurance that He will not *raphah* (רפה), or fail, us. It is interesting that the word *raphah* (רפה) is in a hiphal (causative) form, indicating that nothing will cause God to fail us—no lack of strength or desire. No matter how rotten and low-down we are, it will not cause Him to give up on us.

While Harold was in the hospital, I could not reassure him that he was not failing his Daisy, because, in effect, he was; but I could reassure him that he had not *'azab* (עזב) her, which is the Hebrew word for "*forsake*" or "abandon." *'Azab* (עזב) means to abandon someone and leave them helpless, without any recourse. Daisy was assigned another caregiver while Harold was in the hospital, and Harold insisted that he speak almost hourly with that caregiver, directing her on how to care for his Daisy. So, even though Daisy was now under the care of someone else, Harold was still directing that care. Even though Harold was not physically able to be with his wife, Daisy knew her Harold was still watching out for her. Then, when Harold went to be with the Lord, Daisy must have felt *'azab* (עזב), or "abandoned," so that she lost her will to live.

God Will Never Abandon Us

If God could *raphah* (רפה), or *fail*, us by growing weary or tired, we might still manage somehow. But if He were to *'azab* (עזב), or *abandon* us, well, I don't know about you, but that would be something I could not handle. As expressed in the quote at the beginning of this word study by a woman named "Lil K," who grew up in foster care, "Anything is better…than abandonment." The thought of being abandoned by God is more terrifying to me that the idea of His failing to heal me or to rescue me from financial disaster. I could handle something like that. I could endure having a broken body or having to stand on a street corner with a paper cup asking for money to survive. But if God *abandoned* me, then all I would have is despair.

So, God promises not to *raphah* (רפה), or *fail*, us, and that is good news—but it gets even better. He also promises never to *'azab* (עזב), or *abandon* us, and that is life-giving news!

Study 88

(God Is) Singing to Us: *Zimarath* (זמרת)

"*Thou* {pushed me hard and I nearly fell}:
but the Lord *helped me. The* Lord *is my strength and song,*
and is become my salvation."
—Psalm 118:13–14

The syntax in Psalm 118:14 is open to debate. The Hebrew word for "*song*" is pointed up in the Masoretic text as a noun. However, the more I examine it, I believe that the ancient Jewish sages who lived hundreds of years before the Masoretic text had it right in the first place. They indicated the writer intended the word translated as "*song*" to be a participle. That would render the verse as follows: "The Lord is my strength, and He is *singing to me* because He is my salvation."

Does it seem strange to you that God would sing to David? Everything in nature has a certain rhythm, reflecting the design and musicality of God. I remember listening to an interview with Andraé Crouch, the legendary gospel singer and songwriter. He told how a woman came up to him and said she did not like his music because of the beat, or rhythm, that he used. He said, "Oh, you mean a rhythm like this?" He began to play a certain rhythm on the piano, and the woman said, "Yes, that's it, that rhythm and beat, that's of the devil." Andraé Crouch replied, "That's strange, because that is the rhythm of your heartbeat."

Singing in Harmony with God

The context of Psalm 118 may be that of David being tempted by the enemy to kill Saul (see 1 Samuel 24) and then Nabal (see 1 Samuel 25:2–35)—which he almost did—but the Lord helped him. The Lord delivered David by strengthening him and also perhaps by singing a song to him. The Hebrew word for *"song"* is *zamar* (זמר), a term that is also used to describe pruning or cutting. My study partner helped to shed new light on this word for me, which is why I also included the previous verse, Psalm 118:13, as part of our study text. The sages teach that God sang a song to David to cut away his *yetzer hara* (יצר הרע), or his "evil inclinations." As I've noted in previous studies, the Hebrew word *tov* (טוב), meaning "good," also signifies "to be in harmony with God." As the Lord sang to David, and as David sang to God in harmony, the enemy no longer had an opportunity to overcome David with temptation.

What? Do you really think that God is merely sitting up there in heaven with His arms folded and His legs crossed, listening to us sing our praises to Him while we worship? I mean, are we singing our praises to Him during our worship services just to entertain Him? Is He evaluating us like some judge of an amateur show? My singing voice is so bad that when I sing, I can make Sparky, my neighbor's pit bull, howl. (That is how I get my revenge on him.) But I know there is one Person who can sing in harmony with me, and that is God. When I sing to Him, it is not to entertain Him. Rather, it is like what you see in those old-time movies you can watch on YouTube where two lovers are singing to each other. I watched a segment of an old movie the other day, and I could see the appeal to the romantics of the 1930s. As the two sang to each other, it was if their harmonization created a bond and oneness between them.

God Rejoices Over Us

In contrast to Psalm 118:14, there is no mistaking the syntax in Zephaniah 3:17, which says that God will rejoice over us with *"singing."* He will actually sing over us! The Hebrew word for *"singing"* there is *ranan* (רנן), which is *a song of praise*. There are many different songs—songs of praise, songs of devotion, songs of correction, songs of pruning, and so forth. Do you ever find yourself suddenly just singing some song of praise or worship? Perhaps we can compare this to another of those old movies where the hero is wandering in the forest searching for his beloved, and he hears her singing off in the distance. He begins to follow her voice, singing back to her. They continue singing to each other until the hero finds his beloved—who has been tied up by some villain. The hero appears in all his splendor, and the villain cowers and flees from him, leaving him alone with his beloved.

God is singing out to you, searching for your heart. When you sing back to Him, He begins to resonate with you, and you start to sing in harmony with Him. When that happens, the villain (the enemy) flees from you—from the presence of God. Thus, when we resonate with God, singing in harmony with Him, the enemy doesn't stand a chance to succeed in his temptations.

As you worship God, do you hear Him singing to you? Have you ever considered singing back to Him or in harmony with Him, rather than just singing to Him?

Study 89

To Fear (God): *Yara'* (ירא)

"The fear of the Lord is clean, enduring for ever."
—Psalm 19:9

I recently read a story about a pastor in Uzbekistan who preached from Hebrews 10:34, even though not a single person was listening to his sermon. Nobody was listening because no one else was even present—his congregation was too afraid of being arrested to attend church. But this pastor was called to preach, so he preached to a congregation of one—himself.

If God has called you to preach or to teach, it doesn't matter if you have a congregation or a classroom; you will preach or teach just for the joy of proclaiming the Word of God in some overt way. The dashboard on my blog indicates that I have hits from over two hundred countries around the world; nevertheless, I approach my studies every day with this thought: *Well, I am certainly not going to send this one out.* But I usually do. After I read over what I have written, I think that I might as well hit the "send" button. However, writing these little studies under the impression that no one will really read them gives me the freedom to express my thoughts without fear of offending someone.

There are various kinds of fear—the fear of offending people with one's ideas; the fear of being arrested and persecuted for one's faith; and many more. But in this study, we're going to focus on a particular kind of fear, the "*fear of the Lord.*" The fear of the Lord is a topic I have tackled on a number of occasions, but I have done so under the general assumption that I had a congregation of one—myself. Yet what I write in this study is in response to a question from someone who actually does read my studies online and wanted to know what it means to "fear" the Lord.

Perceiving God as a Threat to Us

I personally believe that the use of the word "*fear*" in Psalm 19:9 is an unfortunate rendering. This is because, in the English language, the word *fear* has gone through an evolutionary process in the last five hundred years. Speaking of evolution, it was Charles Darwin who helped to establish our modern definition of the word *fear* through his book *The Expression of the Emotions in Man and Animals*, published in 1872. Even before this, by the early part of the nineteenth century, the definition of *fear* in English had narrowed to mean *an emotional response to a perceived threat.* Thus, since then—for most of the nineteenth century, through the twentieth century, and now into the twenty-first century—Christians have mainly viewed the phrase "the fear of the Lord" as conveying the idea that God is a threat to us. (It appears that old Charlie Darwin may have damaged Christianity more with his definitions than with his theories.)

Moreover, the Old English word for *fear* is *fryhto*, which means "an awe-inspiring event." By the time of the King James Version, the meaning of the word *fear* in English was a combination of an awe-inspiring event and a terrifying event. As the church depended heavily on fear to keep its members in line, English translators found the word *fear* to be quite an adequate translation for the Hebrew word *yara'* (ירא). Consequently, we understand fear as an emotional response to a danger or a perceived threat, and "to fear the Lord" means to see God as a danger or a threat—that is, as the Judge who will punish us if we sin. The end result is that we tend to avoid sin out of a fear of God's lightning bolts rather than out of a fear of wounding His heart. Fortunately, many modern translations are dropping the word *fear* in favor of the word *honor* or *respect*, which is more in line with the Hebrew word *yara'* (ירא). Still, we cannot adequately translate the word *yara'* (ירא) into English using just one word.

Accepting God's Power, Love, and Heart

So, let's explore the meaning of *yara'* (ירא), which is spelled yod (י), resh (ר), aleph (א). First, the yod (י) is actually the word for "hand" and represents *the complete power of God*. As I mentioned in an earlier study, in ancient times, it was believed that the heart rested in the palm of one's hand, and the hand is the part of the body that one views the most. Additionally, *yara'* (ירא) is rooted in an ancient Akkadian word. In its Semitic root, to fear one's god was *to take the hand of* one's god. That meant to accept his power to go into battle. Therefore, for us to fear God would mean that we accept *His power, His love,* and *His heart*.

Second, the letter resh (ר) represents the head—leadership or authority. Accordingly, to fear the Lord also means to accept God's *leadership, headship,* and *authority* in our lives. The final letter, aleph (א), represents *unity*, and *oneness with God*.

Thus, the built-in commentary in the word *yara'* (ירא) tells us that to fear the Lord means *to accept His power, His love, and His heart; to let His hand rest upon us; and to submit ourselves to His authority and become one with Him*. Now, if we are to look for one English word to fit *yara'* (ירא), don't you think that the word *honor, respect,* or *reverence* would be a better match than *fear*, as we use it in the twenty-first century?

Fearing to Wound God's Heart

But soft: there is an additional element to the word *yara'* (ירא) in its Semitic root, one that we have previously discussed. It originates with Assyrian mothers tattooing their sons' names on the palms of their hands. This practice demonstrated *honor, respect,* and *love* for their sons—but also something else. An Assyrian mother recognized that her son was going off to war to protect her and the rest of the family. She knew that because her son was fighting, she was safe. There was no threat to her, but the threat was to her son, and therefore her fear was not for her own safety but for his.

Yes, the word *yara'* (ירא) can mean to be afraid or to feel a threat, yet it is not a threat to us but to the one whom we love. To fear God means to fear that we may in some way be a threat to Him—the God whom we love, the God who is protecting us. There is only one thing that can harm God, and that is if we betray our love for Him, if we abuse His love and break His heart. With this understanding, we do not keep from sin because we fear that God will punish us. We avoid sin because we fear we may wound God's heart.

Oh, by the way, Psalm 19:9 tells us that *"the fear of the Lord"*—that is, the fear of wounding God's heart—*"is clean."* The word for *"clean"* is *tahar* (טהר), which means "purifying." The fear of wounding God's heart will purify all our motives for serving God and avoiding sin.

Study 90

This, Too, Shall Pass: *Gam Zah Yavur* (גם זה יעבור)

"And he changeth the times and the seasons: he removeth kings, and setteth up kings: he giveth wisdom unto the wise, and knowledge to them that know understanding."
—Daniel 2:21

"This, too, shall pass."
—Attar of Nishapur

Attar of Nishapur, a Persian Sufi poet, told the story of a great and powerful king who assembled all his wise man and demanded that they create a ring with an inscription that would make him happy when he was sad and sad when he was happy. After some deliberation, the sages handed the king a ring with this inscription: THIS, TOO, SHALL PASS. It is believed that this story is a reference to King Nebuchadnezzar and Daniel. Although this account is not found in Scripture, I thought I would deviate from my usual examination of biblical words in this last word study to examine the old Hebrew phrase *Gam zah yavur* (גם זה יעבור), or "This, too, shall pass," which is so engrained in the Jewish culture.

God's Love and Protection in the Midst of Great Changes

In Jewish folklore, it is told that Solomon was humbled when this phrase was passed to him. Throughout Jewish history, as the people of God have gone through various periods of captivity and persecution, and even the Holocaust, the phrase *Gam zah yavur* (גם זה יעבור) has been spoken and often inscripted with just the first letter of each word—gimmel (ג), zayin (ז), yod (י). I once read how a rabbi expanded on this proverb by giving the meaning behind each letter. The gimmel (ג) represents the loving-kindness of God, the zayin (ז) denotes the protection of God, and the yod (י) signifies that radical changes are beginning to take place.

The context of our Scripture text, Daniel 2:21, is that Daniel was living in captivity. He had been a prince and a noble from Israel, of the house of Judah, in the line from which the kings of Judah came. But the Babylonians conquered Judah, and Daniel was carried off to Babylon, removed from his family, his position, and—worst of all—the beloved temple where the presence of God rested. He was forced to serve and train in the court of the pagan King Nebuchadnezzar, with the idea that he would eventually return to his homeland to be a puppet governmental leader for the king, to do his bidding and to turn the Hebrew culture into a Babylonian one. However, God afflicted King Nebuchadnezzar with illness, domestic problems, and foreign invasion to prevent this from happening.

Still, in the midst of all this, things got worse for Daniel. Nebuchadnezzar had a dream that no one could describe or interpret, so he gave the order to kill *"all the wise men of Babylon"* (Daniel 2:12)—which included Daniel and his friends, who were also Hebrews. But they prayed, and God not only revealed the dream to Daniel but also its interpretation. What Daniel saw and what he related to King Nebuchadnezzar was, in a sense, *Gimmel zah yavur* (גם זה יעבור), "This, too, shall pass." God was planning to make great changes, and no matter how powerful the king might be, he would be unable to prevent them from taking place.

In the revelation Daniel received, he saw the rise of the Persian Empire, which would bring an end to the Babylonian Empire; he saw the rise of the Greek Empire, which would bring an end to the Persian Empire; he saw the rise of the Roman Empire, which would bring an end to the Greek Empire; and he saw the fall of the Roman Empire, which would be brought down by God Himself. Technically, the Roman Empire never really fell. Even today, the government of the most powerful nation on earth, the United States, is based on the governmental system of the Roman Empire. It wasn't so much the empires themselves that were being brought down but the governmental systems that man had created in order to rule and to control. In the final days, after man has had the opportunity to establish the best possible governmental systems, God is going to come along and set up His own governmental system that will be perfection against man's imperfection.

God's Perfect Government Is Coming

Today, as we look at the news and grumble about all the events going on in our government, we should never lose sight of *Gam zah yavur* (גם זה יעבור), "This, too, shall pass." Yes, God will eventually bring even our own governmental system down, but one day He will establish His perfect government. Second Timothy 2:12 tells us that in that government, we will rule and reign with Him, if we endure the sufferings we are going through now.

So, the next time your car breaks down, your job disappears, or a bill comes due that you can't pay, just remember: *Gam zah yavur* (גם זה יעבור), "This, too, shall pass." But more important, remember the following from the meaning of the first letters of each word: gimmel (ג), the loving-kindness of God, will zayin (ז), protect and defend you, until the yod (י), or great changes that God is planning, take place.

Glossary

Aramaic: A sister language of Hebrew that has many dialects. Hebrew essentially became a dead language during the time of the Babylonian captivity circa 597 BC. The Hebrew of the Jews was blended into the Aramaic, which was the language of the Babylonians. Then, when the exiled Jews returned to Palestine, Aramaic became their national language, with Classical Hebrew remaining only as a ceremonial language. Various dialects of Aramaic were in use during Jesus' day. Most likely, Jesus spoke the Northern, or Old Galilean, dialect, which was very idiomatic, while those in Jerusalem spoke the Southern dialect that was more formal. (See also **Classical Hebrew.**)

chiriq: A vowel with a long *e* sound, as in *teeth.*

Classical Hebrew: Classical Hebrew is the language in which the Old Testament was written. Also known as biblical Hebrew, it is an archaic form of the Hebrew language that existed as a spoken language until the time of the Jews' captivity by Babylon, circa 597 BC, after which it was blended with and replaced by the Aramaic language. Many scholars believe that Classical Hebrew essentially became a dead language at this time and that, by the first century AD, it existed only as a ceremonial language. Although Modern Hebrew developed from Classical Hebrew, the two forms have many differences.

cohortative: A verbal form that can express self-encouragement; a wish; or a plea, request, or permission. (See also **verbal form.**)

conjunction: A part of speech that connects words, clauses, phrases, and sentences. The conjunction in Hebrew is signified by the letter vav (ו), which can be rendered as *and*, *or*, or *nor*. Deciding which English word to apply in a particular sentence depends upon the context.

construct form: A very common grammatical form in Semitic languages. Nouns are placed in a construct form when they are modified by another noun in a genitive (showing possession) construction.

cuneiform abtar: One of several of the earliest known systems of writing in which the scribes used a blunt reed as a stylus, pushing the reed into a soft, clay tablet to make a wedge-shaped mark. Many Semitic languages used this form of writing, including the Akkadian, the Sumerian, the Hittite, the Ugaritic, and the Old Persian languages. (See also **Ugaritic.**)

Dead Sea Scrolls: Also known as the Qumran Caves Scrolls, the Dead Sea Scrolls are a collection of 981 different texts discovered between 1946 and 1956 in eleven caves near the ancient settlement at Khirbet Qumran in the West Bank, a few miles from the shore of the Dead Sea and thirteen miles east of Jerusalem. The collection has proven to be of great religious and linguistic significance, as it includes the second-oldest known surviving manuscripts of works that were included in the Hebrew Bible. Fragments of every book in the Old Testament, with the exception of Esther, have been identified in the scrolls. The Isaiah scroll is relatively intact and is one thousand years older than any previously known copy of the book. The collection also contains prophecies by Ezekiel, Jeremiah, and Daniel, as well as psalms attributed to King David and to Joshua, that are not found in the Hebrew Bible. Also found in the scrolls but not in the Hebrew Bible are the last words of Joseph, Judah, Levi, Naphtali, and

Amram, who was the father of Moses. Most important, the Dead Sea Scrolls predate the Masoretic text, thus shedding new light on the accuracy of that text, which is the basis for most English Bible translations and is the standard text used in Bible colleges and seminaries. (See also **Masoretes.**)

final form: Also known as a *sofit letter.* Five of the twenty-two letters of the Hebrew alphabet are formed differently when they appear as the last letter of a word. In the original Hebrew text, there were no spaces between words. The reader could know only from his personal knowledge where one word ended and where the next word began. However, five letters did have a different appearance when they were found at the end of a word, indicating that the next letter was the first letter of a new word. These five letters are the following: kap (כ), with a final form of (ך); mem (מ), with a final form of (ם); nun (נ), with a final form of (ן); pe (פ), with a final form of (ף); and sade (צ), with a final form of (ץ). (See also **Hebrew alphabet.**)

Gematria: A practice in which Orthodox rabbis, using the numerical value of a Hebrew word, would seek to find a relationship between it and other Hebrew words that shared the same numerical value. This method is not to be confused with numerology, which places a mystical meaning on numbers. It was simply a teaching tool to guide one into a deeper understanding of the Scriptures. (See also **numerical value.**)

Greek: The Greek of the New Testament is called Koine Greek and was the universal language of people living in the Eastern Mediterranean region under the Roman Empire.

Hebrew alphabet: The Hebrew alphabet consists of twenty-two consonants. Four of these letters—aleph (א), hei (ה), vav (ו), and yod (י)—are also used interchangeably as vowels. Writing in Hebrew is read from right to left. (See also **Classical Hebrew.**)

Hebrew: See **Classical Hebrew.**

hiphal: A verbal form expressing a causative action, as in "I will cause my voice to be heard." (See also **verbal form.**)

hithpael: A verbal form that is reflexive, as in "I will cause myself to hear my voice." (See also **verbal form.**)

holem: A vowel making a long *o* sound, as in "*row* a boat."

idiom: An idiom is a language, dialect, or style of speaking peculiar to a people. For instance, in the Southern dialect of Aramaic, the term "born again" means being born a second time physically. However, in the Northern, or Old Galilean, dialect of Aramaic, "born again" is an idiomatic expression that could mean either a spiritual rebirth, a physical rebirth, or even an entering into a new faith or a new philosophical understanding. Someone from Judah who spoke the Southern dialect of Aramaic, as did the Pharisee Nicodemus, would likely not immediately pick up on the idiom spoken by Jesus, who was from Galilee and spoke the Northern dialect. (See John 3.)

imperative: A verbal form expressing a command or a supplication, as in "Hear my voice, O Lord." (See also **verbal form.**)

infinitive: Hebrew has two infinitives: an infinitive absolute and an infinitive construct. The infinitive absolute is used for focus or emphasis. The infinitive construct is used after prepositions and has a pronominal ending to indicate its subject. (See also **preposition** and **pronominal.**)

interrogative: A word that introduces a question, such as *who, what, where*, or *why.*

lexicon: A wordbook, or dictionary, of an ancient, dead language, such as Latin, ancient Greek, or Classical Hebrew.

lexicographer: A compiler and/or writer of ancient words and their meanings that are included in a lexicon.

Masoretes: A group of Jewish scribe scholars who worked between the sixth century and the tenth century AD. They were responsible for compiling a system of pronunciational and grammatical guides in the form of diacritical notes on the external form of the biblical text in an attempt to establish an authoritative fix on the pronunciation of the Hebrew Bible, as well as on paragraph and verse divisions. At this time, the Jews were scattered throughout the world, and Hebrew had become essentially a dead language, surviving only with ceremonial usage. With six centuries of Jews living in foreign nations and learning to speak many different languages, there was a fear that the original pronunciation of the Hebrew language would be lost without some indication of vowels in the written text. The Masoretes took it upon themselves to add these vowels, which are still widely used today. The resulting Masoretic text of the Old Testament is the standard Hebrew Bible used in today's Bible colleges and seminaries and among Bible translators.

messianic passage: A passage of Scripture from the Old Testament that is believed to be a reference to Jesus.

minyan: A quorum of ten Jewish adults required for public prayer, or a gathering of Jews to perform religious obligations.

Midrash: "A Hebrew word referring to the exposition, or exegesis, of a biblical text. The term can also refer to a specific compilation of midrashic teachings. The two basic types of midrash are known as *Midrash Aggadah*, regarding the ethical or spiritual exposition of a text, and *Midrash Halakhah*, referring to the exegesis of biblically-related Jewish law." (See http://www.newworldencyclopedia.org/entry/Midrash.)

Mishnah: See Talmud.

motif: A dominate idea in an artistic or literary composition. For instance, Psalm 23 follows a shepherd motif.

niphal: A verb that denotes a passive or reflexive voice, as in "My voice was heard by me."

numerical value: This term refers to a quasi-decimal numbering system using the letters of the Hebrew alphabet in which every word is assigned a numerical value. For instance, the word for "weeping" in Hebrew is *baki* (בכי). Beth (ב) represents the number 2, kap (כ) represents the number 20, and yod (י) represents the number 10. Since the total of these three numbers is 32, the numerical value of the word *baki* is 32. Some Orthodox Jews, in order to express a spiritual truth, sought to find relationships between Hebrew words that have the same numerical value. For instance, the word for "heart" is lev (לב). Lamed (ל) is the number 30, and beth (ב) is the number 2. So, the word for "heart," *lev* (לב), has a numerical value of 32, the same value as the word for "weeping," *baki* (בכי). The Orthodox rabbis would use this numerical equivalency to illustrate that all weeping comes from the heart. (See also **Gematria** and **Orthodox Jews.**)

Orthodox Jews: "Judaism that adheres to the Torah and Talmud as interpreted in an authoritative rabbinic law code and applies their principles and regulations to modern living." (See *Merriam-Webster's 11th Collegiate Dictionary.*)

paragogic: This term refers to a grammatical form that is debated among Hebrew scholars. Generally, it is believed that the practice of adding the letter nun (נ) or hei (ה) to a word indicates emphasis, though some scholars believe that these letters may refer to different parts of speech and that they do not signify emphasis.

participle: As with the English language, the Hebrew participle is a verbal adjective—it functions like an adjective but is constructed from a verb. In English, a participle usually ends with *ing*, indicating a present state of action. Although there are no tenses in Hebrew, the Hebrew participle often reflects a present tense.

Phoenician: The ancient Phoenician alphabet is also known as the Proto-Canaanite alphabet. It is sometimes referred to as Ancient

Hebrew but is more accurately described as the Paleo-Hebrew script. It was used in the Hebrew language prior to the development of the square script. The Phoenician alphabet is consonantal, having been derived from Egyptian hieroglyphics. Many of its symbols are based on pagan gods and goddesses. (See also **square script.**)

piel: A verbal form showing intensity, as in "My voice was profoundly heard." (See also **verbal form.**)

play on words: A play on words, or a wordplay, is the use of a single word to bear two meanings in the same context. There are numerous wordplays in the Hebrew Bible. For instance, in Genesis 1:1, we find the first play on words: *"In the beginning God created...."* The word *"beginning"* is translated from the Hebrew *bereshit* (בראשׁית), and the word *"created"* is translated from *bara'* (ברא). When God constructed the story of creation, He twice used the same three letters (ברא) that form the root word of the verb "to create," which is so crucial to the entire story.

prefix: All root words in Hebrew can be built upon by using a prefix (an additional letter or letters at the beginning of a word) or a suffix (an additional letter or letters at the end of a word) to indicate person, gender, singular or plural, pronoun, article, preposition, or conjunction. (See also **article, conjunction, pronoun, preposition,** and **triliteral root.**)

preposition: As in the English language, a Hebrew preposition shows a noun's relationship to another word. In English, prepositions include words such as *from, in, on,* and *unto.* In Hebrew, a preposition is often attached to a word as a prefix. (See also **prefix.**)

pronominal: A pronoun that is attached to the end of a word as a suffix. (See also **pronoun** and **prefix.**)

pronoun: A word that stands in place of a noun, such as *me, he,* or *she.* In Hebrew, a pronoun can be a separate word, or it can be built into a word as a suffix. (See also **prefix** and **pronominal.**)

qal: A simple verb in an active voice, as in "His voice was heard."

rabbinic literature: The entire spectrum of rabbinic writings throughout Jewish history. The term is also used more specifically to refer to literature during the Talmudic era after AD 200.

remez: This word literally means "a hint." In rabbinic teaching, the teacher would use a part of a Scripture passage or a story from oral tradition in a discussion, assuming that his hearers' knowledge of the Scripture passage or story would allow them to deduce a fuller meaning in the teaching. For example, in one of His parables, Jesus spoke of the *"pearl of great price,"* asking the people, in essence, "Would a man not sell all he owns to possess a pearl of great price?" (See Matthew 13:45–46.) Jesus did not tell the entire story about the pearl of great price from oral tradition, knowing that everyone listening had already heard it, possibly by their mothers as a bedtime story when they were children. It was the story of a merchant who was told by a prophet that God would take away his wealth because he was dealing in pearls that were unclean. Out of fear of losing his wealth, he searched the world for a *pearl of great price*, and when he found it, he rejoiced and sold everything he owned to purchase this pearl so that he could hold his entire wealth in his hand, and no one could take it away from him. Jesus' use of the words *"pearl of great price"* was a *remez*, or a hint, that He was offering His audience a deeper meaning in His teaching than the story alone.

scribes: A group of Palestinian scholars and teachers of Jewish law and tradition who were active from the sixth century BC to the first century AD. As well as being authorities on the law, they could read and write, and they often transcribed, edited, and interpreted the Bible.

segol: A vowel making a short *e* sound, as in *red*.

secondary rendering: A secondary rendering is also known as an "alternative rendering." It is a translation from the ancient language that is grammatically and linguistically correct but not commonly accepted by church tradition. For instance, in Judges 11:31, Jephthah makes a vow to God, saying, *"Then it shall be, that whatsoever cometh forth of the doors of my house to meet me, when I return in peace from the children of Ammon, shall surely be the LORD's, and I will offer it up for a burnt offering."* When Jephthah's daughter comes out to greet him, he does according to his vow. (See verses 35–38.) The word *"and"* in verse 31 is the conjunction *vav*, which could also be rendered as *or*. Traditionally, we render the *vav* as *and*, which would mean he offered his daughter up as a burnt offering. A secondary, or alternative, rendering would use the conjunction *or*, which would then indicate an option to either give something to the Lord or offer it up as a burnt offering, suggesting that Jephthah did not offer his daughter as a burnt offering but rather dedicated her to the Lord for life.

Semitic root: All Semitic languages have root words. Among these Semitic languages are the Akkadian language; the Assyrian language; the Aramaic language, which was the language of the Babylonians; the Persian language, from which present-day Arabic developed; the Canaanite language; and the Phoenician language. These languages are interrelated through words whose roots are common among the Semitic languages. For this reason, we can often gain insight into a Hebrew word by examining its origins in other Semitic tongues. (See also **triliteral root**.)

Septuagint: The Septuagint is also known as the Greek Old Testament. It is a translation of the Hebrew Bible into Koine Greek, or an Egyptian Greek. It derives its name (often identified by the Roman numerals LXX), from the seventy Jewish scholars who completed the translation circa the second century BC. The Septuagint is often quoted in the New Testament, particularly by the apostle Paul in his letters. The story behind the Septuagint centers on Ptolemy II, who was king of Ptolemaic Egypt from about 283–246 BC. He was the promoter of the Library of Alexandria and reigned during the height of the literary splendor of the Alexandrian court. Greek literature from that time reflects quotations from

Jewish law, and possibly from this Jewish influence, as well as from the fact that the Hebrew language was quickly becoming extinct, Ptolemy commissioned seventy Jewish scholars to translate the Old Testament into Koine Greek. It is believed by many (although it is disputed among some scholars who consider it legend) that these seventy scholars were forbidden to consult with each other during the translation process and that when they concluded their translations, all seventy were in perfect agreement. Recent discoveries from the Dead Sea Scrolls have shown that the Septuagint carries a higher degree of accuracy than the Masoretic text.

shureq: A vowel making a long *u* sound, as in *true.*

square script: Square script is also known as block script. Used in Hebrew writing today, it came into existence around the time of the Jewish captivity period in the sixth century BC. It is believed by some that it was developed by the scribe Ezra to replace the Phoenician script that was used prior to this time in Hebrew writing. This theory carries the idea that the letters in the Phoenician script were rooted in pagan symbols used in idolatry, and Ezra and his scribes sought to develop a script that would be free of any pagan influences.

suffix: See **prefix**.

syntax: This term refers to the arrangement of words to form a sentence. In English, much depends upon word order, but in the Hebrew language, the order of the words is not as important. For example, in English we say, *"In the beginning, God created…the earth"* (Genesis 1:1). We know by the placement of the verb *"created"* that God created the earth—not that the earth created God. However, in the Hebrew, this meaning isn't as apparent by the word order; therefore, the Hebrew word designating *"the earth"* is preceded by an *'eth* (את), which is not an actual word but rather a symbol for a direct object, indicating that God is doing the action, and the earth is the direct object receiving the action. Some people have argued that Hebrew has no set rule of syntax, so that we must depend upon the context alone to determine the word order. However, most scholars disagree with that theory.

Talmud: A collection derived from oral tradition and commentaries, consisting of the Mishnah (oral laws) and Gemara (commentaries). There are two editions of the Talmud. One was produced in Palestine around AD 400. The other, which is the most commonly used, was produced in Babylonia around AD 500, and is written in Tannaitic (Mishnaic) Hebrew and Aramaic.

Torah: The word *Torah* is sometimes used for the first five books of the Tanach, or Old Testament, known as the Pentateuch. Other times, it refers to the Old Testament as a whole. The term is also used to refer to the parchment scroll on which the Pentateuch is written, or even to denote the entire body of Jewish religious literature and teaching contained in the Old Testament and the Talmud. Like many words in Hebrew, the meaning changes according to the context in which it is used.

triliteral root: The majority of Hebrew words are built upon a three-consonant root word that contains the very basic meaning of the Hebrew word. Hebrew words were developed by adding various vowels and any of numerous prefixes and suffixes to the root word. From a cluster of consonants, any number of words can be derived that share the same root.

Ugaritic: A Northwest Semitic language that was rediscovered in 1928 in the ruined city of Ugarit, Syria, which was destroyed circa 1180–1170 BC. It is one of the oldest phonetically-based languages written in a cuneiform abjab (alphabet without vowels) on clay tablets, and was used around the fifteenth century BC. It is also the oldest example of the family of West Semitic scripts that was used for the Phoenician, Hebrew, and Aramaic languages. Its grammatical features are highly similar to that of the Hebrew grammar. The Ugaritic language has been used by scholars of the

Hebrew Bible to clarify biblical Hebrew texts. (See also **Aramaic**, **cuneiform**, **Hebrew**, and **Phoenician**.)

verbal forms: Verbal forms are also referred to as the grammatical properties of a verb, which must be considered in the translation process. These properties indicate person, number, gender, voice, mode, and tense, as well as whether the verb is weak or strong.

vowel pointings: Vowel pointings are also known as *niqqud*. In rabbinic Hebrew, the consonants aleph (א), hei (ה), vav (ו), and yod (י) may also serve as vowels. Around the sixth century AD, the Masoretes created a system of diacritical signs used to represent vowels or to distinguish between alternate pronunciations of letters in the Hebrew alphabet. This system of vowel pointings is used today in modern Israeli orthography for specialized works, such as dictionaries, books of poetry, or texts for children and new immigrants to aid in learning to speak the language. (See also **Masoretes**.)

Hebrew–English Index

'alal (אלל): no; not; a negative word (Study 42)

'amad (עמד): standing or pausing to contemplate (Study 41)

'aman (אמן): to stand firm, immoveable (Study 41)

'amaquth (עמקות): deep things; that which is unsearchable (Study 3)

'amar (עמר): sheaves; stalks of grain tied together; people who are self-seeking (Study 13)

'amar (אמר): to speak; a word; ordinary conversation (Study 24)

'anah (ענה): to be humbled (Study 8)

'anah (ענה): to make; to produce something; to create something (Study 70)

'anah (אנה): to sigh or express deep feelings of relief (Study 36)

'aneph (אבף): anger; expressing strong emotion; the snorting of a camel (Study 12)

'apar (עפר): dust; young man (Study 53)

'arak (ארך): health; to restore; to cure, in the sense of creating longevity (Study 20)

'aram (עירם): naked (questionable root); to act prudently, wisely, or cautiously (Study 55)

'arar (ארר): curse; cursed; to be without protection (Study 23)

'asar (אצר): storehouse; treasures that are laid up but not hidden (Study 38)

'aterat (עטרת): a crown, one which encircles the head (Study 77)

'ashar (אשר): blessing; happiness; moving in the direction of peace and happiness (Study 33)

'atar (עתר): to entreat; to show favor (Study 35)

’atsab (עצב): to worship with sorrow (Study 10)

’atsah (עצה): twig; stick; branch; tree trunk; tree (Study 27)

’aval (איל): horned animal; any animal with horns—a goat, a deer, a ram, or a horned bull (Study 61)

’avar (אבר): feathers (Study 40)

’aveq (אבק): to wrestle; to get dusty; dust; fragrant powder (Study 22)

’ayakah (איכה): “Where are you?”; a cry of grief and mourning; a lamentation (Study 55)

’ayar (עיר): to be in agony, as in the agony of death (Study 55)

’azavu (עזבו): to leave behind; to forsake; to step back from (Study 57)

baali (בעלי): my master, as to a slave; a husband in a loveless marriage or a marriage of convenience (Study 11)

badad (בדד): to be alone, solitary, separated (Study 22)

baka’ (בכא): to weep over one’s own grief (Study 86)

bakah (בכה): to weep in the presence of someone (Study 86)

bakal (בכל): with all (Study 42)

baqash (בקשׁ): to seek; to ask; can be an act of worship when used in relation to God; a longing (Study 35)

bara’ (ברא): to create; to form something brand new (Study 20)

barak (ברך): to be blessed; to make happy (Study 33)

basar (בשׂר): flesh; to seek the counsel of man (Study 23)

batsa’ (בצע): to plunder; to gain at the expense of another (Study 18)

basur (בצור): rock (Study 30)

batach (בטח): to trust; to cling or adhere to something; to be welded to something (Study 23; Study 51)

batsar (בצר): a pruning (Study 1)

bo' (בוא): coming into; being a part of; having intercourse with (Study 26)

chakah (חכה): to wait; to be patient; to hold back (Study 33)

chalah (חלה): to be exhausted; to be diseased; to be weak; to be feeble; to be afflicted; griefs; physical sickness and pain; mental anguish (Study 8, Study 80)

chalam (חלם): dream (Study 25)

chamah (חמה): barrier; wall of defense (Study 60)

chamor (חמר): donkey; fermenting; foaming (Study 28)

chamor (חמר): standing in fear (Study 41)

chanan (חנן): gracious—carrying the idea of compassion and favor (Study 33)

chaqaq (חקק): to imprint; to engrave; to tattoo; to imagine (Study 60)

chasad (חסד): loving-kindness; mercy (Study 17; Study 79)

chasah (חסה): to trust; a shelter, a place of protection (Study 24)

chasak (חשׂך): that which is restrained (Study 3)

chashak (חשך): darkness (Study 3)

chasith (חסת): refuge (Study 37)

chatan (חתן): bridegroom; marriage (Study 67)

chatsav (חצב): devices; thoughts; ideas; imaginations; desires (Study 71) *chav* (חב) [Aramaic]: a common word for love; a love that is given but not necessarily returned (Study 4; Study 82)

chayah (חיה): to give life; to live; to become strong; food; restored from sickness (Study 47; Study 85)

chazah (חזה): to see; to perceive (Study 7)

chazaq (חזק): stout; stubborn; strong (Study 18)

chul (חול): to be in pain; to tremble; to shake (Study 8)

dalaph (דלף): to melt; to shed tears; to weep; raindrops; rain (Study 47)

dama' (דמא): to weep over the suffering/grieving heart of another person (Study 86)

daresh (דרש): to seek; to consult an oracle (Study 42)

derek (דרך): a journey, either spiritual or physical; a way or path; possibly crossroads in a plural form (*derekim*) (Study 34; Study 41)

devar (דבר): to speak; to say; a word; words spoken from the heart (Study 16; Study 18; Study 41; Study 47; Study 69; Study 83; Study 85)

devek (דבק): to cling; to embrace; to hug (Study 5)

dodi (דודי): beloved, as in spousal love (Study 4; Study 32)

'Elohim (אלוהים): God; the word is in a masculine form, showing the masculine nature of God as Protector, Provider, and Disciplinarian; the plural form of the word represents that God is pluralistic in majesty and is the ultimate or supreme God (Study 73; Study 77)

'eth (את): This term has no meaning as a word but is a sign of a direct object. (Study 49)

'even (אבן): stone (Study 21)

'ezer (עזר): helper; helpmeet; one who helps someone to understand something (as in one who helps another to understand the love and nature of God) (Study 73)

gadar (גדר): hedge, fence, or wall (Study 19)

galah (גלה): to reveal a secret (Study 3)

galah (גלה): to open; to lay bare; to reveal; to be intimate with; to have intercourse (Study 25)

galal (גלל): to discover (Study 3)

gamal (גמל): to mature; a ripened fruit; being nourished until completely ripe; a child weaned from its mother (Study 85)

garam (גרם): to be strong; to gnaw at a bone and lick it clean; cleansing through affliction (Study 28)

gavar (גבר): mighty man; leader (Study 23)

gozel (גזל): nesting bird; pigeon; to pass over (Study 68)

gil (גול): to rejoice (Study 36)

ha'or (האור): light (Study 3)

hadar (הדר): glory; beauty; majesty; splendor (Study 79)

hafak (הפך): turn; the word gives the impression of ruin, being overthrown, being destroyed; it is also the word for being imprisoned or put into stocks; additionally, it expresses a tumbling or churning.(Study 50)

hagah (הגה): to meditate (Study 36)

halah (הלה): praise; the term from which we get the word *hallelujah*, meaning "praise the Lord" (Study 36)

hamishepethaim (המשפתים): two burdens (Study 28)

kavas (כוס): cup; pelican or stork (Study 42)

kavod (כבוד): heaviness; burdensome; grievous; heavy burden; glory (Study 44; Study 79)

kebes (כבש): yearling sheep; lamb (Study 63)

ketam (כתם): to be hidden (Study 37)

ki (כי): for; because (Study 17; Study 84)

lan'ar (לנער): young woman (Study 53)

layan (לין): to murmur; to remain; to stay (Study 59)

lev (לב): heart; the source of all passions (Study 23; Study 86)

levav (לבב): heart; understanding; thought; reasoning; judgment; kindly (Study 2; Study 9; Study 31; Study 62; Study 83)

livabethini (לבביני): to ravish the heart; to pull the bark from a tree (Study 2)

linethiboth (לנתבות): paths; difficult paths (Study 41)

ma'aq (מעק): pressed; burdened with pain (Study 13)

magan (מגן): shield; to tend (Study 24)

magen (מגן): gardener (Study 24)

manach (מנח): offering; gift (Study 58)

matsa (מצא): to find; to discover hidden knowledge or secret knowledge (Study 64)

melekah (מלכה): a queen; royal; royalty (Study 77)

melek (מלך): a king (Study 12)

michtam: see *miktam*

midbar (מדבר): wilderness (Study 47; Study 83)

miktam (מכתם): from gold; from the hidden; "Poem of Gold" (Study 37)

minchcath (מנחת): oblations; offerings; tribute; gifts (Study 58)

misetarim (מסתרים): secret places (Study 38)

mitspah (מצפה): watchtower; indicates a close bond between two people who protect each other's hearts while they are apart (Study 45)

mogan: to deliver; to set up to examine and regard (Study 50)

Moloch (מלך): a notorious false god that demanded human sacrifice (Study 12; Study 23)

mot (מוט): to fall down; to collapse (Study 75)

moth (מות): death (Study 3; Study 27; Study 75)

nacham (נחם): repentings; a turning away as a result of sorrow or grief (Study 50)

nakach (נכה): to be smitten; to be struck down (Study 48)

nakon (נכון): to be fixed; to be established or directed (Study 44)

naphal (נפל): inferior; to fall; to surrender; to give up (Study 31)

nasa' (נשׂא): to be made high or exalted; also expresses the idea of to bear or to carry away (Study 80)

nasah (נסה): to try; to tempt; to probe; to test; also denotes "to write an essay" (Study 57)

nathan (נתן): to give (Study 27; Study 43; Study 50; Study 75)

nathav (נתב): a path of uncertainty (Study 41)

navch (נוח): rest; implies a rest that comes from just lying down or being in repose (Study 43; Study 58) *nephesh* (נפש): the soul; one's physical life; free will; the central area of the will, emotions, and passion (Study 14)

neshamah (נשמה): soul (Study 36)

neshimah (נשמה): breath (Study 36)

nesor (נשׂר): eagle or vulture; sawing or ripping apart (Study 40)

netsor (נצר): diligence; to keep watch, as in "to guard and conceal" in order to scrutinize (Study 9)

noam (נעם): beauty; pleasure (Study 79)

pa'al (פעל): working for a reward or a commission; work; activity; deeds; what one has done (Study 70; Study 79)

pa'ar (פאר): beauty, glory and/or honor; a green bough or branch (Study 77)

pala' (פלא): hard; something wonderful or marvelous (Study 69)

palal (פלל): to pray; to offer supplication to God; to offer humble praise to God (Study 36)

pani (פני): face; God's presence (Study 7; Study 43; Study 65)

paqad (פקד): to punish; to examine (Study 83)

paras (פרץ): a gap; to break, tear down (Study 19)

pathah (פתה): to allure; to seduce; to open wide (Study 83)

pavak (פוך): antimony; fair colors; eyeliner; eye paint (Study 21)

qatal (קטל): to slay; a physical killing; a killing of the spirit; a killing of all hope; can also denote to make small or to be of little value (Study 78)

qatsar (קצר): to be impatient; to be discouraged; to cut down; to reap; grieved; unable; short; deficient; passionate (Study 34) *qavah* (קוה): to wait; making rope; looping rope; binding together (Study 33; Study 40)

qum (קום): to strengthen; to arise (Study 47)

quts (קוץ): to awaken from sleep or from death (Study 7)

quwam (קום): rising up to stand (Study 41)

ra'a' (רעע): evil, with the sense of brokenness (Study 71)

ra'ah (רעה): brotherly love; friendship; friend; "my love"; a consuming passion; shepherd; evil, in the sense of a consuming passion for something that is not of God; trouble (Study 4; Study 30; Study 32; Study 43; Study 59; Study 63)

ra'ah (ראה): to appear; to see with the physical eyes; to see spiritually (Study 12; Study 14; Study 41; Study 49; Study 76)

rachab (רחיב): to enlarge; an enlargement of understanding (Study 84)

racham (רחם): tender mercies; romantic love; [Aramaic] love that is returned (Study 4)

rachaq (רחק): from afar; to be far off; to be far away (Study 76)

raga' (רגע): a rest that comes suddenly after one has gone through a turbulent time (Study 41)

ragam (רגם): to cleanse through stoning (Study 28)

rakak (רכך): to be tender or delicate of heart; to be delicate, dainty, gentle, and feminine; can carry the idea of nurturing (Study 54; Study 62)

rakav (רכב): chariot (Study 39)

ranan (רנן): a song of praise (Study 88)

rapha' (רפא): to cure; to heal; to restore; to repair; to forgive; to pardon; to render whole; to sew or weave; prosperity (Study 20) *ratsach* (רצח): murder; physical killing, intentional or premeditated (Study 78)

rova' (רבע): fourth part; four (Study 53)

sagav (שׂגב): refuge; to be high (Study 1)

sakal (שׂכל): to prosper (spiritually); to understand (Study 8)

saphir (ספר): sapphire stone; lapis lazuli; a deep, rich blue (Study 21)

satar (סתר): to hide; a hiding place; to conceal; to be secret (Study 30; Study 38; Study 65)

sava (שׂבע): satisfied; seven; complete filling; completeness (Study 7)

saval (סבל): to carry; porter; one who carries a heavy load for another person (Study 80)

savek (סבך): thicket; to entwine; an entwining vine, tree, or bush (Study 61)

shabah (שׁבה): to return; to turn back (Study 81)

shabbat (שׁבת): to rest; to cease (Study 6; Study 73)

shachah (שׁחה): to worship; to bow down; fall prostrate; [Ugaritic]: a god sharing his or her passion with a human being, and the human sharing his or her passion with the god (Study 10)

shachar (שׁחר): early; black, as in night, dawn, or early morning (Study 64)

shagah (שׁגה): to wander; to stray; to be hindered; to sin or err out of ignorance (Study 42)

shakach (שׁכח): to forget; to neglect; to leave behind (Study 60)

shalak (שׁלך): gives the idea of a flower being blown away from its plant by the wind (Study 75)

shaleg (שׁלג): snow (Study 26)

shamar (שמר): to keep; to watch over; to guard; to beware; to preserve; to watch closely; to observe; watchtower (Study 9, Study 37, Study 85)

shaphaya (שפיא) [Aramaic]: a sharp splinter (Study 74)

shaqar (שקר): to feign; to be deceptive (Study 81)

sharak (שרק): to hiss; whistle; signal; comes from a Semitic root that was used for a musical instrument like a pipe or a flute (Study 46)

shavach (שבח): to sooth; to calm; to relax (Study 6)

shavah (or *shabah*) (שבה): to take as captive (Study 6; Study 81)

shavak (שבכ): to mingle; to interweave; to have intercourse (Study 6)

shaval (שבל): to grow (Study 6)

shavar (שבר): to examine in order to make pure (Study 6)

shavat (שבט): to measure (Study 6)

shavats (שבצ): to weave or intermingle together to create something beautiful (Study 6)

shavav (שבב): to kindle a fire (Study 6)

shave (שוא): vain; to make a worthless noise (Study 18)

shavuh (שוה): to make oneself like another (Study 81)

Shekinah (שכינה): dwelling; settling; often used to denote the dwelling or settling of the presence of God; it is in a feminine form and represents the feminine aspect of God, such as gentleness, nurturing, and caring (Study 32; Study 64)

shikachah (שכחה): forgetfulness (Study 26)

shur (שור): song, specifically a song of peace, joy, and celebration of the power of God (Study 8) *shuv* (שׁוב): to return; to restore (Study 73)

sukkah (סכה): pavilion; dwelling; covering of protection (Study 30)

tahar (טהר): clean; purifying (Study 89)

taman (טמן): to hide; to keep in reserve (Study 38)

tavar (תור): turtledove; to go around; to spy; to investigate; to explore; denotes searching out one's heart to discover the truth (Study 68)

tela' (טלא): lamb; to be blemished, spotted, or wounded (Study 63)

tov (טוב): good; to be in harmony with God; to prosper (Study 15; Study 37; Study 41; Study 54; Study 56; Study 88)

tsachaq (צחק): to laugh (Study 69)

tsalach (צלח): to prosper, in the sense of moving forward, making progress (Study 49)

tsalal (צלל): shadow (Study 3)

tsalemaveth (צלמות): shadow of death (Study 3)

tsamah (צמא): to be thirsty; to have an overwhelming desire for something (Study 29)

tsaphan (צפן): to hide; the hiding of treasure or precious gems (Study 30)

tsaraph (צרף): pure; refine (Study 24)

tsarar (צרר): trouble, in the sense of being bound up (Study 1)

tsava' (צבא): [Aramaic form for the Hebrew *tsavah* (צוה)]: want; desire; to serve in the temple; to go forth to war; warriors, soldiers; commander in chief. This word also carries the idea of "to will," "to find pleasure," or "to choose," denoting divine design. (Study 42)

tsavah (צוה): commandments (has the idea of appointing or making a decree or a commission); to go forth to war; military service;

trial; struggle; affliction; to serve in the temple; monument; pillar; signpost (Study 42)

tsenif (צניפ): diadem; turban; to wrap around (Study 77)

tsiphar (צפר): a bird that is happily chirping and dancing; can also signify a humble or soft voice that brings the presence of the Holy Spirit (Study 68)

tsum (צום): to fast; to put a cover over one's mouth (Study 35)

y'ash (יאשׁ): "no hope"; to be despondent; to be in despair (Study 71)

ya'al (יעל): to receive; to profit; to benefit (Study 40)

ya'ats (יעצ): to consult (carries the idea of deliberating or taking counsel); counselor (Study 17; Study 72)

yachal (יחל): to trust; to have an expectant hope (Study 78)

yad (יד): hand; a symbol of power and/or protection (Study 17; Study 32; Study 77)

yadiyad (ידיד) beloved (Study 32)

yagah (יגה): heaviness; oppressiveness (Study 47)

yagun (יגון): grief; pain, sorrow, or misery; comes from a Semitic root word for a horse that has such pain in its hoof that it has become lame (Study 74)

yahab (יהב): to give, with the idea of a giving of responsibility (Study 75)

yara' (ירא): to fear, as in terrorized or scared to death; to fear for the safety or well-being of another person (Study 14; Study 89)

yasad (יסד): foundation; intimacy; intercourse (Study 21)

yasadithike (יסדתיך): to lay a foundation (Study 21)

yasur (יסר): to turn away; to withdraw; to pervert (Study 23) *yashab* (ישב): to dwell (Study 81)

yasta' (יצא): issues; seasons, particularly springtime (Study 9)

yastar (יצר): a pure, shining oil; an anointing oil; an essential oil used to anoint a wound (Study 11)

yatsab (יצב): a standing to be seen (Study 41)

YHWH (יהוה): Lord; God's name *Jehovah*; comes from a root word meaning "to exist," "to be." YHWH represents the feminine nature of God, reflecting His mercy, His loving-kindness, and His nurture of us. (Study 49; Study 73)

yisemah (יצמא): to thirst (Study 29)

yisrael (ישראל): prince of God; Israel, the name of the Jewish nation (Study 50)

zamar (זמר): a song of praise that comes when one is being pruned or tried by God; a joyful but focused praise; cutting; pruning (Study 8; Study 44; Study 88)

zarar (זרר): arm, representing the primary source of nourishment or financial security (Study 23)

English–Hebrew Index

be: *hayah* (היה): to come; to be; to become; to exist (Study 16)

beauty: *hadar* (הדר): glory; beauty; majesty; splendor (Study 79)

beauty: *hod* (הוד): beauty; brilliance (Study 17)

beauty: *noam* (נעם): beauty; pleasure (Study 79)

beauty: *pa'ar* (פאר): beauty, glory and/or honor; a green bough or branch (Study 77)

because: *ki* (כי): for; because (Study 17; Study 84)

behold: *hen* (הן): though; often translated as "behold" (Study 78)

beloved: *dodi* (דודי): beloved, as in spousal love (Study 4; Study 32)

beloved: *yadiyad* (ידיד): beloved (Study 32)

bird: *tsiphar* (צפר): a bird that is happily chirping and dancing; can also signify a humble or soft voice that brings the presence of the Holy Spirit (Study 68)

blessed: *barak* (ברך): to be blessed; to make happy (Study 33)

blown: *shalak* (שלך): gives the idea of a flower being blown away from its plant by the wind (Study 75)

breath: *neshimah* (נשמה): breath (Study 36)

bride: *kallah* (כלה): bride (Study 67)

bridegroom: *chatan* (חתן): bridegroom; marriage (Study 67)

brilliance: *hod* (הוד): beauty; brilliance (Study 17)

capture: *shavah* (or *shabah*) (שבה): to take as captive (Study 6; Study 81)

carry: *saval* (סבל): to carry; porter; one who carries a heavy load for another person (Study 80)

crown: *'aterat* (עטרת): crown, one which encircles the head (Study 77)

cry of grief and mourning: *'ayakah* (איכה): "Where are you?"; a cry of grief and mourning; a lamentation (Study 55)

cup: *kavas* (כוס): cup; pelican or stork (Study 42)

cure: *'arak* (ארך): health; to restore; to cure, in the sense of creating longevity (Study 20)

cure: *rapha'* (רפא): to cure; to heal; to restore; to repair; to forgive; to pardon; to render whole; to sew or weave; prosperity (Study 20)

curse: *'arar* (ארר): curse; cursed; to be without protection (Study 23)

curse one's soul: *'alah* (אלה): these; to worship and adore; to swear; to curse one's soul; to be fat, or stout (Study 15; Study 31)

darkness: *chashak* (חשך): darkness (Study 3)

death: *moth* (מות): death (Study 3; Study 27; Study 75)

deceptive: *shaqar* (שקר): to feign; to be deceptive (Study 81)

deep things: *'amaquth* (עמקות): deep things; that which is unsearchable (Study 3)

deliver: *mogan*: to deliver; to set up to examine and regard (Study 50)

despair: *y'ash* (יאש): "no hope"; to be despondent; to be in despair (Study 71)

devices: *chatsav* (חצב): devices; thoughts; ideas; imaginations; desires (Study 71)

diadem: *tsenif* (צניפ): diadem; turban; to wrap around (Study 77)

diligence: *netsor* (נצר): diligence; to keep watch, as in "to guard and conceal" in order to scrutinize (Study 9)

direct object (in Hebrew grammar): *'eth* (את): This term has no meaning as a word but is a sign of a direct object. (Study 49)

evil: *ra'ah* (רעה): brotherly love; friendship; friend; "my love"; a consuming passion; shepherd; evil, in the sense of a consuming passion for something that is not of God; trouble (Study 4; Study 30; Study 32; Study 43; Study 59; Study 63)

exalted: *nasa'* (נשׂא): to be made high or exalted; also expresses the idea of to bear or to carry away (Study 80)

examine: *mogan*: to deliver; to set up to examine and regard (Study 50)

examine: *shavar* (שׁבר): to examine in order to make pure (Study 6)

exist: *hayah* (היה): to come; to be; to become; to exist (Study 16)

extol: *harim* (הרם): to extol (Study 36)

face: *pani* (פני): face; God's presence (Study 7; Study 43; Study 65)

far off: *rachaq* (רחק): from afar; to be far off; to be far away (Study 76)

fast: *tsum* (צום): to fast; to put a cover over one's mouth (Study 35)

fear: *yara'* (ירא): to fear, as in terrorized or scared to death; to fear for the safety or well-being of another person (Study 14; Study 89)

feathers: *'avar* (אבר): feathers (Study 40)

find: *matsa* (מצא): to find; to discover hidden knowledge or secret knowledge (Study 64)

fixed: *nakon* (נכון): to be fixed; to be established or directed (Study 44)

flesh: *basar* (בשׂר): flesh; to seek the counsel of man (Study 23)

for: *ki* (כי): for; because (Study 17; Study 84)

forget: *shakach* (שׁכח): to forget; to neglect; to leave behind (Study 60)

forgetfulness: *shikachah* (שׁכחה): forgetfulness (Study 26) forsake: *'azavu* (עזבו): to leave behind; to forsake; a stepping back (Study 57)

foundation: *yasad* (יסד): foundation; intimacy; intercourse (Study 21)

four: *rova'* (רבע): fourth part; four (Study 53)

gap: *paras* (פרץ): a gap; to break, tear down (Study 19)

gardener: *magen* (מגן): gardener (Study 24)

gift: *'Issachar* (ישׂשׂכר): comes from the Hebrew root word *shacar* (שׂכר), which means a reward; a gift; intoxication (Study 28)

give: *nathan* (נתן): to give (Study 27; Study 43; Study 50; Study 75)

give: *yahab* (יהב): to give, with the idea of a giving of responsibility (Study 75)

glory: *hadar* (הדר): glory; beauty; majesty; splendor (Study 79)

glory: *kavod* (כבוד): heaviness; burdensome; grievous; heavy burden; glory (Study 44; Study 79)

God: *'Elohim* (אלוהים): God; the word is in a masculine form, showing the masculine nature of God as Protector, Provider, and Disciplinarian; the plural form of the word represents that God is pluralistic in majesty and is the ultimate or supreme God. (Study 73; Study 77)

God sows: *Jezreel* (יזרעאל): God sows (Study 11)

gold: *miktam* (מכתם): from gold; from the hidden; "Poem of Gold" (Study 37)

good: *tov* (טוב): good; to be in harmony with God; to prosper (Study 15; Study 37; Study 41; Study 54; Study 56; Study 88)

gracious: *chanan* (חנן): gracious—carrying the idea of compassion and favor (Study 33) griefs: *chalah* (חלה): to be exhausted; to be diseased; to be weak; to be feeble; to be afflicted; griefs; physical sickness and pain; mental anguish (Study 8; Study 80)

griffin: *karv* (כרב) [Akkadian Persian/Assyrian]: a mythical creature that was considered a form of deity; also known as a *simurgh* (Study 39)

grow: *shaval* (שבל): to grow (Study 6)

grow up: *'alah* (עלה): to mount up; to ascend; to grow up (Study 40; Study 85)

guard: *netsor* (נצר): diligence; to keep watch, as in "to guard and conceal" in order to scrutinize (Study 9)

hand: *kap* (כפ): the palm of the hand (Study 77)

hand: *yad* (יד): hand; a symbol of power and/or protection (Study 17; Study 32; Study 77)

happiness: *'ashar* (אשר): blessing; happiness; moving in the direction of peace and happiness (Study 33)

hard: *pala'* (פלא): hard; something wonderful or marvelous (Study 69)

harmony: *tov* (טוב): good; to be in harmony with God; to prosper (Study 15; Study 37; Study 41; Study 54; Study 56; Study 88)

heal: *rapha'* (רפא): to cure; to heal; to restore; to repair; to forgive; to pardon; to render whole; to sew or weave; prosperity (Study 20)

health: *'arak* (ארך): health; to restore; to cure, in the sense of creating longevity (Study 20)

heart: *lev* (לב): heart; the source of all passions (Study 23; Study 86)

heart: *levav* (לבב): heart; understanding; thought; reasoning; judgment; kindly (Study 2; Study 9; Study 31; Study 62; Study 83)

heaviness: *yagah* (יגה): heaviness; oppressiveness (Study 47)

husband: *'ishi* (אִשִׁי): my husband, in a love relationship (Study 11)

imitate: *shavuh* (שׁוה): to make oneself like another (Study 81)

impatient: *qatsar* (קצר): to be impatient; to be discouraged; to cut down; to reap; grieved; unable; short; deficient; passionate (Study 34)

imprint: *chaqaq* (חקק): to imprint; to engrave; to tattoo; to imagine (Study 60)

Israel: *yisrael* (ישראל): prince of God; Israel, the name of the Jewish nation (Study 50)

Jehovah: *YHWH* (יהוה): Lord; God's name *Jehovah*; comes from a root word meaning "to exist," "to be." YHWH represents the feminine nature of God, reflecting His mercy, His loving-kindness, and His nurture of us. (Study 49; Study 73)

journey: *derek* (דרך): a journey, either spiritual or physical; a way or path; possibly crossroads in a plural form (*derekim*) (Study 34; Study 41)

keep: *shamar* (שׁמר): to keep; to watch over; to guard; to beware; to preserve; to watch closely; to observe; watchtower (Study 9, Study 37; Study 85)

kill: *qatal* (קטל): to slay; a physical killing; a killing of the spirit; a killing of all hope; can also denote to make small or to be of little value (Study 78)

kindle: *shavav* (שׁבב): to kindle a fire (Study 6)

kindle: *kamar* (כמר): to kindle, as in making a fire; smoldering (Study 50)

king: *melek* (מלך): a king (Study 12)

lamb: *kebes* (כבשׂ): yearling sheep; lamb (Study 63)

lamb: *tela'* (טלא): lamb; to be blemished, spotted, or wounded (Study 63)

lamentation: *'ayakah* (איכה): "Where are you?"; a cry of grief and mourning; a lamentation (Study 55)

laugh: *tsachaq* (צחק): to laugh (Study 69)

lay a foundation: *yasadithike* (יסדתיך): to lay a foundation (Study 21)

leader: *gavar* (גבר): mighty man; leader (Study 23)

leave behind: *'azavu* (עזבו): to leave behind; to forsake; to step back from (Study 57)

light: *ha'or* (האור): light (Study 3)

live: *chayah* (חיה): to give life; to live; to become strong; food; restored from sickness (Study 47; Study 85)

Lord: *'adoni* (אדני): master; guide; instructor; lord (Study 37; Study 73)

Lord: *YHWH* (יהוה): Lord; God's name *Jehovah*; comes from a root word meaning "to exist," "to be." YHWH represents the feminine nature of God, reflecting His mercy, His loving-kindness, and His nurture of us. (Study 49; Study 73)

love: *'ahav* (אהב): the most common Hebrew word for love; comes from a Semitic root that has the idea of a heart that is full and satisfied (Study 4; Study 64; Study 76)

love: *chav* (חב) [Aramaic]: a common word for love; a love that is given but not necessarily returned (Study 4; Study 82)

love: *racham* (רחם): tender mercies; romantic love; [Aramaic] love that is returned (Study 4)

loving-kindness: *chasad* (חסד): loving-kindness; mercy (Study 17; Study 79)

majesty: *hadar* (הדר): glory; beauty; majesty; splendor (Study 79) make: *'anah* (ענה): to make; to produce something; to create something (Study 70)

make oneself like another: *shavuh* (שוה): to make oneself like another (Study 81)

man: *'adam* (אדם): man that is of the earth, or flesh (Study 23)

man: *'ish* (איש): a man; a spiritual man or a spiritual presence (Study 22)

manslaughter: *harag* (הרג): manslaughter; physical killing, accidental or unintentional (Study 78)

master: *baali* (בעלי): my master, as to a slave; a husband in a loveless marriage or a marriage of convenience (Study 11)

master: *'adoni* (אדני): master; guide; instructor; lord (Study 37; Study 73)

mature: *gamal* (גמל): to mature; a ripened fruit; being nourished until completely ripe; a child weaned from its mother (Study 85)

measure: *shavat* (שבט): to measure (Study 6)

meditate: *hagah* (הגה): to meditate (Study 36)

melt: *dalaph* (דלף): to melt; to shed tears; to weep; raindrops; rain (Study 47)

mercy: *chasad* (חסד): loving-kindness; mercy (Study 17; Study 79)

mighty man: *gavar* (גבר): mighty man; leader (Study 23)

mingle: *shavak* (שבכ): to mingle; to interweave; to have intercourse (Study 6)

Moloch: *Moloch* (מלך): a notorious false god that demanded human sacrifice (Study 12; Study 23)

pavilion: *sukkah* (סכה): pavilion; dwelling; covering of protection (Study 30)

pelican: *kavas* (כוס): cup; pelican or stork (Study 42)

pigeon: *gozel* (גזל): nesting bird; pigeon; to pass over (Study 68)

pleasure: *noam* (נעם): beauty; pleasure (Study 79)

plunder: *batsa'* (בצע): to plunder; to gain at the expense of another (Study 18)

porter: *saval* (סבל): to carry; porter; one who carries a heavy load for another person (Study 80)

praise: *halah* (הלה): praise; the term from which we get the word *hallelujah*, meaning "praise the Lord" (Study 36)

praise: *hodu* (הודו): a praise of thanksgiving (Study 17)

praise: *ranan* (רנן): a song of praise (Study 88)

pray: *palal* (פלל): to pray; to offer supplication to God; to offer humble praise to God (Study 36)

perceive: *chazah* (חזה): to see; to perceive (Study 7)

pressed: *ma'aq* (מעק): pressed; burdened with pain (Study 13)

prince of God: *yisrael* (ישראל): prince of God; Israel, the name of the Jewish nation (Study 50)

profit: *ya'al* (יעל): to receive; to profit; to benefit (Study 40)

prosper: *tsalach* (צלח): to prosper, in the sense of moving forward, making progress (Study 49)

prosper: *sakal* (שׂכל): to prosper (spiritually); to understand (Study 8)

pruning: *batsar* (בצר): a pruning (Study 1)

punish: *paqad* (פקד): to punish; to examine (Study 83)

sapphire: *saphir* (ספר): sapphire stone; lapis lazuli; a deep, rich blue (Study 21)

satisfied: *sava* (שׂבע): satisfied; seven; complete filling; completeness (Study 7)

seasons: *yasta'* (יצא): issues; seasons, particularly springtime (Study 9)

secret: *satar* (סתר): to hide; a hiding place; to conceal; to be secret (Study 30; Study 38; Study 65)

secret places: *misetarim* (מסתרים): secret places (Study 38)

security: *zarar* (זרר): arm, representing the primary source of nourishment or financial security (Study 23)

see: *chazah* (חזה): to see; to perceive (Study 7)

see: *ra'ah* (ראה): to appear; to see with the physical eyes; to see spiritually (Study 12; Study 14; Study 41; Study 49; Study 76)

seek: *baqash* (בקשׁ): to seek; to ask; can be an act of worship when used in relation to God; a longing (Study 35)

seek: *daresh* (דרשׁ): to seek; to consult an oracle (Study 42)

seize: *'achaz* (אחז): to seize; to grab hold of (Study 7)

set up to examine and regard: *mogan*: to deliver; to set up to examine and regard (Study 50)

shadow: *tsalal* (צלל): shadow (Study 3)

shadow of death: *tsalemaveth* (צלמות): shadow of death (Study 3)

sheaves: *'amar* (עמר): sheaves; stalks of grain tied together; people who are self-seeking (Study 13)

sheep: *kebes* (כבשׂ): yearling sheep; lamb (Study 63)

shepherd: *ra'ah* (רעה): brotherly love; friendship; friend; "my love"; a consuming passion; shepherd; evil, in the sense of a consuming

stand: *quwam* (קום): rising up to stand (Study 41)

stand: *yatsab* (יצב): a standing to be seen (Study 41)

step back: *'azavu* (עזבו): to leave behind; to forsake; to step back from (Study 57)

stick: *'atsah* (עצה): twig; stick; branch; tree trunk; tree (Study 27)

stone: *'even* (אבן): stone (Study 21)

storehouse: *'asar* (אצר): storehouse; treasures that are laid up but not hidden (Study 38)

strengthen: *qum* (קום): to strengthen; to arise (Study 47)

strong: *garam* (גרם): to be strong; to gnaw at a bone and lick it clean; cleansing through affliction (Study 28)

strong: *chayah* (חיה): to give life; to live; to become strong; food; restored from sickness (Study 47; Study 85)

stork: *kavas* (כוס): cup; pelican or stork (Study 42)

stubborn: *chazaq* (חזק): stout; stubborn; strong (Study 18)

surrender: *naphal* (נפל): inferior; to fall; to surrender; to give up (Study 31)

tattoo: *chaqaq* (חקק): to imprint; to engrave; to tattoo; to imagine (Study 60)

tender mercies: *racham* (רחם): tender mercies; romantic love; [Aramaic] love that is returned (Study 4)

tender: *rakak* (רכך): to be tender or delicate of heart; to be delicate, dainty, gentle, and feminine; can carry the idea of nurturing (Study 54; Study 62)

tent: *'ahal* (אהל): a tent or tabernacle (Study 30)

thanksgiving: *hodu* (הודו): a praise of thanksgiving (Study 17)

two burdens: *hamishepethaim* (המשפתים): (to carry) two burdens (Study 28)

understand: *sakal* (שׂכל): to prosper (spiritually); to understand (Study 8)

unsearchable: *'amaquth* (עמקות): deep things; that which is unsearchable (Study 3)

"Until when?": *'ad mati* (עד מתי): "Until when?"; a cry of a broken heart (Study 59)

vain: *shave* (שׁוא): vain; to make a worthless noise (Study 18)

wait: *chakah* (חכה): to wait; to be patient; to hold back (Study 33)

wait: *qavah* (קוה): to wait; making rope; looping rope; binding together (Study 33; Study 40)

want: *tsava'* (צבא) [Aramaic form for the Hebrew *tsavah* (צוה)]: want; desire; to serve in the temple; to go forth to war; warriors, soldiers; commander in chief. This word also carries the idea of "to will," "to find pleasure," or "to choose," denoting divine design. (Study 42)

watch closely: *shamar* (שׁמר): to keep; to watch over; to guard; to beware; to preserve; to watch closely; to observe; watchtower (Study 9; Study 37; Study 85)

watchtower: *mitspah* (מצפה): watchtower; indicates a close bond between two people who protect each other's hearts while they are apart (Study 45)

way: *derek* (דרך): a journey, either spiritual or physical; a way or path; possibly crossroads in a plural form (*derekim*) (Study 34; Study 41)

weak: *chalah* (חלה): to be exhausted; to be diseased; to be weak; to be feeble; to be afflicted; griefs; physical sickness and pain; mental anguish (Study 8; Study 80)

worship: *'alah* (אלה): these; to worship and adore; to swear; to curse one's soul; to be fat, or stout (Study 15; Study 31)

wrestle: *'aveq* (אבק): to wrestle; to get dusty; dust; fragrant powder (Study 22)

young man: *'apar* (עפר): dust; young man (Study 53)

young woman: *lan'ar* (לנער): young woman (Study 53)

About the Author

Chaim Bentorah teaches biblical Hebrew, Aramaic, and Greek to lay teachers and pastors in the metro Chicago area through Chaim Bentorah Ministries. He and his study team also conduct regular Sunday services and Bible Studies at area nursing homes.

Chaim Bentorah has a bachelor of arts degree in Jewish Studies from Moody Bible Institute, a master's degree in Old Testament and Hebrew from Denver Seminary, and a PhD in Biblical Archaeology. All of his Hebrew professors in college and graduate school were involved in the translation of the *New International Version* of the Bible. In their classes, he learned of the inner workings involved in the translation process. In graduate school, he and another student studied advanced Hebrew under Dr. Earl S. Kalland, who was on the executive committee for the translation work of the *New International*. It was this committee that made the final decisions on the particular renderings used in the original *NIV* translation.

Having done his undergraduate work in Jewish Studies, Chaim was interested in the role of Jewish literature in biblical translation. Professor Kalland encouraged him to seek out an orthodox rabbi and discuss the translation process from a Jewish perspective. From this experience, he discovered many things about the Hebrew language that he had not learned in his years of Hebrew studies in a Christian environment. Later, from his contact with Jewish rabbis and his studies in the Talmud, the Mishnah, and other works of Jewish literature, as well as his studies in the Semitic languages, Chaim began doing Hebrew word studies as devotionals and sending them out by e-mail to former students whom he had taught in his thirteen years as an instructor in Hebrew and Old Testament at World Harvest Bible College, as well as those he taught through Chaim Bentorah Ministries.

After self-publishing several books of Hebrew word studies and related topics, Chaim chose ninety word studies to create *Hebrew Word Study: Revealing the Heart of God*, which is his first book with Whitaker House. He believes that if we take the time to study the Hebrew language, we can see the true beauty of God's Word and come to know God and His heart in a much deeper way.

Chaim Bentorah Biblical Hebrew Studies
www.chaimbentorah.com
chaimbentorah@gmail.com